THE CRUNK FEMINIST COLLECTION

EDITED BY

**Brittney C. Cooper, Susana M. Morris,
and Robin M. Boylorn**

**FEMINIST
PRESS**
AT THE CITY UNIVERSITY
OF NEW YORK
NEW YORK CITY

Published in 2017 by the Feminist Press
at the City University of New York
The Graduate Center
365 Fifth Avenue, Suite 5406
New York, NY 10016

feministpress.org

First Feminist Press edition 2017

 This book was made possible thanks to a grant from New York State Council on the Arts with the support of Governor Andrew Cuomo and the New York State Legislature.

First printing January 2017

Cover design by Elise Peterson
Text design by Sarah Evelyn Castro

Library of Congress Cataloging-in-Publication Data is available for this title.

For our mamas, our homegirls, and each other

CONTENTS

RACE AND RACISM: ALL BLACK LIVES MATTER

FAMILY AND COMMUNITY: CHOOSING FAMILY

GIRLS STUDIES: BLACK GIRLS ARE MAGIC

POLITICS AND POLICY:
THE PERSONAL IS POLITICAL

IDENTITY: INTERSECTIONALITY FOR A NEW GENERATION

SISTERHOOD: SHE'S NOT HEAVY, SHE'S MY SISTER

SELF-CARE: THUS SAITH THE LORDE

The Crunk Feminist Collective Mission Statement

The Crunk Feminist Collective (CFC) will create a space of support and camaraderie for hip hop generation feminists of color, queer and straight, (with)in the academy and without, by building a rhetorical community, in which we can discuss our ideas, express our crunk feminist selves, fellowship with one another, debate and challenge one another, and support each other, as we struggle together to artic-ulate our feminist goals, ideas, visions, and dreams in ways that are both personally and professionally beneficial.

The CFC aims to articulate a crunk feminist consciousness for women and men of color who came of age in the hip hop generation by creating a community of scholar-activists from varied professions who share our intellectual work in online blog communities, at con-ferences, through activist organizations, and in print publications, and who share our commitment to nurturing and sustaining one an-other through progressive feminist visions. This collective is a forum where we seek to speak our own truths and to both magnify and en-courage the feminist credos that shape and inform our lives and that we use to engage and transform our world. Crunk feminism is the animating principle of our collective work together and derives from our commitment to feminist principles and politics and also from our unapologetic embrace of those new cultural resources, which provide or offer the potential for resistance. Crunk(ness) is our mode of resistance that finds its particular expression in the rhetorical, cul-tural, and intellectual practices of a contemporary generation.

Beat-driven and bass-laden, crunk music blends hip hop culture and Southern Black culture in ways that are sometimes seamless but more often dissonant. Its location as part of Southern Black culture references the South both as the geography that brought many of us together and as the place where many of us still do vibrant and important intellectual and political work. The term "crunk" was initially coined from a contraction of "crazy" or "chronic" (weed) and "drunk" and was used to describe a state of *uber*intoxication, where a person is "crazy drunk," out of their right mind, and under the influence. But where merely getting crunk signaled that you were out of your mind, a crunk feminist mode of resistance will help you *get your mind right*, as they say in the South. As part of a larger women of color feminist politic, crunkness, in its insistence on the primacy of the beat, contains a notion of movement, timing, and of meaning-making through sound that is especially productive for our work together.

Percussion by definition refers to the "sound, vibration, or shock caused by the striking together of two bodies." Combining terms like "crunk" and "feminism" and the cultural, gendered, and racial histories signified in each is a percussive moment, one that signals the kind of productive dissonance that occurs as we work at the edges of disciplines, on the margins of social life, and in the vexed spaces between academic and nonacademic communities. Our relationship to feminism and our world is bound up with a proclivity for the percussive, as we divorce ourselves from "correct" or hegemonic ways of being in favor of following the rhythm of our own heartbeats. In other words, what others may call audacious and crazy, we call *crunk* because we are drunk off the heady theory of feminism that proclaims that another world is possible. We resist others' attempts to stifle our voices, acting belligerent when necessary, and getting buck if and when we have to. Crunk feminists don't take no mess from nobody!

—The Crunk Feminist Collective, 2010

Hip Hop Generation Feminism: A Manifesto

We are hip hop generation feminists. We unapologetically refer to ourselves as feminist because we believe that gender, and its construction through a White, patriarchal, capitalist power structure, fundamentally shapes our lives and life possibilities as women of color across a range of sexual identities. We are members of the hip hop generation because we came of age in one of the decades, the 1990s, that can be considered post-soul and post–civil rights. Our political realities have been profoundly shaped by a systematic rollback of the gains of the civil rights era with regard to affirmative action and reproductive justice policies; the massive deindustrialization of urban areas; the rise and ravages of the drug economy within urban, semiurban, and rural communities of color; and the full-scale assault on women's lives through the AIDS epidemic. We have come of age in the era that has witnessed a past-in-present assault on our identities as women of color, one that harkens back to earlier assaults on our virtue and value during enslavement and imperialism. Our era has likewise been marked by an insidious reimagining of earlier forms of violence to include the proliferation of stereotypes, both from the public sphere and from our communities, which have now named us welfare queens, quota queens, baby mamas, hoochies, gold-diggers, wifeys, bitches, hoes, and tricks, along with a range of (un)creative rhetorical permutations.

We identify with hip hop because the music, the culture, the fashion, and the figures provide the soundtrack to our girlhood and our young womanhood. Our coming-of-age happened in the linguistically and rhetorically rich cultural milieu and transformation that was the 1990s, the decade of the woman, but also the decade of the female emcee: Queen Latifah, MC Lyte, Da Brat, Left Eye (and TLC),

Foxy Brown, Lil' Kim, and Lauryn Hill. We not only jammed to new jack swing, we reveled in the beats of new jill swing too, because we understood what Queen meant when she sang, *"In a nineties kind of world, I'm glad I got my girls."* We witnessed Puffy "invent the remix," Mary J. Blige pioneer hip hop soul as she looked for a "real love," and FUBU start a global Black fashion trend that was for us by us. We were captured by Darius and Nina falling in love, breaking up, and falling in love again, even as we observed that the art of *Boyz n the Hood* and *Jason's Lyric* imitated a side of life and death seen too often in our communities. We grooved to sounds of the G-funk era and wept at the murders of Tupac Shakur and the Notorious B.I.G. We are hip hop's middle children, folks who fell in love with hip hop at the tail end of what Jelani Cobb identifies as the "Golden Age," came of age during the "Modern Era," and find ourselves increasingly concerned with the gender and race politics of hip hop in the "Industrial Era." We unapologetically blend the terms "hip hop" and "feminism" like our hip hop feminist big sister Joan Morgan did more than a decade ago when she invited us to "fill in the breaks, provide the remixes, and rework the chorus." So we call ourselves hip hop *generation* feminists because while many of us appreciate the culture and the music, we do not have a blind allegiance to it, nor is our feminism solely, or in many cases even primarily, defined by hip hop. Yet our connection to hip hop links us to a set of generational concerns and a community of women, locally, nationally, and globally.

We also recognize the hip hop generation as a community of men, some progressive, but many, many more who are not. Our brothers are either with us or they are not. If you are with us, your life and your politics—and not just your rhetoric—will reflect a commitment to the health and wholeness of women, not just as sisters, as wives, as mothers, or as daughters. We don't need protectors or providers; we need partners in (the) struggle. We will not be battered or bruised by your words, forced into submission by your accusations of racial disloyalty, or tolerant of your homophobia, transphobia, or religio-patriarchal zealotry. Neither will we be silent in the face of rape, sexual abuse, intimate partner violence, and/or the psychic and rhetorical violence that daily reduces us to both sexual objects and objects of scorn. We welcome thinking brothers who appreciate thinking sisters, brothers committed to strategizing with us for a gender-inclusive world.

We spent our twenties negotiating the uncompassionate conservatism of the Bush era, with its brand of fascism masquerading as patriotism. We entered the workforce en masse in the era of boom and bust laissez-faire capitalism, where we are still paid less than our White sisters—when we are employed at all—and where our places of employment still operate under a politics of surveillance and containment, many times rendering us "outsiders within." Daily, we negotiate our work lives in places meant to discredit our truths about the operations of racism, sexism, and heterosexism and to disregard our attempts to resist the power of those forces in our lives. Whether we identify as activists, academics, health-care professionals, spiritual leaders, caregivers, or any of the above, we eschew any false divide between public and private, as we hold dear the principle that the personal is indeed political. We claim the right to resist the forces of racist, sexist, heterosexist domination by any means necessary. Through our written and spoken words, our activism, our collective work, and our support of one another, we will act up, turn it out, set it off, bring wreck, talk back, go off, or get crunk whenever and wherever necessary. These are the strategies of survival for a generation of women never meant to win, and who yet survive.

While our declaration of feminism pays homage to our feminist foremothers and big sisters, hip hop generation feminism is not just a remix but also a remake that builds on the beats and rhythms from the tracks already laid down, but with a decidedly new sound, for a new era. This, in other words, ain't ya mama's feminism. This is next generation feminism, standing up, standing tall, and proclaiming, like Celie, that we are indeed Here. We are the ones we have been waiting for. We love ourselves even when we get no love. We recognize that we are our own best thing, our own best argument, and patriarchy's worst nightmare.

—The Crunk Feminist Collective, 2010

Intro: Get CRUNK!

In the beginning, we got CRUNK. At house parties at Susana and Crunkista's place. In the club. And in the classroom. Crunkness was energy and life, fire and resistance, swagger and verve, going off and showing out. But it was also about showing up, for ourselves and for each other, in spaces that didn't love us. This was the purpose of the initial iteration of the Crunk Feminist Collective, back when Crunk-adelic (Susana), Crunktastic (Brittney), and Crunkista were in grad school together in 2004.

Six years later, when Brittney and Susana decided to revive the Collective, their hope was that they could get that old thing back, that feeling, that hopefulness—the lightness and fun that had sustained them through graduate school. They were two working-class, first-generation college graduates and academics, trying to be well as they navigated the tough and taxing spaces of academe. They used the tools they had, each other, and a gift for writing to convene a group of Black feminists with about a decade's difference in age range. Their work? To create space where Black and Brown chicks who loved hip hop but didn't love sexism could say what needed to be said. Bridging crunk with feminism seemed like an unnecessary project to some, but building off the work of hip hop feminists like Joan Morgan and Gwendolyn Pough, they knew that not only could it be done, it had to be done.

Crunk music is Southern hip hop filled with bass and hard-driving beats. Feminism is theory and praxis that aims to get us free. Crunk feminism, then, is the partnership of two warring ideals that come together to make a hot beat. Our work is fueled by the notion of the percussive—when you put crunk beside feminism you don't get a sweet melody but rather a productive and compelling dissonance.

1

Brittney and Susana wanted to take the best of what they had learned (in their homes, in their communities, in the streets, and in their classes) and make something beautiful. And they knew that in order to do it, what they needed was a crew. There is no hip hop without crew, clique, posse.

"Who you wit? GET CRUNK!!! Who you wit?!"

There's no Black feminism without crew either. Combahee taught us that in love and war, you always need somebody to have your back.

So Brittney and Susana invited feminists of color of various backgrounds and similar politics to join them, and the Crunk Feminist Collective was reborn, inaugurated on March 1, 2010 (Women's History Month). Our collective was comprised of community activists, allies, rising scholars, wives, partners, hetero, queer, and questioning folk of color invested in creating the world we wanted to see. It was important to us as a crew that our group be inclusive, to represent a range of identities, perspectives, standpoints, and experiences. It was also important for us to make space for difference and debate, to be accountable to and for one another, and to show up. For us, the strength in a collective is the collaboration and opportunity to be changed and challenged. We worked together to build consciousness and awareness around issues we were passionate about, bucked at systems of social injustice and inequality, and offered accountable and loving critique when we witnessed so much bullshit. We were committed to doing the work of being visible and vocal Black feminists and cultivating a space where feminism—specifically crunk feminism—wasn't an overly theoretical concept held hostage by the academy. We needed a home(girl) feminism that we could take home and that could be used in our lives.

When the blog first began in 2010, we posted twice a week, sometimes more. We had a lot to say and we blogged about everything. We reviewed shows, films, and books. We talked about our family and dating experiences. We responded to acts of injustice and invisibility. We wrote about our jobs and the movement. And even though many of us wrote under pseudonyms, we felt raw and vulnerable sharing our stories and perspectives. We understood the political risk and reward of Black feminist praxis and were determined to give visibility to issues we found to be disappeared in media. Almost immediately, our stories and feminist analyses were met with understanding, enthusiasm, and affirmation by our readers.

We were excited to have an audience. Our online community wrestled with the issues in the comments and clapped back when trolls came to visit. When we started our Facebook page and got to seventy-five likes, we couldn't believe it. Our blog had seventy-five readers! We continued to feel honored as the numbers grew from a few to a thousand to tens of thousands.

After blogging at breakneck speed for several years, experiencing a host of personal and professional challenges, and the reconfiguration of the Collective after some growing pains, the CFC reemerged in the fall of 2013 with a renewed vision and sense of purpose. What started as a collective of fourteen became a group of eight. What remained was our commitment to each other and to the larger goal and vision of putting crunk feminism into practice. We learned we were more interested in creation than critique. We decided that we wanted to be revolutionary rather than reactionary.

The goal is not and was never to be a homogenous group of feminists with identical views and values. We don't all think alike, do feminism alike, get crunk alike, or approach this work alike. The book you are reading is only one part of our work together. Some of us have chosen to focus on raising crunk, politically aware, radical babies. Some of us get crunk while changing the landscape of our disciplines in the academic institutions where many of us work. Some of us get crunk through our commitment to organizing. Some of us get crunk by working to preserve community institutions that share our radical vision of the future. Some of us get crunk by working with girls and young women, helping them hone a feminist sensibility that will serve them equally well on the block and in the boardroom.

We share some things in common, but in other things we challenge each other, disagree with each other, and at times walk away from each other. In the end, we come back to the table. That has been our agreement and commitment—that before we stand in solidarity with anyone else, we stand in solidarity with and among ourselves.

These kinds of solidarities are harder to forge than many might imagine in the age of digital feminism. Unfortunately, some mistake the mean-spirited, shady, and highly public forms of calling out and clapback emboldened by Twitter for integrity, righteous indignation, and "wokeness." Sometimes calling out and clapping back is necessary. Don't get us wrong. And to be clear, we think we are some of the best to ever do it. (Ask Talib. Ask Tyler. Ask all manner of errant White girls.) However, some of that shit is just mean and lacking in generosity. *We* wouldn't be crunk if we didn't call out the manner in which some folks use the language of social justice to disguise the emotional work they haven't done. There is a rush to *perform* radicalism in the avatar-selves that anyone can carefully curate on-line. But the day-to-day work of living in a socially just manner is far slower, requires far more forgiveness, and even more patience. But if clicks and likes are what you are in it for, this kind of care work is easy to miss. Our commitment to a feminist ethic of care far exceeds any performance you may see from the easy clickable, consumable personae folks create online. Doing this work has taught us to never forget the difference.

Our feminism is a living, evolving project. We didn't know all that we know now when we began in 2010. Some things we have kept, some things we have picked up, some things we have chosen to discard. One thing we have committed not to discard is the women in hip hop who made it possible for us to do this work. We know, for instance, that despite their indisputable flyness, the sisters on the cover of this book don't in any guise identify as feminists. In fact, quite a few of them (here's looking at you, E. Badu) say some antifeminist shit on the regular. We want y'all to know we know. But here's the thing: the swag, the confidence, the bravado, the lack-of-fucks-to-give that these sisters brought to hip hop is a resistance practice. The unapologetic ways they came to tell us the truths they have told over the more than twenty-five years that they have been in the game created a blueprint for all us Black and Brown girls who had some shit to say when the brothers were crowding the mic. Their presence and visibility in hip hop, in the very moment we were budding Black feminists, was substantial and substantive. We rock the feminist label proudly cuz we 'bout this life, which is to say we 'bout this fight for a better world for women and girls of color. In the words of Master P, we "been 'bout it." But we know that Black women's resistance comes in all kinds of packages, and we aren't interested in making Erykah or Lauryn or Queen rock a label that they refuse. This book, and in particular its cover, simply acknowledge that without them showing up and laying the groundwork for younger sisters like us, *there is no us.* Crunkness and feminism, you should know by now, ain't a label so much as a lifestyle.

We are because they are. That is the principle of collectivity.

And this, right here, right now? This is not easy, clickable *unity.* This is *collectivity.*

A gathering place. A cypher. A collection of peoples, ideas, experiences, and feelings that, if shared and grappled with in community, can help us get closer to being free.

So what we share with you here is both collection and collectivity.

Our blogs-turned-essays are love letters and labors of love. We wrote them for you, for ourselves, for our daughters and sons, for educators, for haters, for imitators (who wish they could be duplicators), for the uninitiated, for elders, for lovers, for friends, for the curious, for the questioning, and for those who already know—the choir.

The Crunk Feminist Collection is an assemblage and revision of some of the most popular, provocative, and crunk posts from our blog from 2010 to 2015. We created themes that emerged from our collective work as crunk feminists and our commitment to unapologetically, critically, theoretically, and ethically engage each other and our community. We hope this book inspires dialogue, debate, understanding, clarity, questions, answers, unanswerable questions, and the bravery to embrace (y)our contradictions. We hope this book offers visibility to (personally) vocal but (politically) voiceless Black and Brown girls who are seeking to learn, like we did, how to reconcile a love for hip hop culture alongside a love for themselves, flaws and all. The following essays demonstrate the continued importance of these conversations and revelations in classrooms, book clubs, barber and beauty shops, activist gatherings, churches, and across kitchen tables, which are the varied kinds of spaces that we imagine this book might travel.

Get CRUNK!

—Brittney, Susana, and Robin, 2016

GENDER: @#$% THE PATRIARCHY

Introduction

The essays in this section confront the numerous and varied ways patriarchy and gender norms marginalize women, girls, trans folk, and all things feminine. While patriarchy ultimately harms everyone, cisgender men and boys are rarely forced to reckon with the ways their lives, experiences, and concerns are valued at the expense of others. Our formal education does not teach us what is at stake for folk who are gender fluid, gender nonconforming, gender neutral, or same-gender loving. As crunk feminist Eesha Pandit has noted, "Sex and gender are different and there are more genders than two," but in a patriarchal culture that privileges masculinity and maleness, binary categorization reinforces the hegemonic harms linked to the social construction of gender and the hegemonic harassment that insists masculinity be given social capital.

Just as gender is not synonymous with sex, it is not preoccupied with femininity. We approach gender as a contrived system designed to dictate how women and men (including trans and intersex folk) negotiate their roles and performances, in public and private. Many of us found feminism after recognizing and/or resisting the blatantly sexist and misogynist cultural expectations of how we were supposed to think, act, dress, and behave. The strict confines of gender scripts failed to represent the hybrid, fluid, androgynous spectrum of gender expression we experienced and witnessed in our lives. Gender was invented to restrict the performance of women and men to conservative and traditional behaviors, punishing nuances such as female masculinity or androgynous femme.

These limitations of gender are particularly problematic in Black communities because of the residue of Moynihan's matriarchy thesis,[1] the nuanced negotiation of gender in Black households, and the vulnerability of Black masculinity due to limited resources and opportunities linked to racism. Even though our social circumstances, allegiances to Black men, and devotion to Black churches have often complicated our relationship to raced gender performance, Black women can rarely afford to hold conservative or traditional attitudes about gender, which were designed with White women in mind. Because Black women are framed by images of independence, strength, and resilience, their gender performance, unlike White women's, has often been read as an assault on Black manhood and evidence that Black women are inherently more masculine and, therefore, don't deserve or require the same protection and provision as White women. Thus, Black feminism recognizes and calls out the racist agenda of gender categorization, particularly the ways it polices the bodies and actions of Black women.

Our work seeks to further complicate the already problematic relationship Black women have to the patriarchy, a relationship that is both abusive and one-sided. While we understand the myriad ways Black men are targeted for their own negotiation of gender, we refuse to prioritize the needs of men over women or to overlook the investments *all* men have in patriarchy because of their inherent privileges. We understand gender to be a social construction created to limit our options and access.

As crunk feminists we embrace the possibilities of gender performance, insisting that Black women and women of color be given the room and agency to make sense of who we are, outside of stereotypes. As women of color, we are intimately aware of the politics of identity, the role of racism in the ways our gender is read and understood, and the interconnection of our race, gender, sex, ability, sexuality, and class. Our allegiance to Black men—we are allied—is not an investment in patriarchy, because our feminism pushes us to challenge the status quo and demand equal standards.

We envision an understanding of gender that is inclusive and nonhierarchal; we imagine relationships that are reciprocal and not violent. We are also invested in the lives and experiences of our com-

---

1. The controversial Moynihan Report, written in 1965, concluded that the high rate of Black families headed by single mothers would greatly hinder the progress of Black communities toward economic and political equality.

munity and siblings, including all sexes and genders, and we are deeply invested in and committed to shifting our language practices and social justice commitments to be more gender inclusive.

Black women and girls are not generally offered the luxury of femininity. Women of color are faced with more than sexism in our homes, jobs, and communities. We face criticism when we express our independence from and solidarity with men, and receive backlash when we express our disappointment and frustration with their flagrant disregard for our lives and well-being. Many of us grew up witnessing our foremothers and other women in our lives demonstrate strength and independence out of necessity, never given the luxury or opportunity to be "kept women." Places we were told to revere like churches and schools, as well as intimate spaces like our homes and bedrooms, were privately, if not publicly, sexist. We were encouraged (by women and men alike) to accept these unfair and unjust practices as normal.

The absence of men was never an absence of possibility. We were raised to be feminists (what our mamas called "having our own," outside of a man), to get educated, to be capable of achieving our goals, to understand the function and functionality of female friendships, especially in households that were largely matriarchal. Still, the absence of men was never an absence of male reverence. Patriarchal influences permeated our lives and we, like Black feminists before us, had to learn and understand that our allegiance is to ourselves and that we cannot afford to be invested in patriarchal norms.

Feminism, which ultimately seeks equal rights and recognition for women and girls, and crunk feminism, which unapologetically and actively resists patriarchy by practicing, being, and performing "crunkness," inform the impetus of this section. As crunk feminists, we are not invested in being polite, respectable, or politically digestible—because our very lives are on the line.

Women and girls are perpetually reminded that *their* lives are not valued, that their testimonies (against men) will not be believed, and that their well-being is unimportant when masculinity (including ego) and patriarchy are at stake. This was reinforced, for example, when the Black women assaulted by former police officer Daniel Holtzclaw said they felt that reporting him would be futile, and when the more than fifty women who have come forward as rape victims of Bill Cosby are framed as "accusers," not victims. It is also reiterated through the documented double standard of the wage gap and the fact that Black women and trans women of color are disproportionately affected by violence that ends in death.

Patriarchy is invested in the normalization of masculinity in all of its manifestations (including rape culture and violence) and the silence and invisibility of women, especially women of color. The patriarchy tells us that women should stay in their place and not challenge authority. The patriarchy wants us to be misguided and misinformed. The patriarchy wants us to be defeated and disenchanted. Our essays on gender demonstrate resistance and refusal to comply with traditional, irrational, and patriarchal bullshit. Fuck the patriarchy!

Dear Patriarchy

Crunkista

Dear Patriarchy,

This isn't working. We both know that it hasn't been working for a very long time.

It's not you . . . No, actually, it is you. This is an unhealthy, dysfunctional, abusive relationship—because of you. You are stifling, controlling, oppressive, and you have never had my best interests at heart. You have tricked me into believing that things are the way they are because they have to be, that they have always been that way, that there are no alternatives, and that they will never change.

Anytime I question you or your ways, you find another way to silence me and coerce me back into submission. I can't do this anymore. I've changed and in spite of your shackles, I've grown. I have realized that this whole restrictive system is your own fabrication and that the only one gaining anything from it is you. You selfish dick.

I will not continue to live like this. I will not continue to settle. I know now that there is a better way.

Before you hear about it from one of your boys, you should know that I have met someone. Her name is Feminism. She is the best thing that has ever happened to me. She validates and respects my opinions. She always has my best interests at heart. She thinks I am beautiful and loves me just the way I am. She has helped me find my voice and makes me happier than I have ever been. We have made each other stronger. Best of all, we encourage and challenge each other to grow. And the sex . . . Well, the sex is so much hotter.

I'm leaving you. You're an asshole. We can never be friends. Don't call me. Ever.

Never again,
Crunkista

On Black Men Showing Up for Black Women at the Scene of the Crime

Brittney C. Cooper

In 2013 I showed up to the Brecht Forum in Brooklyn ready to have a conversation about what we mean when we say "ally," "privilege," and "comrade."

I showed up to have that discussion after months of battle testing around those issues in my own crew. Over the years, I've learned that it is far easier to be just to the people we don't know than the people we do know.

So there I sat on a panel with a White woman and a Black man. As a Black feminist, I never quite know how political discussions will go down with either of these groups. Still, I'm a fierce lover of Black people and a fierce defender of women.

The brother shared his thoughts about the need to "liberate all Black people." It sounded good. But since we were there to talk about allyship, I needed to know more about his gender analysis, even as I kept it real about how I've been feeling lately about how much brothers *don't* show up for Black women, without us asking, and prodding, and vigilantly managing the entire process.

In a word, I was tired.

I shared that. Because surely a conversation about how to be better allies to each other is a safe space.

This brother was not having it. He did not want to be challenged, did not plan to have to go deep, to interrogate his own shit. Freedom talk should've been enough for me.

But I'm grown. And I know better. So I asked for more.

I got cut off, yelled at, screamed on. The moderator tried gently to intervene, to ask the brother to let me speak, to wait his turn. To model allyship. To listen. But to no avail. The brother kept on screaming about his commitment to women, about all he had "done for us," about how I wasn't going to erase his contributions.

Then he raised his over-six-foot-tall, large, Brown body out of the chair and deliberately slung a cup of water across my lap, leaving it to splash in my face, on the table, on my clothes, and on the gadgets I brought with me.

Damn. You knocked the hell out of that cup of water. Did you wish it were me? Or were you merely trying to let me know what you were capable of doing to a sister who didn't shut her mouth and listen?

Left to sit there, splashes of water, mingling with the tears that I was too embarrassed to let run, because you know sisters don't cry in public, imploring him to "back up," to "stop yelling," to stop using his body to intimidate me, while he continued to approach my chair menacingly, wondering what he was going to do next, anticipating my next move, anticipating his, being transported back to past sites of my own trauma . . .

I waited for anyone to stand up, to sense that I felt afraid, to stop him, to let him know his actions were unacceptable. Our copanelist moved her chair closer to me. It was oddly comforting.

I learned a lesson: everybody wants to have an ally, but no one wants to stand up for anybody.

Eventually three men held him back, restrained him, but not with ease. He left. I breathed. I let those tears that had been threatening fall.

Then an older Black gentleman did stand up. "I will not stand for this maligning of the Black man . . . ," his rant began. While waiting for him to finish, I zoned out and wondered what had happened here.

Did this really happen here? In movement space?

Tiredness descended. And humiliation. And loneliness. And weariness. And anger at being disrespected. And embarrassment for you. And concern for you and what you must be going through—to show your ass like that. And questioning myself about what I did to cause your outburst. And checking myself for victim blaming myself. And anger at myself for caring about you and what you must be going through. Especially since you couldn't find space to care about me and what I must be going through.

Later, with my permission, you came in and apologized. Asked us to make future space for forgiveness. I didn't feel forgiving that day. I don't feel forgiving today. I know I will forgive you though. It's necessary.

After being approached at the end by a Gary Dourdan–looking macktivist, who couldn't be bothered to stand up to the brother screaming on me, but who was ready to "help" me "heal the traumas through my body"—as he put it (yes, you can laugh)—I grabbed my coat and schlepped back to Jersey.

On the long train ride home, and in the days since, I was reminded that that was not the first time I had been subject to a man in a movement space using his size and masculinity as a threat, as a way to silence my dissent. I remembered that then as now, the brothers in the room let it happen without a word on my behalf.

Why?

Is it so incredibly difficult to show up for me—for us—when we need you? Is it so hard to believe that we need you? Is solidarity only for Black men? As for the silence of the sisters in the room, I still don't know what to make of that. Maybe they were waiting on the brothers, just like me.

I do know I am tired. And sad. And not sure how much more I want to struggle with Black men for something so basic as counting on you to show up.

The Evolution of a Down-Ass Chick

Robin M. Boylorn

> Down-Ass Chick: a woman who is a lady but can hang with thugs. She will lie for you but still love you. She will die for you but cry for you. Most importantly she will kill for you like she'll comfort you. She is a ride-or-die bitch who will do whatever it takes to be by your side. She'll be your Bonnie if you are her Clyde.[1]

I taught a class on Black masculinity that covered everything from Black man stereotypes and the patriarchal requirements of Black masculinity to big Black penis myths, homophobia, and hip hop. One of our classes on romantic relationships between heterosexual Black women and men inspired an interesting conversation that stayed for days. Forgive me for a quick (perhaps academic) summary.

Several Black women scholars (including Patricia Hill Collins and bell hooks) tell us that Black love is an act of rebellion. In a culture that claims Black women are unlovable and undesirable, and Black men are violent and irredeemable, it is considered "rebellious" when Black men and women love each other. Further, Black male scholars

---

1. This definition comes from Urban Dictionary's entry for "down ass bitch." The term "chick" is often substituted for "bitch" in hip hop culture, mainly as a radio-edit option so songs with explicit language can be played on air.

(like Mark Anthony Neal, Michael Eric Dyson, Byron Hurt, and Michael Jeffries) have discussed the ways thug (or hip hop) masculinity makes room for romantic love, and how patriarchy (and hip hop) promotes a binary perception of women as either "good" or "bad." In other words, heterosexual romantic love relationships between Black women and men are complicated. And hip hop culture situates Black women as either a ride-or-die chick and/or a wifey (but not a wife) or a disposable woman, used for sex and a good time. I wasn't feeling either one of those options.

As a self-proclaimed "good girl," I have always found it problematic that "good girls" are punished for being good. While we may be the ones men claim to "want," most of the good sisters I know are situationally single. The good girl is put in the pocket while the other woman gets the attention, affection, love, sex, and children. Alternatively, if good girls become ambivalent about this wait-and-see kind of love, and if they transform themselves into the version of themselves that men will pay attention to, they will no longer be seen as "good" and therefore no longer be desired. Ain't that some shit? Patriarchy at its finest.

When I was seventeen years old, in the mid-1990s, I aspired to be a down-ass chick. I was into pseudothugs and pretty boys, or any combination of the two, and (would have) gladly compromised my dignity and self-esteem to be "down."

A down-ass chick was loyal, sexual, willing to lie, die, fight, or steal for her ni**a. She kept her mouth shut and legs slightly open, but only for her dude. She was supportive and submissive, and essentially self-sacrificing. She was glamorized in music and films and always got the dude—whether he was worthy of being had or not.

At the time, the promises of the down-ass chick were intoxicating, seemingly liberating. Mind you, I was nowhere near being a feminist when I was a teenager, and like most of the other Blackgirls I knew, I was trying to get chose. But that was then. Now that I can carefully critique the role, I realize that being a down-ass chick makes it nearly impossible for a Black woman to measure up. For example, while hip hop thug masculinity acknowledges that "thugs need love too," it is a particular kind of love that cannot be accomplished by one woman. A thug needs polyamorous love that can simultaneously feed his ego and his reputation. Women have to be conflicted and oxymoronic to be "enuf." For example, you need to be good, but willing to participate in criminal activity; you need to have your own, but let him take care of you; you need to be virginal, but sexually talented enough to keep him satisfied; you need to be faithful to him, but willing to tolerate his infidelity; you need to be masculine enough to kick it with the fellas, but feminine enough to be sexually desirable. Being a down-ass chick was a paradoxical proposition and damn near impossible.

When we went around the classroom, quizzing each other on our "down-ass-chick-ness" (or desire to have a down-ass chick) I responded, "Hell nah!" My interpretation of a down-ass chick (the ride-or-die chick who is willing to sacrifice herself, sit idly by while being disrespected and dismissed, and tolerant of emotional and physical abuse and infidelity) is not desirable to my grown-woman sensibilities. The seventeen-year-old in me was saying yes, but the grown-ass, thirty-something feminist woman with things to lose said, "Hell nah."

When I said I was NOT a down-ass chick the Black men in the room were visibly disappointed. I don't think they saw down-ass-chick-ness as something linked to maturity, education, or *knowing better therefore doing different*. For them, the fact that I was cool and cute, and had been unapologetically vocal about my love and advocacy for Black men, should have made me automatically down. For me, I was too old for that shit. Grown women don't do down-ass chick.

Over the next few days I began to imagine an evolution of the down-ass chick, since I had willfully outgrown the original version.

I decided that a grown-up version of a down-ass chick should evolve based on the types of relationships she invites into her life. As a feminist woman, my aspiration for down-ass-chick-ness involves being in partnership with someone I can build with. I see a grown-up down-ass chick as someone who is not a liability and brings something (other than just herself) to the table. But a grown-ass down-ass chick is not looking for love in all the wrong places, not sacrificing herself or her dignity for a relationship, not tolerating disrespect or infidelity, and regularly calls her partner out for their bullshit. Fuck silent complicity. I get crunk.

A grown-ass down-ass chick is loyal, has sex for her own pleasure, is a truth teller and a truth seeker, and is not interested in a man (or woman) who would require or ask her to sacrifice herself for them. She speaks her truth and her mind, sits wide legged or with her legs crossed (depending on how she feels), and owns her own sexuality confidently. She is supportive, but not submissive, and seeks a relationship that is mutually beneficial with someone who gives as good as they get. She wants to be down for a man (or woman) who wants to be down for her, who wants to dream with her, who wants to build with her. She shows up in music and films, usually as Miss Independent, and is sometimes (most of the time) single.

Being a down-ass chick isn't bad, but it requires a reimagining of what progressive relationships look like. Being a grown-ass down-ass chick should be inclusive of nonheterosexual partnerships, resist patriarchal and hierarchal roles in relationships, and encourage independence and individuality. Being a grown-ass down-ass chick shouldn't require you to compromise or settle or lose your self-esteem. Being a grown-ass down-ass chick should allow you to be fully yourself and fully feminist. For that, I might be down.

How Did I Become a Feminist?

Eesha Pandit

Instead of fitting into a neat narrative, my feminism came in fits and starts. My feminism was inspired by teachers and friends and wonderful family, by poets and writers who spoke my own internal fears and hopes back to me, and by musicians that sang my dreams to me. So in homage to the work of the Crunk Feminist Collective, and the legacy of feminists from which we come, here are just a few snapshots of the moments I became more and more feminist. It's not a complete list by any means, and my feminism is forged daily, but these were pivot points in my life.

1. **High school, Friendswood, Texas:** I skipped last-period English class to help a classmate find out where the local Planned Parenthood clinic was. She was terrified. We weren't really even friends. We happened to be in the bathroom together and she was crying, and I had no idea what to do. Unprepared to offer anything but my research skills, I told her to meet me in the computer lab to find out whatever we could. That afternoon, she said something to me that I'll never forget: "This should be something my mom or my best

friends can help me with, but I can't even imagine talking to them about it. Ever. For the rest of my life." It would be many years before I would take my first job working in the reproductive justice movement, but that was the day that I first understood the injustice of shame and fear.

2. **Sophomore year in college, in a class called Modern Philosophy:** The class covered major enlightenment thinkers and, demonstrating the power of a women's college education, my professor added a text to our syllabus called *Women Philosophers of the Early Modern Period.* The book included a series of letters written by sisters, aunts, friends, and lovers of the early modern philosophers we were reading in the course. In the letters, these women share ideas and help to refine the ideas of the men with whom they correspond. For example, Descartes's *The Passions of the Soul* derives from his conversations with Elisabeth of Bohemia. And Leibniz wrote, "My philosophical views approach somewhat closely those of the late Countess of Conway." Yet these women are not taught in most philosophy classes. I was struck, too, by the awareness that these women were wealthy, European, and White. In that moment, despite my unabashed love for the discipline of philosophy, I understood the systemic erasing of women, their thoughts, and their contributions to intellectual history.

3. **Senior year of college, upon reading *Toward a Feminist Theory of the State* by Catharine MacKinnon:** Read as part of an independent study on feminist theory, this book changed the way I think about power and the law. I carried it around for weeks reading and rereading passages. But I didn't see myself in it—not fully, at least. There is a paragraph (maybe two) in the book in which MacKinnon refers to women of color and the divergent experiences they have. She admits that her perspective and narrative is limited, without making any serious effort to address this limitation. It was a heart-swell and a heartbreak in a matter of moments. It was then that I understood the difference between the second wave and the third wave of feminism, in a visceral way. I read bell hooks and Arundhati Roy in the weeks following, and I found a deep and resonant solace in their words and methods.

4. **First summer after college, spent doing research on human rights in Cambridge, Massachusetts:** In retrospect, I learned a lot about human rights and international law that summer, but it's the poetry that stands out. Having zero dollars of discretionary income and armed with a Harvard Library card (everyone should be so lucky for at least some part of their lives), I lurked around the poetry room in Widener Library every evening and most weekends. That was the summer of Audre Lorde's *Sister Outsider* and Adrienne Rich's *The Dream of a Common Language.* I almost cried when the latter was recalled, and I might still have my copy of *Sister Outsider* somewhere (shhh!).

5. **Traveling to India for the 2005 International Women and Health Meeting in New Delhi:** I went with colleagues to share our work on reproductive justice activism in the US. I met feminist activists from all over the world, and was moved by their persistence in the face of terrible state oppression. But it was the informal conversations with Indian feminists that are seared into my memory, conversations about advocating for reproductive rights and choices in an international context, about femicide and transnational surrogacy. I felt embraced, validated, and nourished by those women and those conversations. We talked about feminism within the South Asian community in the US and my experiences in India. We spoke in Hindi and English, alternating between the two without noticing. We shared stories of giddy victories and shattering losses, both personal and political. There I began to fully understand the power of history, legacy, and the achingly long line of feminists and freedom fighters from which I come.

Now here I find myself—with these and dozens of other transformative moments that comprise my trajectory, alongside a group of feminist friends (sisters, really) who are unrelentingly present in my life, offering constant love, support, and intellectual fuel (because feminists get tired too, y'all). Without them, I wouldn't be nearly as comfortable in my skin and in my mind as I am today.

On we go.

Do We Need a Body Count to Count?
Notes on the Serial Murders of Black Women

Aisha Durham

> Number 47 looks like my second-grade teacher. Number 83 re-
> sembles one of my daughters. Number 66 calls to mind my chil-
> dren's grandmother. And although some faces were cropped from
> near-naked bodies, others were shot outdoors, wearing boots and
> jackets.
>
> — LA Times *reporter Sandy Banks, commenting on*
> *photos of unidentified Black women*

Debra Jackson. Click. Henrietta Wright. Click. Barbara Ware. Click. These are some names of Black women who were sexually assaulted, drugged, murdered, and dumped in LA alleys and backstreets by a former city trash collector. As news broke about a serial killer dubbed the "Grim Sleeper," I found myself at the computer clicking on the still images of 180 nameless, numbered Black women and girls first published by the *LA Times* in 2010. I sat with each photo picturing each life—and remembering the life of my aunt who was murdered years ago.

For women who are poor, who are Black, who are substance abusers, who are single/mothers, who are sex workers, and for wom-en who possess no Olan Mills yearbook portrait like that of Natalee Holloway, how do we make sense of their lives? Do we see them?

The national news coverage of the 1985–2007 Los Angeles mur-ders was sensational. It created a weeklong media event where im-ages of rape survivors, recovering addicts, missing persons, family, friends, and kinfolk served as a collective spectacle to construct a gritty drama about Lonnie Franklin Jr., the accused killer cast as the Grim Sleeper. The first *LA Times* web photo of an unidentified Black woman, for example, included a star rating (the star rating, three out of five, has been removed from the photo, and women who've con-firmed their identity with the LAPD have had their photos removed from the site). The CNN online reporting resembled a movie trailer or a television crime series such as *CSI*.

Buried beneath the news headlines and hidden between police press releases was the actual story: the Black male serial killer. I am unsure if the public was as appalled by the dead Black women as we were fascinated by Franklin because he represented the methodical efficiency usually assigned to White male serial killers. The Franklin case prompted me to think about other news stories reporting updates or new cases about serial murderers Walter Ellis and Jason Thomas Scott, who targeted Black women and girls in Wisconsin and Maryland.

You would think the separate news stories about the systematic killing of Black women and girls in different regions would launch a national conversation about gender violence in Black communities. In the same week that a major network news station reported the LA murders, it also celebrated the number-one YouTube video called "Bed Intruder." The video had been watched more than fifty-four million times by December 2010. It uses actual news footage of Antoine Dodson, a concerned brother who reports on the attempted rape of his sister Kelly. I remain dumbfounded by the complete thematic disconnect and the utter disregard for the actual loss of Black girls and women. It is as if media makers and the consuming public are unable to see Black women unless we are repackaged as entertainment.

I began thinking about writing this piece and imagined there were other stories to tell that would not sour our holiday eggnog. Then, I listened to the interview by Stephanie Jones, who created MOMS (Missing or Murdered Sisters) to raise money and national awareness about the serial murders of poor Black women in Rocky Mount, North Carolina, and how she had to rent a billboard to attract local media attention. Then, after watching the morning news about another serial murderer in Kensington, Philadelphia, I could not look away. At a press conference, Philadelphia Mayor Michael Nutter announced a $37,000 reward (from the city and police fraternal organizations) for the arrest of the "Kensington Strangler," a Black man accused of killing three non-Black women. No such reward was offered in 1998 when my aunt, Mildred Darlene Durham, lay dead from gunshot wounds in the Kensington area of Norfolk, Virginia.

At the end of group sessions at an Illinois collective called SOL-HOT (Saving Our Lives, Hearing Our Truths), Black feminist Ruth Nicole Brown used to invite me and other members to light incense to recall another person or to remember ourselves. We stood face-to-face so that we might see each other. One by one, we would say the names of a loved one so she/we would not be forgotten.

This essay is my virtual incense to my aunt Mildred Darlene Durham and every other Black woman whose face has been etched in my memory.
I do see you. You have not been forgotten.
You are loved. You are missed.

What Does Black Masculinity Look Like?

Robin M. Boylorn

In 2014, in the midst of discussing, debating, and dreaming about the possibility for fluidity in raced gender performance, I listened to a Black man weep and express his platonic love for his teammates (Kevin Durant's NBA MVP acceptance speech); watched a Black man kiss a man, full lips, on live television in celebration (draft coverage of Michael Sam, the first openly gay football player drafted to the NFL, on ESPN); and relished the Pepto-Bismol-pink Cadillac a Black man gave to his mother, a breast cancer survivor, to fulfill a childhood promise (*Teddy Bridgewater: A Promise to Rose*, a short documentary by Spike Lee). In addition to being feel-good, rags-to-riches stories about Black male athletes, the narratives of Durant, Sam, and Bridgewater center the extraordinary escape from difficult circumstances and highlight the generosity, humanity, and possibility of Black manhood. These stories resist the stereotypic representations of Black masculinity that saturate the media and often limit Black men, especially in professional (and college) sports, as commodities and bodies. In these stories, we see Black men as sons and brothers, same-gender-loving, promise-keeping, goal-setting men who cry, tell their truths, and love their mamas.

There are three lessons that can be gleaned from these representations of Black masculinity.

LESSON #1: Black men can (only) talk about loving other men within the context of sport, brotherhood, and heterosexuality without (social and cultural) punishment.
While I enjoyed and appreciated the vulnerability and honesty with which Durant expressed himself in his acceptance speech, I couldn't help but think about the politics of representation and how Michael

Sam, a Black man who is attracted to men, could never give the same speech without critique and discomfort. As a heterosexual man, Durant has the flexibility of expressing himself and his love, appreciation, and affection for other men on his team without contempt. However, outside of that context, his words of admiration and genuine care would have been problematic. The only time a Black man can admit to loving another Black man is if it is seeped in testosterone. And while the patriarchy is detrimental to everyone equally, racism makes men of color peculiarly susceptible to mischaracterization and emasculation, so they have more to prove, more at stake when expressing love, which is seen as a weakness or vulnerability. We need an intervention.

LESSON #2: Black men who identify as gay must uniquely negotiate their performances of masculinity because of homophobia.
Football is the most aggressive and hypermasculine sport one can play, and while it has always been true that nonheterosexual men are fans and players of the sport, there are stereotypical assumptions that it is a "straight man's sport," a "manly man's sport." Michael Sam's outness is brilliant in that it outs the ignorance around homophobia and stereotypes by proving that all gay men are not feminine and that sexual orientation does not limit or dictate one's physical or athletic ability or talent.

I find the brevity of discussion around the hyperhomophobia in Black communities interesting and troubling, especially when it is within that framework that Michael Sam is being viewed. His bravery and willingness to sacrifice money (many speculate that he compromised his earning potential by coming out) to avoid sacrificing himself is commendable, and with an already troubled relationship with his family there should be more discussion about what it means to be an out gay Black man. There are unique circumstances and risks, which is why the DL continues to be "a thing." We need an intervention.

LESSON #3: Black men can love (and generously love on) their (Black) mamas, but what about Black women in general?
Teddy Bridgewater is two things that I like: country and a mama's boy. Black men loving their mothers, especially when/if their fathers are absent, is expected and celebrated in the Black community. Even the music of self-described thugs puts their mamas on a pedestal.

Baby mamas? Not so much. Your everyday around-the-way girl that might be kicking it at the mall or sitting on the stoop? Not so much. I wish there were more examples of Black men fiercely loving, fiercely defending, and fiercely holding down Black women who didn't carry them in their wombs, but do carry them on their backs sometimes. Black women are perpetually defending, protecting, and covering Black men but teach themselves not to expect the same in return. I know hella dudes who respect the hell out of their mamas but have no love for women they don't know, which is a problem because loving your mama is not the same thing as loving women.

There is a way in which our skewed understanding of Black masculinity limits the possibilities of Black love—love that is and can be both revolutionary and unreasonable. Unfortunately, culture teaches Black men to love their mamas but be suspicious of other women. We need an intervention.

Salvation comes in different forms. Durant credits God, his teammates, and his family for his success, Sam credits football and his chosen family, and Bridgewater credits his mother.

When it comes to considerations of Black masculinity the easy answer is not always the right answer. It is easy to blame Black men for their circumstances without critiquing the system designed to fail them, designed to make them fail. Racism, homophobia, and poverty are real, everyday issues that impact the performative possibility of Black masculinity. Survival should not be an exception. We need an intervention.

I have reflected on the ways the world has forever changed in the months and years since we lost Black men in training like Trayvon Martin, Jordan Davis, Tamir Rice, and countless others taken by racism and irrational fear, remembered in eulogy, stripped of the space and opportunity to grow into men. We owe it to them and ourselves to intervene, when and where possible, to make the world a safer space for Black boys and men to see Black masculinity beyond a cool pose. And we owe it to ourselves and them to require and expect more from what Black masculinity looks like.

My mama didn't birth any boys, but I grew up surrounded by masculinity, both by the women in my household who adopted the mannerisms and characteristics out of forced habit and by the men who sometimes failed and sometimes thrived on being cool. My intervention is in seeing Black masculinity as bigger than the box culture tries to put it in. The more variety we see in terms of who Black men are, and can be, the better. There needs to be more visibility of trans men, men with disabilities, men who are present and responsible fathers, men who identify as feminist, men who are active in their communities, men who are nonmisogynist, nonhomophobic, nonaggressive, and antiviolent. We need to see Black feminist men (outside the academy) to know they exist. They need to see each other to know they exist. Progressive and fluid—that's what Black masculinity should look like.

Eight Reasons Why Formenism Can Ruin Your Love Life

Brittney C. Cooper and Susana M. Morris

Despite the fact that "How Feminism Is Ruining Your Love Life" (an article published on *MadameNoire* in the summer of 2011) traffics in the worst kind of stereotypes around Black feminism, we want to respond in the spirit that we'd like to think the original piece was intended. The stated goal of the article is to help sisters—albeit those who have "misguidedly" used "radical Black feminism" and, as a result, are single, or rather, man-less. Unfortunately, in the guise of helping folks who have been led astray, this piece will undoubtedly lead some sisters down a road to perdition and to a world of hurt. When it comes to sisters' lives, we don't play. And for that reason, we are also gonna keep it *crunk* with our response list.

1. Not all women want a man. Some of us want women. Some of us want (multiple) men. Some of us want to be, and are, gloriously single. We can experience intimacy in multiple ways. Black women are complicated. And, low key, calling single sisters "mules" because they are holding it down by choice or circumstance—well, that ain't what Mother Zora had in mind.
2. Femininity? How about femininities (and masculinities)? There are multiple ways to be a Black woman. See #1. (Also, 1892 called. They want their old-ass notions of Black womanhood back.)

3. It takes a village, not only to raise a child, but also to be(come) a fully actualized human being. Perhaps sisters wouldn't have to work so hard if we got rid of this patriarchal hierarchy in which female friendships come last. Sisterfriends and other forms of family need not necessarily compete in one's life. (Relationships should, in fact, *not* be *user*-friendly. Beware of any sister that puts her girls on a DVR plan—pauses them at will, fast-forwards through the inconvenient parts, and makes time for them only when she has nothing better to do on a Saturday night.)

4. The "How to Get a Man Checklist Meme" = #Fail. Like majorly—and if a list about finding a partner doesn't include attention to things like shared interests, politics, goals, etc., but is (yet another) checklist on what sisters don't (read: never) get right and what we need to fix about ourselves then, frankly, it's the last thing sisters need. Can a day go by when there is not a pejorative list of dos and don'ts for Black women? (Seriously, this author sounds like the love child of Shahrazad Ali and Steve Harvey; T. D. Jakes is the godfather, and Daniel Patrick Moynihan officiated at the shotgun wedding, where Tyler Perry was the videographer.)

5. Formenism = #Setup; feminism = #ComeUp. For*men*ism is the misguided belief (read: sexist man's wet dream) that giving in to every traditional and stereotypical gender role for women will guarantee that you get a man and live happily ever after. That is, you will happily submit while T.I.'s "Whatever You Like" plays in the background. There is, however, a catch . . .

6. It's hard to yell when the bed rail's in your mouth! (We told y'all it was a setup!) So, um, yeah, giving women contradictory messages ("a ho is a ho is a ho" but don't be a prude) about sex is unhelpful. No one is saying go fuck with reckless abandon. But don't abandon your desires when you fuck. We advocate responsible, fulfilling sexual activity. Why? Cuz we grown. And cuz sex is not just for men. Women want it too. And they should be able to get it on their own terms. No apologies. Wonder how that "hey, you should just conform to the sexist sexual double standard cuz that's how it is" would've worked on the whole slavery and

racism thing? And in case you hadn't heard, Black feminist sex is the best sex ever. Even scientists agree.

7. For the record: there are plenty of sisters out here looking for a dude to be the head of her family while she serves as his willing "helpmeet," and she isn't having any more luck than the rest of us. Can't blame that on feminism. Try again.

8. *MadameNoire* might as well be called "misogynoir" if it's gonna publish this kind of ish, which promotes dangerous messages about Black women in the name of our welfare. We deserve better. #ShutItDown

Real talk: we acknowledge that the original piece speaks to a sort of disgruntled feminism, the kind that might occur among sisters who played all their feminist cards right and still don't have the (progressive) man to show for it. We feel your pain, truly. But asking us to turn a caustic, critical gaze back on Black women—rather than to take a good hard look at the systems that perpetuate patriarchy, sexism, and the like—is unfair and damaging. As crunk feminist Eesha Pandit put it, "Feminism is not about 'living your best life.' It's about decentering yourself so that we can all live our best lives."

At the end of the day, advocating that sisters seek out traditional marriage roles denies the fact that Black women and their partners, be they men and/or women, have been creating multiple models of partnership, family, and love for a very long time. Going backward to a way *we never were* is not an option; as Renina Jarmon says, "Black girls are from the future."

On Being Called Out My Name

Robin M. Boylorn

When I was working on my PhD, I swore that I would not be one of those people who tripped every time someone didn't greet them with the proper title. I didn't think I would be easily offended or bothered by someone's failure to acknowledge my qualifications. I didn't expect that my identity as a young professional and first-generation college student would dictate, almost require, that I be seen and acknowledged as an authority figure. I didn't recognize the politics of naming that works for and/or against women who are highly credentialed. I didn't know that not using the proper title for a woman was a slight, and I didn't realize failing or refusing to refer to a woman with a PhD as "Doctor" is often used as a way of throwing shade at and undermining women of color in the academy.

However, it did not take long for me to feel some kind of way about the failure of colleagues and students to refer to me by proper title. While I understand that students are far less pressed with being politically or socially correct with professors these days, I can't help but take issue when I am called by my first name in a professional context, without permission. When this happens I feel uncomfortable and uneasy, as if I am being undermined and thrown the shadiest of shade.

Many times the lack of formality and the assumption of casual interaction feel disrespectful. It is as if regardless of my training and background, some students assume I can't possibly know more than them, resulting in the academic equivalent to the infamous childish rant, "You ain't my mama, you don't tell me what to do" ("You are a Black woman, you can't tell/teach me shit").

This is textbook intersectionality. When this happens, I find myself in a conundrum, wondering if this presumed informality is based on my race, gender, age, or some combination of the three. I can't help but think about how Black women have historically been seen as not worthy of particular social etiquette or respect simply because they were Black. In the Jim Crow South, while White women were referred to as "ma'am" by Black children and adults, Black women were called by their first names, even by White children, even if they were elders. White children were allowed to reinforce, literally, that Black women (and men) garnered less regard and respect than they did. I think about these things and wonder, when I am called by my first name, instead of Doctor, is it a slight, a mistake, a social miscue, or a reminder to put me "in my place"?

Some faculty members are automatically given the courtesy of title acknowledgment. I remember sitting in a professional meeting with staff members and professors across campus, seated next to another faculty woman of color (we were the only two people of color in the room). Throughout the meeting, staff members referred to the White male professor in the room as Dr. ____, while calling me and my colleague by our first names. Don't get me wrong, in professional contexts, with other professionals, I don't expect to be called Doctor, but it seems to mean something when I am called by my name while the White man in the room, whose credentials are no higher than mine, is addressed as Doctor. There was a distinction being made, making me feel like my PhD was illegitimate or irrelevant—and that the same could be said for me.

There are politics in naming, and as a Black woman with a PhD who juggles racial micro- and macroaggressions every day of my life, I don't want to wonder what is meant when informality is assumed. In professional contexts it is important that boundaries and distinctions of relationship are clear. Because I don't meet the stereotypical standards of a professor (or a PhD), it can be problematic and uncomfortable when I am not acknowledged in the same way other professors are.

I realize that there are exceptions to this rule. For example, as a PhD student I was encouraged (and given permission) to interact with and engage my professors by their first names. (However, depending on my relationship/s with them, I sometimes still reverted to formal titles.) And some academic and departmental cultures are intentionally informal in an attempt at being egalitarian, encouraging students and professors to interact on a first-name basis. I don't have a problem with these generalized and understood preferences. It is the pick-and-choose naming based on skin color or gender that I take issue with.

I personally think students should always be formal with their professors (those they work with and those they don't know, both in person and in digital communication) unless and/or until they are given permission not to be. Being informal without permission can be interpreted as disrespectful, presumptuous, and unprofessional (when coming from a student), especially for faculty who are sometimes so easily dismissed as authority figures. My colleagues of color who are men or masculine of center don't report the same liberties being taken that I have experienced. My sista-docta colleagues do. That tells me there is something to being called out our name(s).

Jesus Wasn't a Slut Shamer, or How Conservative Theology Harms Black Women

Brittney C. Cooper

I'm a feminist who believes in God. Raised Christian, I still attend church. But what I am not is a person who will willingly check her brain, political convictions, or academic training at the door in order to enter the house of God or to participate in a community of faith. Express homophobic views, tell me that God requires me to let a man rule my house because I have a vagina, or spout a prosperity theology premised on the idea that poor folks are poor because they lack faith, and you are likely to see me get up and walk out.

I love Jesus, and I remain a person of faith because I know, to put it in the parlance of the Black churches of my youth, how good God has been to me. And while that kind of God-talk doesn't play well in secular academic contexts, it doesn't have to. My Christianity isn't about trying to save anyone else's soul but my own. I know that's not what a good evangelical is supposed to say, but if you haven't figured it out yet, a good evangelical is not what I'm trying to be.

Black women are the most religious demographic in this country, and most of that religious identification falls within the bounds of Christianity. But if Black feminism does not grapple with the fact that Black women still love the Black Church, and still sustain that institution in startling numbers, it will miss a significant segment of the population. And that is untenable because conservative evangelical Black churches are one of the central places that Black women pick up harmful gender ideology.

In 2014 Toni Braxton, the daughter of a preacher and product of a conservative Christian family, released a memoir in which she discusses her one-time belief that her son's autism was a punishment from God for having an abortion. Luckily she has revised her thinking, no longer seeing autism as a form of God's judgment.

Autism is not a punishment. It is a different way of learning and being and encodes different kinds of ability. Disability is not a punishment. Disability is a fact of life. And it is an opportunity, if we are mindful, to think about how to make our built and lived worlds more hospitable for each and every person that has to live in it.

As for abortions, we really need to think about whether a loving God wants women to have children that they don't want to have or can't afford to have. We need to ask ourselves if God conscripts women's wombs in service of His purposes (sorry for the gendered language but evangelical God is always male). And if God does such things, as the story of Jesus's mother kinda suggests, we need to ask ourselves if we have the right to disagree. (Like what if Mary had said no when the angel came to her?) We need to think about whether God actually dictates that a fetus's life is more important than its mother's life. We need to ask ourselves if God values our reproductive capacity over us.

Moreover, abortion ethics in the church are steeped in shame, shaming women for having sex outside of marriage, while assuming married women don't have or need abortions. But it is clear to me from the biblical story of the woman caught in adultery, a woman who Jesus saved from being stoned, that Jesus was not a slut shamer. He didn't permit his community to cast stones at a woman because of her sexual practices, but he invited that community to consider their own practices. And in so doing, that story demonstrates, among many other things, that our impulse to judge and harm others is fundamentally about all the things we don't want to confront in ourselves.

Conservative theology, of the evangelical sort, is rooted in a view of God as a great judge who metes out divine retribution for our sins. Because of Jesus's crucifixion and resurrection, we are allowed to have a personal relationship with this God, but we better toe the line. God loves us and forgives us, but we better be in a continual state of confession, repentance, and trying to live right. Otherwise, our sin will bring us terrible consequences because even though God loves us, the divine Homie don't play that.

"Sin" is a word that is used often in conservative evangelical churches. There's a whole lot of talk about individual sin, the preponderance of which seems to be of a sexual nature. A whole lot of talk, a lot of fear, and a lot of guilt. Individual sin, in this theological reckoning, separates us from God and puts us outside the realm of God's blessing, puts us beyond the "hedge of protection," where all manner of evil will befall us. And it's all our fault because of our failure to deal with our pesky sin.

We don't talk much though about the sins of capitalism or racism or sexism or homophobia or militarism or the evils of the prison industrial complex. We tell women to wear longer dresses and boys to pull up their pants. We seem to believe that if we merely conquer our individual sins, God will protect us from the effects of all the other "isms." We in the Black Church have allowed church philanthropy to take the place of radical social critique. It's incredibly shortsighted.

From this angle, punishment looks like God holding us from achieving the very societal ideals that these systems hold up as carrots—a fancy house and car, a beautiful partner, lots of money. Instead of questioning our investments in these systems, we think serving God will give us greater success within them.

So many of us have a faith built on theologically thin terrain.

This brings me to Sherri Shepherd, former cohost of *The View*. Back in 2010 and 2011, I watched fascinated as she candidly discussed her courtship with Lamar Sally and her choice to remain celibate until she married him. She routinely expressed shame over the multiple abortions she had in her youth. Her deeply conservative evangelical commitments made her and Elisabeth Hasselbeck unlikely bedfellows on the show.

According to conservative evangelical scripts, Sherri Shepherd "did it God's way." She courted Lamar properly, waited until after marriage for sex, and should now be on her way to happily ever after.

But she isn't.

In 2014 Sally filed for separation papers, prompting Shepherd to file for divorce. In a bizarre addendum to their prenuptial agreement, Sally made several troubling demands of Shepherd. The revised agreement included statements like:

> I, Sherry Sally, am a happy, godly, attractive, and sexy wife. I provide a peaceful and pleasant haven for my husband to come home to. I respect my husband's opinions and recognize him as the leader of our home. I always speak well of my husband to others and look for specific ways to compliment his fine character and behavior. I enjoy having sex with my husband. I crave intimacy with him and want to be uninhibited and free in our lovemaking together. I care about my appearance and take effort to look attractive and stay fit. I am a fun person who loves to laugh.

It goes on to say:

> It is my joy to submit to my husband as a way to honor God. Even if my husband doesn't respond the way I'd like, I will respect him and be loyal to him.

Say what now?

So you need a prenup to tell your wife that she enjoys sex with you? You need a prenup to ensure she gives you compliments? And you need a prenup to make her "joyfully submit" to you?

My head aches. And so does my ass.

All of this language is straight out of conservative Christian theological doctrine. In fact, it reminds me of an unfortunate experience I had in a class I took at my former church several years ago called Marriage without Regrets. When the author of the study, famed Christian writer Kay Arthur, started railing against wayward women who had stepped out of their rightful place, causing the downfall of society, I knew that something had gone incredibly wrong.

But what was more striking was the fact that the Marriage without Regrets class was overwhelmingly populated by single women, all hoping to prepare and position themselves for a "godly mate." In order to do so, we were supposed to endure sixteen weeks of study about "what the Bible says about marriage" and how to style our lives to meet such goals. I dropped out at week three, right around the time that the facilitator told us that as women we were "biblically mandated" to manage a household.

My household-management skills suck. And since I'm utterly uninterested in the domestic arts, I don't anticipate that they will get any better.

Moreover, to riff on Dr. Renita Weems, one of my favorite womanist preachers, I already have a head. I'm not looking for a man to provide me one. Or, as I've heard more than one popular Black minister put it, I'm not interested in letting him be the head while I be the neck. What the entire . . . ? (Well, I'm talking about Jesus things, so let me not show out with the profanity).

But I know a whole lot of women who think like Sherri Shepherd. I used to roll hard with chicks like Sherri Shepherd. They have this view that celibacy and proper courtship are "God's way." They have a view that following this plan to marriage will ensure God's blessings and a happily ever after.

In the case of Lamar Sally, it seems that all this God-talk covered up the screwed-up beliefs of a deeply controlling man who sees women as property, views sex as being primarily for his pleasure, and thinks women serve the ornamental function of looking pretty and keeping him happy.

I wonder how much better our relationships and partnerships might be if churches spent less time regulating our intimate space and more time dealing with the lack of emotional and spiritual maturity that plagues so many unions.

Moreover, I long for the church as an institution to stop touting this biblical literalism and biblical inerrancy madness. It encourages a shallow faith, grounded in false notions of security, propped up by people who have been discouraged from thinking for themselves.

When I see the way the Old Testament demands that women marry their rapists, I have a problem with that.

When I see the ways in which the Old Testament seems to sanction genocide so a chosen group can get to their "Promised Land," I have a problem with that.

When I see the proscriptions Paul or the Pauline writers place on women in the New Testament, the calls for silence and submission, I take issue with that.

When I see discussion of queer people as an "abomination," I disagree.

And when Paul tells slaves to "be kind to your masters," I wholeheartedly reject such thinking. And I'm so glad Harriet Tubman and Harriet Jacobs and Frederick Douglass and all the rest rejected it, too.

The idea that we can't struggle with the biblical text, that we have to agree with and live by everything it says, is not only impossible but unhealthy. For Black women to agree to live by it all is for us to sign up for silence, submission, and slavery. Literally. And that would mean that the Bible and Christianity offer us no greater alternative than what White folks dreamed for us when they dragged us to these shores.

We deserve more than that. And God wants more for us than that. And that means that we have to stop letting these preachers toss the Bible in our face as a rule book. We have to stop letting them manipulate us with fear of divine punishment for asking questions and coming to different conclusions. Based on this conservatism, the church exploits and appropriates Black women's time, labor, and money, while giving back to us a theology that does not serve us well. I'm not denying Black Christian women's agency, experiences of God, or accusing them of false consciousness. I'm saying that we have bought into some ways of thinking that don't serve us well, that limit us spiritually, and that often do us harm.

At my most conservative, I was incredibly resentful and angry with God because I felt I could never live up to the standard. I suffered perpetual guilt and anxiety and got little joy. I know better now.

Now I view the Bible as an invitation. An invitation to come to the table equipped with stories of other people's faith journeys and to use their stories to grapple with my own journey with God. I come able to see and call out racism, sexism, patriarchy, and homophobia in the text. While we will never live in a faith journey outside of these contexts, the text becomes instructive for thinking about who we are, what we're capable of, what we want to be, and what we don't want to be. And we learn about ways in which God showed up for generations prior to us and are perhaps encouraged that God will show up for us, too.

So many Black women have full-bodied commitments to church—we give our mind, heart, spirit, body, time, labor, and money to the church. We deserve for it to serve our needs. We deserve for the theologies we hear to be liberatory. We deserve for those theologies to help us to create healthy, full, loving lives, whether we have partners or not, whether we want marriage or not, children or not, sex or not.

Bad theology is harmful. It misrepresents who God is and who we are. But we must give ourselves permission to construct a new way to live if spiritual matters are going to retain their importance to us. I am actively in the process of reconstructing an informed theology that works for my life by reading people like Delores Williams and Katie Cannon and Wil Gafney and Rachel Held Evans and Brian McLaren and Jay Bakker. And if you didn't know, it's in our spiritual Black feminist legacy to do exactly that. I'll end with one of my favorite quotes from Anna Julia Cooper:

> And I do not mean by faith the holding of correct views and unimpeachable opinions on mooted questions, merely; nor do I understand it to be the ability to forge cast-iron formulas and dub them TRUTH. For while I do not deny that absolute and eternal truth *is*— still truth must be infinite, and as incapable as infinite space, of being encompassed and confined by one age or nation, sect or country— much less by one little creature's finite brain. To me, faith means *treating the truth as true.*

Figure out what is true for you and have enough faith in yourself and your God to treat those truths as true.

RACE AND RACISM: ALL BLACK LIVES MATTER

Introduction

When Trayvon Martin was killed in February of 2012, the precarity of Black life became real again in the most visceral of ways. Slain just a few months before the reelection of President Barack Obama, Trayvon's death ended any fleeting optimism we might have retained about the possibilities of Black life and racial progress under an Obama presidency. Seventeen months later, when his killer, George Zimmerman, was acquitted at trial, we were reminded in a most violent way that having a Black man at the head of global empire still could not guarantee justice for a young Black boy walking home with a bag of Skittles and a can of iced tea.

We followed the lead of the radical Black feminist women Alicia Garza, Patrisse Cullors, and Opal Tometi, who began to proclaim after the acquittal of George Zimmerman that Black Lives Matter. This current movement is rooted in the most radical dimensions of Black feminist politics, particularly in its insistence on fighting for the liberation and safety of all Black lives, including those of queer and trans Black people.

We know that for too many Black people, violence and surveillance are routine aspects of daily life. That a run to the corner store for snacks during the game can end with a young man bleeding to death alone on a street corner makes clear the extent to which regular movement through time and space is, for Black people, always tethered to the possibility of violence, a potential moment where one's humanity is challenged.

For Crunkista, that moment came when she went to Sears for a day of retail therapy, only to be accused of shoplifting by mall security. Black and Latinx people do not have the luxury of being presumed innocent as they shop, walk, talk on the phone, drive to their destination, sit at their desks at school, attend pool parties, or ride the train in wine country with friends. All of these incidents have led to humiliating encounters with law-enforcement officers, broadcast in the media, in the years since Trayvon Martin was killed.

Though much of the current movement found its moment after Michael Brown Jr. was unceremoniously slaughtered by a Ferguson, Missouri, police officer in August 2014, the moment that we began to collectively decry the taking of Black lives with impunity was with Trayvon.

How do we write and articulate our experiences as women of color living under these kinds of conditions? How do we articulate that our Black lives, our Latinx lives, our South Asian lives matter, in the context of US imperialism that frequently fails to concede this as a foregone conclusion?

It is hard to stand committed to a critique of anti-Black US state violence and the many violent incursions of the state into the lives of people of color when US Black politics is still inclined to center the experiences of violence against young men like Michael Brown and Tamir Rice, rather than the killings of Rekia Boyd and Aiyana Stanley-Jones.

To be a Black feminist in this moment is to have to continually negotiate the problem of rampant police brutality against Black communities, the regular killing of unarmed young Black men, while vigilantly proclaiming that "Black women's lives matter too." And when we say Black women's lives matter, we don't just mean cisgender Black women. In 2015 more than twenty trans women of color were murdered in the United States. In very few cases were the killers of these sisters brought to justice. This, too, this killing of trans women with impunity, is state-sanctioned violence.

As a collective of cisgender women of color, we stand in solidarity with trans women and fully acknowledge the perspectival limitations of writing about what feminism means solely from the perspective of cisgender women. For *all* Black lives to matter, we all have to be willing to refuse complicity in a system that says that only certain experiences are worthy of protection. Traditional gender categories of womanhood and ladyhood won't protect any of us.

But the work of making Black Lives Matter does not just happen in the streets. It happens in community. As Sheri Davis-Faulkner reminds us, we must "address oppression in community." We write and think together as a collective about feminism and the problems of patriarchy, capitalism, heterosexism, and White supremacy because there is accountability in community. There is, if you do it right, shared labor in community. There is, if you do it right, care in community. In community, it becomes clear that We Got Us.

Thinking about how to build across difference, and very specifically to build with White allies, is work that many feel is antithetical to the proclamation that Black lives matter. Many hear that proclamation as being fundamentally anti-White. Many people, it remains clear, don't read enough or know their history. Being anti–White supremacy is not the same as being anti–White people. If White people want to help dismantle White supremacy, they are welcome at the table.

The CFC is composed of all kinds of women of color. We are not all Black, but we are all Brown-skinned girls writing and riding for freedom. And we are all deeply rooted in the foundational texts of Black feminism, because in them we see a foundation for solidarity and the work of justice across our respective racial backgrounds. When we secure the integrity of Black lives, particularly the lives of transgender and cisgender Black women, we will have created a foundation in which all people can be free. All lives matter, but that proposition only works if *all* Black lives are included.

Thus, when Brittney Cooper critiqued the racial politics of Slut-Walks back in 2011, she was challenging this necessary antirape movement to think about what it would mean to articulate an anti-rape framework that acknowledged the particular precarity that Black women face. She asked whether the reclamation of "slut" really can do the kind of cultural work that SlutWalk organizers claimed. A racially conscious antirape agenda is all the more urgent in this moment where we have learned of Bill Cosby's numerous alleged rapes, primarily of White women, and where we have witnessed Daniel Holtzclaw in Oklahoma be convicted of the rape of several Black women, whom he victimized and exploited because they were sex workers confronting poverty and addiction.

This group of essays demonstrates that the perennial battle of Black feminism remains the same—demanding both that mainstream feminist movements don't elide Black women's struggles and that mainstream Black politics don't forget Black women either.

Can we live? This is the question that Eesha Pandit asks when she challenges the gaze of the White photographer, snapping pictures of Indian people going about their daily lives. Can we live without being surveilled as we shop for clothes at the mall, walk home from the store, or sell our wares in the marketplace? Can we live without being raped and then blamed for wearing the wrong thing?

That we are perpetually "waiting to exhale" is not just some throw-away line from a 1990s Black rom-com. The constriction of Black breath, the stealing of Black lives by those sworn to protect them, has become as much a part of the history of the twenty-first century as the storied narrative of the first Black president.

It boggles the mind. It fucks with the heart.

Our chests constricted with fear as we watched police smother Eric Garner on a Staten Island street corner as he repeatedly cried out, "I can't breathe."

Our hearts ached when we watched a police officer threaten to tase twenty-eight-year-old Sandra Bland after pulling her over for fail-ure to signal. We still scratch our heads wondering how she died in a jail cell, just a few miles away from her new dream job.

Her anger and Serena William's anger, profiled in this section, may have had different targets, but they were rooted in the same cry—the demand to be treated with dignity and respect.

Can we live?

And can we breathe?

Refereeing Serena: Racism, Anger, and US (Women's) Tennis

Brittney C. Cooper

Yesterday I tuned in, as I have done nearly every summer since I was nine or ten years old, to watch the finals of the US Open. Serena Williams was vying for her fifteenth Grand Slam title against Australian player Sam Stosur.

As I tuned in, I steeled myself for the endless stream of racist commentary from the sportscasters.

All honest tennis players and fans will admit that the Williams sisters have transformed the game of women's tennis. They have brought power and speed to bear in ways that used to be relegated to the men's game. With their power serves, speed, and willingness to chase down and make impossible shots, the sisters also upped the physical fitness requirements for champions.

When asked three years ago how the Williams sisters had transformed the game, Darren Cahill offered rather hesitantly, "They have opened the doors to people from all walks of life." Really? That's it? Tennis is more colorful now that the Williams sisters have been a part of it? Thanks for the magnanimity, Darren.

But it is the female commentators who make me want to spit nails. Mary Carillo and occasional commentator and tennis legend Chris Evert are the worst of them all. Mary Carillo vacillates between loving Serena—now, anyway—and criticizing her. In the early part of their careers, the sisters' winning game was attributed to their powerful bodies. But they were frequently accused of "lacking strategy," "not thinking about their shots," and "relying on their natural athleticism." When they started coming to the net and winning, their success was attributed yet again to their "natural athletic ability." The Williams sisters were represented as hypermasculine, unattractive women overpowering dainty White female tennis players (although Jennifer Capriati, Svetlana Kuznetsova, Kim Clijsters, and Justine Henin are anything but dainty). These narratives about Black bodies as "naturally athletic," "more powerful," "more wild," "less thoughtful," and "less strategic" and Black female bodies as "(un)naturally strong," "invulnerable," and "unattractive" are central to Western narratives of White racial superiority.

I knew the hateration would be back in full force this year when I tuned in to watch Donald Young, a Black male wild-card player in an early round match.

As Young played, Patrick McEnroe went on a diatribe about how "undisciplined" Young is and how the US Tennis Association (USTA) has had "problems" with him. Young stopped training at the USTA's tennis academies and has instead chosen to let his parents train him at the facility they opened in Atlanta. But if Black players continue to defect from the formal ranks of the USTA, to train by themselves, perhaps the issue is not with the players or their "lack of discipline" but rather with the USTA itself. Perhaps the *problem* is with a tennis system that largely sees Black players as a "problem."

How does it feel to be a problem?

Still, it is the Williams sisters who bring to the surface most of the problems with racism in US tennis. After losing the first set to Sam Stosur, Serena hit a winner at 30–40 in the first game of the second set. Trying to pump herself up, she yelled out, "Come on!" before Stosur hit the ball, apparently violating a little known "point hindrance" rule. The point, played at 30–40 on Serena's racket, was taken away, giving Stosur the first game. The ref had the discretion to call for replay of the point or take it away if it was deemed intentional. Clearly, it was unintentional.

Serena gave the ref the business for the next three games. She accused her of being the ref "that screwed me over last time," remarking, "That is so not cool." Turns out, the ref was not in fact the same person. Then during two changeovers Serena mocked the referee, telling her that she was "unattractive inside." As she insulted the ref, Serena told her, "Don't even look at me. I am not the one!"

Serena's outbursts could be costly. At the 2009 US Open, she was fined $82,500 and put on probation for threatening to shove a ball down the throat of a referee who kept giving her poor calls. After yesterday's show of anger, she could be banned altogether. That move would be unfortunate, unfair, and costly for the game of women's tennis.

Yes, Serena lost yesterday's match because Sam Stosur played better. But I must point out that Serena played the semifinal until almost midnight on Saturday evening, only to have to turn around and play the finals match at 4:30 p.m. Sunday. The tennis officials capitalized on the Williams sisters' prime-time appeal by making Williams play her match after the two men's semis. The move makes no sense (why split up the women's semis?) unless we consider what the Williams sisters mean for the US Open's bottom line.

And frankly, I see Serena's outburst as understandable and amusing. Call me a Williams stan if you want to. It's true. But this is not about simple loyalty.

Yes, I'm aware of all the ways in which her acts in this moment reinforce stereotypes of the angry Black woman. However, we cannot use our investment in a respectability politic that demands that Black women never show anger or emotion in the face of injustice to demand Serena's silence. Resistance is often impolite, and frequently it demands that we skirt the rules.

Even so, when asked about her loss yesterday, Serena, while not remorseful about her exchange with the ref, was nothing but gracious to Sam Stosur on her win.

Moreover, the USTA loves angry, heckling players—as long as they are White men. Early in the tournament, there was a video and interview tribute to Jimmy Connors, a player legendary for his angry outbursts on the court. In the tribute they devoted extended time to showing one of the more famous of these outbursts in a celebratory manner. White anger is entertaining; Black anger must be contained.

Serena continues to disrupt tennis spaces with her dark-skinned, powerful body, her flamboyant sartorial choices, her refusal to conform to the professional tennis obstacle course, and her willingness to get angry and show it.

That disruption is necessary—because however "right" or "wrong" it may technically be—it demonstrates that all is not well racially in tennis. Black folks—men and women—are still largely understood within a narrative of brute, undisciplined physical strength rather than as athletes who bring both physical and intellectual skills to their game. As long as these issues remain, tennis will continue to be "unattractive" from the inside out.

On Kimani Gray, or To Be Young, Guilty, and Black

Susana M. Morris

I've been trying to wrap my mind around the situation with Kimani Gray, but it just doesn't make sense. I mean, considering the unceasing frequency of US police brutality, the story is "simple" enough. Sixteen-year-old Kimani, known as Kiki to his loved ones, was out late, returning from a gathering. While out in East Flatbush, Brooklyn, Kimani and his friends were approached by two men, apparently plainclothes police officers with records of brutality and excessive force, who sidled up in an unmarked van. While those close to Kimani claim the youth was simply adjusting his belt or waistband, the police have claimed that Kimani pulled out a .38, which caused the officers to unload eleven rounds of ammunition into his body, killing him there in the street.

Simple, right? Not even close.

For every Black and Brown person I've spoken with, this is so clearly another example of our communities' ever increasing militarization that, not only marks our bodies as inherently deviant and always guilty, but also is hell-bent on killing and/or imprisoning our people with impunity.

Although they are little more than half the population of New York, African Americans and Latinxs were subject to almost 90 percent of the incidences of stop-and-frisk in the city in recent years. Stop-and-frisk policies are not only morally unsound but statistics have clearly shown that they are also expensive and inefficient. The *New Yorker* reports, "As for the effectiveness of stop-and-frisk, since Bloomberg doubled down on the program, in 2002, murder attempts, robberies, and assaults have fallen by less than one percent. Arrests are made in about six percent of the stops, and a firearm is found in about one percent."

Likewise, Vincent Warren notes on MSNBC.com:

> Every first-year graduate student learns that correlation does not prove causality, but the NYPD routinely claims that the city's falling crime rates are caused in part by their stop-and-frisk practices. There is not a single published study providing evidence for this claim. The truth is that no one knows what has caused the city's drop in crime, but given the fact that only 6% of stops result in arrest and the vast

majority of these are for so-called quality of life violations, it seems improbable, to say the least, that crime rates are going down because of stop and frisk.

Then again, cost is no object in a police state, right?

Reading about Kimani's story takes me back to my own youth in Fort Lauderdale, Florida, where I witnessed police negligence and violence firsthand. While they could never be counted on to come when someone was going upside your head or stealing someone's car, they for damn sure would show up and show out in other moments, making my already unsafe hood even less safe. I learned to be more afraid of the police than of my dope-fiend neighbor who bashed my bedroom window open to steal or the pimps that stood just outside the gate of middle school everyday at 3:00 p.m. They were treacherous, but I knew how to deal with them. But the police—they were a wild card. They could come into your house, disrespect you, put their hands on you, talk to you any kind of way, and you'd just be standing there contemplating the virtues of taking a cast-iron frying pan to their skulls but remembering your duty to your family. But, for some people, sometimes that cast-iron pan would win.

Twenty years ago, something happened with the police that I'll never forget. I was an eighth grader, walking home from school. A big crowd had gathered to watch two girls, two of my classmates in fact, tussle. These sisters were rolling around and around in the dirt. Look, I wasn't a fool. I wasn't really trying to be all up in this altercation, but the crowd was so big that I couldn't get through or around it. So I watched, shaking my head, knowing that one girl was jealous of another and that some knucklehead dude was at the center of this drama. It wasn't until they separated that I saw how horrible the fight had been. The sister that initiated the fight had carried a razor blade in her mouth and sliced the other girl on her face and neck. This young sister stumbled past me, her face and neck swollen and bloodied, her white T-shirt splattered with her own blood.

I could not believe my own eyes. I had just watched someone get slashed with a razor. I was appalled. I was disgusted. I was worried for my classmate. Would she bleed to death? (She did, in fact, live.) She lived a block away from me, but despite her injuries seemed to be making a defiant walk home. I looked around to see if anyone was there to help. There were mostly other teens like myself, standing there with a mixture of curiosity, disbelief, and horror.

Then, I spotted the police. They had been in the background all along. I mean, they were always there along my route home, apathetic observers who never stopped when drug transactions were made brazenly, out in the open, or when twelve-year-old girls were propositioned for sex in broad daylight. But on that day, they really jumped the shark. As I scanned the crowd, looking for an adult to help—my go-to adult helpers have always been older Black women—I saw the police pointing and laughing at my bloodied classmate. I'm not talking about a nervous giggle or an uncomfortable chuckle, but some of that old bent over, clutching your stomach, and wiping your eyes kind of laughter. Rather than going to the aid of an injured young woman (who was wounded by another injured young woman), these fools were laughing. It was as if we were all slaves in a Roman gladiator's ring, killing each other for their amusement. The image of their laughter haunts me to this day.

Years later, when I read Toni Morrison's *Beloved* in college, I came across this line that has stayed with me, haunting me, ever reminding me of the constant dehumanization Blacks endure under White supremacy. After the novel's protagonist, Sethe, is abused by the Whites that run her plantation, she remembers, "They handled me like I was the cow, no, the goat, back behind the stable because it was too nasty to stay in with the horses." I felt that way, felt that way for my classmate, on the day I saw her attacked and no one rushed to help her.

So, when reports allege that Kimani Gray pulled a .38 on the admittedly plainclothes officers, I do not think of Black-on-Black crime or out-of-control urban Black youths that are menaces to society. I think of a kid who lived in a war zone, a kid who not only could not count on those who vow to protect and serve to do either of those things, but who could also expect the police to be the major perpetrators of state-sanctioned terrorism.

Let me be clear. I do not think that systemic violence is strategy that is going to liberate our communities. And I do not actually think Kimani had a weapon. However, I would understand why a kid would think he was in danger if two random dudes rolled up on him in a car and jumped out yelling. And I do understand the pain, anger, and frustration the protestors in East Flatbush have been expressing. And I wish that stories like this were not a constant unbroken loop in our communities, continually traumatizing us into silence and submission.

SlutWalks vs. Ho Strolls

Brittney C. Cooper

SlutWalk Toronto started as an activist response to the ill-informed, misguided words of a Toronto police officer who suggested that "women should avoid dressing like sluts in order not to be victimized." Women in Toronto were enraged, and rightfully so, and Slut-Walks have become a way to dramatize the utter ignorance and danger of the officer's statements. And on that note, it fucks very hard with the concept and with the response, which is creative, appropriate, and powerful.

What gives me pause is the claim in SlutWalk Toronto's mission statement of sorts that because they are "tired of being oppressed by slut-shaming; of being judged by our sexuality and feeling unsafe as a result," they are reclaiming and reappropriating the word "slut." Um, no thank you?

Here's the source of my ambivalence: as I read the mission statement, I was struck by the righteous indignation these women had over being called "slut." While that indignation is absolutely warranted, it also feels, on a visceral level, as though it comes from women who are in fact not used to being fully defined by negative sexual referents.

Perhaps my cynicism reflects my own experience as a Black woman of the hip hop generation in the US, or a Black woman who's a member of the Western world period. It goes without saying that Black women have always been understood to be lascivious, hypersexed, and always ready and willing. When I think of the daily assaults I hear in the form of copious incantations of "bitch" and "ho" in hip hop music directed at Black women, it's hard to not feel a bit incensed at the "how dare you" quality of the SlutWalk protests, which feel very much like the protests of privileged White girls who still have an expectation that the world will treat them with dignity and respect.

The first activist response I ever heard to such mistreatment was Queen Latifah's 1993 Grammy-winning song, "U.N.I.T.Y." It energized a community and opened a space for much-needed conversation. But sisters did not line up to go on symbolic, collective ho strolls—for good and, I think, obvious reasons.

So maybe the best way to deal with the debates about reappropriating the term "slut" is the way I deal with the whole N-word debate. As a Black person, who occasionally uses the N-word (with an "a" on the end), I am admittedly ambivalent about whether or not the use of the term among Black people really does constitute a reappropriation. I've heard and read most of the arguments, and I remain . . . ambivalent. Generally, though, I think the word is unproductive.

That said, I balk at older Black folks who act as though the hip hop generation are the first Black people to toss the word around. Read any nineteenth-century Black literature and you'll know different. What I'm clear about, however, is that to use or not to use is a decision that lies solely within Black communities. White people simply don't get a say; the word is off-limits to them. Black folks have surely won the right, long held by White folks, to struggle and determine among ourselves how we will refer to and define ourselves. Period.

For me, so it is with the word "slut." It is off-limits to me. But for those who have been shamed and disciplined and violently abused on the basis of its usage, they have the prerogative to determine whether to reclaim or not. As a word used to shame White women who do not conform to morally conservative norms about chaste sexuality, the term very much reflects White women's specific struggles around sexuality and abuse. Although plenty of Black women have been called "slut," I believe Black women's histories are different, in that Black female sexuality has always been understood from without to be deviant, hyper, and excessive. Therefore, the word "slut" has not been used to discipline (shame) us into chaste moral categories, as we have largely been understood to be unable to practice "normal" and "chaste" sexuality anyway.

But perhaps we have come to a point in feminist movement building where we need to acknowledge that differing histories necessitate differing strategies. This is why I'm somewhat ambivalent about accusing my White sistren of being racist. If your history is one of having your sexuality regulated by the use of the term "slut" for disciplinary purposes, then SlutWalk is an effective answer.

What becomes an issue is those White women and liberal feminist women of color who argue that "slut" is a universal category of female experience, irrespective of race. I recognize that there are many women of color who are participating in the SlutWalk movement, and I support those sisters who do, particularly women who are doing it in solidarity and coalition. But rather than forcing White women to get on the diversity train with regard to the inclusivity of SlutWalk, perhaps we need to redirect our racial vigilance. By that I mean I'd prefer that White women acknowledge that they are in fact organizing around a problematic use of terminology *endemic to White communities and cultures*.

In doing so, this would force an acknowledgment that the experience of womanhood being defended here—that of White women—is not universal, but is under attack and worthy of being defended all the same.

Alice Walker said recently:

> I've always understood the word "slut" to mean a woman who freely enjoys her own sexuality in any way she wants to, undisturbed by other people's wishes for her behavior. Sexual desire originates in her and is directed by her. In that sense it is a word well worth retaining.

Clearly, from a strictly prosex perspective, I could see why it would be attractive to reclaim this word. And within Black communities, certainly there is, like in most other communities, a tacit shaming of "loose women" and a strident investment in women being "good girls and ladies." Still, slut shaming has particular resonance for White women, whose sexuality has largely been constructed based upon middle-class, often Christian, heteronorms of proper chaste womanhood. The positive referent about chastity against which "slut" becomes the negative referent has never been universally available to Black women. A Black woman who "freely enjoys her own sexuality" has been called "jezebel," "hoochie," "hoodrat," "ho," "freak," and, perhaps, "slut." In other words, "slut" is merely part of a constellation of terms used to denigrate Black female sexuality; it is not at the center of how our particular sexuality has been constructed.

But "sluttiness" and "slut shaming" around sexuality are, in fact, central to White women's experiences of sexuality. So to start a movement around that word is to inherently place White women and their experiences at the center. To actually be able to materially reclaim "slut," however much one has been slut shamed, is to have the power to work within a universe of multiple meanings in which both committed chastity and casual coitus, and everything in between, are understood as sexual options. For Black women, our struggles with sexuality are to find the space of recognition that exists between the hypervisibility of our social construction as hoes, jezebels, hoochies, and skanks and the invisibility proffered by a respectability politic that tells us it's always safer to dissemble. To reclaim "slut" as an empowered experience of sexuality does not move Black women out of these binaries. We are always already sexually free, insatiable, ready to go, freaky, dirty, and by consequence, unrapeable. When it comes to reclamations of sexuality, in some senses, Black women are always already fucked.

Thus, the politics of reclaiming "slut" expose the fault lines that exist between the discursive, the material, and the symbolic. And the degree to which reclaiming "slut" will be placed in any of these categories is necessarily determined by the power and privilege that each SlutWalker has. If Black women's discursive acts cannot change our material realities with regard to our sexuality, then our actions become merely symbolic. Our actions will come to exist only in the realm of representation. The truth is probably somewhere in the middle. Black women do have agency. Our voices do matter, and our interventions will contour this mo(ve)ment, though we are unsure yet just what those contours will look like. But our commitment to discursive acts must be measured—by our histories, by our material realities, by the psychic and social costs, and by the attendant benefits of such acts for improving the quality of our (sex) lives. We are long past the point of putting our own bodies on the line for political acts that improve White women's lives while leaving the rest of us in the dust.

Perhaps, also, if White women could recognize SlutWalk as being rooted in White female experience, it would provide an opportunity for them to participate in coalition and solidarity with similar movements that are inclusive and reflective of the experiences of women of color.

One example is the Stop Street Harassment (SSH) movement—a multiracial movement that has led to SSH campaigns throughout the US and abroad. This movement, too, works from the premise that streets and schools should be safe for women, but it recognizes that challenges to that safety, while similar in some respects, can differ across race and class. And as I said earlier, different histories necessitate different strategies. In that regard, I don't think sisters will be lining up to go on a symbolic "Ho Stroll" anytime soon.

Fuck Sears, or When Mall Cops Attack

Crunkista

This weekend I found myself with something beautifully rare: one *whole* day where I didn't have *any* work to do, didn't have any meetings, no pending deadlines, no lunch or dinner plans . . . basically no responsibilities. It felt *amazing.* I could spend an entire day just doing something for *me,* while thinking about the meaning of life. Seriously, what a privilege! On these rare occasions that I have a large block of free time, I like to go to the nearest bookstore, buy a cup of coffee, and just sit down for hours looking through dozens and dozens of fashion magazines. You see, I'm an (affordable) fashion junkie. I know it may seem random for a crunk feminist to love all things gossip and fashion, but it just makes me feel all warm inside to look at the pretty pictures and think about ways I can add different looks to my existing wardrobe. Most of all, sitting down by myself with a warm cup of coffee feels like I am doing something special. Just. For. Me.

While surfing through my Instagram and various fashion blogs, I felt a new surge of inspiration. Today, I was going to find my balance. I was going to write my next CFC post about self-care, fashion, keeping positive, and making the best of what you've got. I thought I should write about all the things we *can* do to find happiness and motivation when we find ourselves in a professional or even emotional rut. Right then, I came across a picture of Khloe Kardashian in a beautiful, fitted, long-sleeved black lace dress. The black dress looked *so* beautiful on her that I decided I should go to the nearest mall and try it on, you know, for *research.* It would be great motivation for my new post about life, love, feminism, fashion, and all things pretty.

I follow the Kardashians and I know that their line can only be found in Sears, so I made my way to the mall. As I walked through Sears, I passed by the electronics and appliances sections and noticed that they had a flat-screen television at a great price, as well as some humidifiers on display. I thought to myself, I have been really good about saving money and those are two things that I actually need for my apartment. I decided that once I was done shopping at the mall, I would exit through this section and purchase those items on my way back home. I went to the women's section and headed straight for the Kardashian Kollection. I quickly found the black lace bodycon dress along with a cute royal-blue blouse to try on. Unfortunately, I was not impressed by the fit of the blouse or the dress. I put my clothes back on and went back to grab the dress in a larger size, just in case it was a better fit for me. While outside of the dressing room, I spotted *another* cute black lace dress to try on. I tried both dresses on and again just wasn't impressed by the fit. I sadly put both dresses back on the clothing rack outside the dressing room and continued to look around the women's section. I wasn't in any rush. I could linger. I had a full day to myself with no plans . . . Why not?

I walked around the women's section and found a really cute pair of Now & Then harem pants that I was searching for on my last trip to New York City. I had been looking for these pants for months now, but I could never find a pair made with decent/quality material. They not only had them in my size but they had them in black and in a cute print. I went back into the dressing room to try these on. Both pants looked fabulous on me: flattering my figure and hugging my curves in all the right places. I went back to the rack to get an additional pair in the olive color because they just looked so darn adorable. To my happy surprise, the pants were on sale! It felt like it was my lucky day. After thinking about it for a while (and doing the calculations about how much I could not spend on groceries this month), I decided that I was actually going to buy *all three* pairs. I deserved a treat yo'self moment. I became really excited just thinking about all of the outfit combinations I would make with these. Maybe I would even add a picture of them to my blog post!

I paid for my purchase and as I happily walked out of Sears, two White people intercepted me outside of the store: a large White man and a young White woman. The young woman said something about working with store security and said that I needed to follow her. I started walking with them in shock and disbelief and said, "There seems to be a misunderstanding."

They just keep walking and motioning for me to follow. I follow them back into the store. The man walks in front of me and says, "Just follow us," while the young woman walks behind me. While we are walking through the store I ask, "Why did you stop me and where are we going?" The young White woman replies, "You went into the dressing room with a Kardashian blue blouse and a dress but you didn't come out with any of those items." I say, "I went into the dressing room twice. Once, with a blue blouse and a black dress and a second time with two black dresses. I left all of the items on the dressing-room rack outside of the room." She continues to walk and says, "Just follow us." I say, "Okay, but where are we going and what happens when you realize you are wrong?" She replies with, "We'll talk more once we are in the office." We go up an escalator and keep walking through the department store to what looks like the back warehouse.

Once we go through the SEARS EMPLOYEES ONLY door, I start feeling really frightened. My spidey senses tell me something is about to go totally wrong. I stop in my tracks and give her the "I am not going any further until you tell me where we are going" look. At this point, I am in full-on panic mode. I am scared. I am sweating. I am confused. I am offended. I think to myself, I don't trust these White people and do not know what they are capable of. I don't really know where I am or what is about to happen to me. My fight-or-flight responses are in full effect and I am having a complete physiological response to this stress. She notices my fear and says, "The office is right here." They both go into the office and I follow them in. All three of us are in the office, when two additional men of color (Et tu, Brute?) immediately walk into the room from another door in the office. I become even more frightened and ask, "Do you have any idea how intimidating this is?" The White man responds with, "We are not trying to intimidate you, ma'am." At this point, the young woman says, "We need you to open your bag."

I put the shopping bag on the table, open my pleather backpack, and take out my knit scarf—showing them an empty bag. "You see, I don't have anything!" I exclaim. Then she asks, "Are you wearing anything?" At this point, I am beyond offended, completely humiliated, and flabbergasted. I yell, "NO!" I start unbuttoning my coat to show them. The White man says, "Ma'am, you don't have to take off your coat." But I want them to see that I don't have *anything*, so I do. Then I say, "You see, I don't have anything! Now what?" At this she responds, "I'm sorry for the inconvenience."

I'm sorry for the inconvenience.

After accusing me of stealing, walking me back through the store like a criminal, frightening me, and causing me all kinds of distress, all she had to say was, "I'm sorry for the inconvenience." I grabbed my scarf, put it in my backpack and walked out of the office. I may have uttered a "fuck you." May have. I was so angry and offended and felt so humiliated that my hands started to tremble. I couldn't hold back the tears.

I quickly remembered my "you got out the 'hood and got an edumacation" privilege when I saw a store clerk outside. I asked them to call a manager for me, immediately. When the manager came to meet me, I told him everything that had happened. He was an older White man who seemed empathetic to my now streaming tears and utter disbelief. He was very nice and very apologetic. He mumbled something about security not being on the same page as everyone else in the store and offered to give me a discount. I said no, and repeated that I wanted to return all of the items I purchased, that I wanted my money back, and that I would not purchase anything else from Sears *again*. I also informed him that I wanted to file a formal complaint. He apologized again, took my credit card, reimbursed the charges, gave me the number to the corporate office, and I left the store, still in tears.

As I left the mall, distraught, I tried to sort through what had just happened. I tried on four pieces and left them in the dressing room, like I was supposed to. If the so-called security had paid attention to the cameras they would have seen the sales associate putting the clothes that I tried on right back on the clothing racks. Store security needs to have a lot more evidence before they are allowed to humiliate someone or accuse anyone of stealing. They need a lot more evidence than the simple fact that they saw a Latina (in a fitted teal peacoat, by the way) shopping in the store. Seriously, what was my crime? Looking fabulous? Wearing a peacoat? Wearing a cute backpack? I've worked in retail. Patrons aren't told to put items back on the sales racks where they found them. Customers are expected to put items back on hangers and leave them outside of the dressing room—on the dressing-room racks—so that sales associates can neatly place them back where they belong. That is exactly what I did. Not only did I do that, but I then continued to shop! Why would anyone steal something from one section and then go and buy three items from another one? Moreover, why would I steal something from Sears? Seriously, *Sears*. It just doesn't make *any* sense. Oh, wait it does.

I, a Latina, had the nerve to go into a department store and try on some cute dresses. My bad.

Let me be clear, I would not have left the mall without spending *at least* another $400 on a flat-screen television and humidifier. Sears not only lost that money today, they lost a customer. They also truly ruined my carefree day.

I called my little brother in tears, telling him what happened to me. In response, he shared an even more frightening profiling experience he had on a recent Delta flight, for which he never had a chance to file a complaint. The thing is, I do not know any people of color who have *not* experienced some type of racial profiling. Oprah had a store clerk refuse to show her a bag in Switzerland because it was "too expensive" and she clearly could not afford such an item; Barneys had a young Black man arrested for buying a $350 Ferragamo belt; and another Black woman was attacked by four NYPD officers for purchasing a $2,500 Céline bag (you guessed it, at Barneys). The moral of this story: this type of shit happens every day.

But it doesn't have to.

So, how can we stay safe as people of color just trying to live? My brother says that it is within my right to refuse to go into any back office with security (whether at the mall or at the airport) and inform them that they can and should indeed call the police. Sadly, given that I am a woman of color in 2013, having them call the police does not console me much or help me feel like it will keep me any safer. However, I am not giving up. I am going to make a big deal out of this. I will write letters, I will email Sears's customer service, and I will be calling their corporate offices. No one should ever have to experience this. No. One.

Re-Nigging on the Promises: #Justice4Trayvon

Brittney C. Cooper

Another Black kid is dead.

This time it's seventeen-year-old Trayvon Martin.

His life snuffed out at the hands of an overzealous, trigger-happy, White neighborhood-watch commander named George Zimmerman, who thought Trayvon looked "suspicious" as he walked back to his father's home in a suburban Florida neighborhood with a pack of Skittles and an iced tea for his little brother. Trayvon was unarmed; Zimmerman was packing a semiautomatic weapon.

How do we make sense of the senseless?

From the facts alone, it is clear that Zimmerman presented the real threat. But it has now been two and a half weeks since the shooting, and the Sanford Police Department has declined to charge Zimmerman with a crime. Law enforcement officials claim they have no evidence to dispute Zimmerman's claim that he acted in self-defense.

Apparently an unarmed dead Black teen is not evidence enough. If this were 1912 and not 2012, we would call a Black man killed by a one-man firing squad with no just cause what it is: a lynching. These days, we search for euphemisms.

Self-defense. That feels so inadequate.

I mean, whose selves really need defending if it is Black selves—primarily Black male selves—that keep being murdered?

It's high time that we started asking some serious questions about how we keep ending up here. Because there is most assuredly a racial logic—an alarming method—to this madness.

So come, let us reason, together. (Yeah, I got biblical, because in times like these we need a savior. Take that as literally or as figuratively as you will.)

In one of the earliest reports I read about this murder, the author felt it important to mention that Trayvon was visiting his father because he had been suspended from school for a week. It infuriated me that this detail was there. It was a subtle way to suggest that this kid didn't have his head on straight, that he had some flaw, that he had already demonstrated himself to be a disciplinary problem.

How does it feel to be a problem? It feels like gunshots, unheard screams, and a lonely, violent death.

It is now statistically documented that Black students are suspended 46 percent more than all other students and account for 39 percent of expulsions, though they only make up 18 percent of the school system. One in five Black boys is subjected to out-of-school suspension. The increase in zero-tolerance policies and automatic referrals to law enforcement are major culprits here. It is beginning to sound like schools have zero tolerance for students of color in general and an aversion to Black boys in particular.

A story.

Years ago, I taught reading to a group of middle schoolers in DC public schools. That year, four of my male students—all African American—were expelled. Three of them were expelled not for selling drugs on the campus but for failing to report that they knew one of their classmates was doing so. As the head of school told me, "We have an honor code and a zero-tolerance policy." Nearly ten years later, I find that decision the most dishonorable of decisions I encountered at that school, and working there was a fairly dishonorable experience for me. What my boss didn't seem (willing) to understand is that these students—while boarding students during the week—returned home on weekends, to the very communities where they lived. To ask these students to put their lives and their families' lives in danger in order to honor our "honor code" was an exercise in missing the point. So the kids were expelled.

I learned a lot then about how the cultures of discipline in public schools fail to honor the very real material realities that shape how kids engage in school. When scholars talk about a school-to-prison pipeline, they are not simply talking about the ways that systematic lack of educational access sets up Black people for a stint in the criminal justice system. They are also pointing to the fact that the very logic of public schools is designed to discipline Americans into a certain model of citizenship—one that helps us to believe in the propaganda of equal rights that we are taught in our social studies classes—while obscuring the systematic inequalities that are on gratuitous display through the treatment of children of color, students with disabilities, and poor students.

I can't help but wonder if it was this kind of *discipline* to which Trayvon had been subjected. School discipline should not be the pathway to a prison sentence or a death sentence.

A Black kid is dead. And blame must be placed somewhere.

I have zero tolerance for a justice system that deputizes overzealous White men and vests them with the power to be judge, jury, and executioner, under the trumped-up guise of self-defense. If this community fails to prosecute George Zimmerman, their silence, their acquiescence, their *approval* will constitute an official sanctioning of his course of action.

I can't help but wonder what Trayvon must have thought as he was confronted for no reason by a White guy with a gun, while he was simply trying to go home.

Eyewitnesses said they heard Trayvon call for help. The police swiftly *corrected* them, letting them know that, in fact, it was the White guy who had called for help. Even with eyewitness testimony, the police seemed incapable of seeing Trayvon as the victim. Young Black men are always the aggressors, right? Not the gun-toting White guy who weighed one hundred pounds more than Trayvon. Not the self-styled neighborhood vigilante with a documented disrespect for law enforcement. Nope. Just the Black kid, whose skin is perceived as a weapon.

Though Zimmerman had been charged in the past with battery on a police officer and resisting arrest, officers told Trayvon's parents that Zimmerman's record was squeaky clean.

What is this peculiar thing about Whiteness, that it makes criminals look like victims and victims look like criminals?

Trayvon's skin, not his actions, not his character, made him a criminal. Blackness always looks suspicious. Whiteness always looks safe.

A history lesson.

In 1857 Justice Roger Taney infamously declared in the *Dred Scott* case that a Black man "had no rights which the White man was bound to respect."

In this most-racial moment (thanks to Rhea Combs for the term), we must seriously reevaluate this narrative of linear historical progress we are beholden to. No, Black men don't routinely find themselves hanging from trees. But that might be less an evidence of progress and more an evidence of White racial adaptation.

"Racial patterns [will always] adapt in ways that maintain White dominance," father of critical race theory Professor Derrick Bell's famous maxim echoes in my ears.

Perhaps a hip hop metaphor is more appropriate. Present White racial violence frequently *samples* its own racial past but packages the narrative in ways that make us think we are making progress, that we are doing a new thing. But this shit ain't original.

The challenge in getting stuck on this show of ignorance is that most racism isn't that visible. And because it isn't, White folks can tell themselves that this is isolated racial ignorance.

They don't have to contend with the ways that our legal system continues to *renege* on its promises of equality and justice for all, through the enactment of supposedly color-blind policies like stricter voter registration laws that are designed to exclude folks of color from voting, through campaign suggestions that racialize the welfare system, and through sentencing disparities that criminalize Black and Brown folks for life. White folks can see this bumper sticker and never think about the ways in which every one of these deadly racial encounters (which seem to be a not-infrequent occurrence in Sanford, Florida) constitutes a "re-nig(gerizing)" of the Black male body.

Trayvon Martin "looked suspicious," Zimmerman told the 911 dispatcher. In fact, to say "suspicious" and "Black man" in the same sentence feels redundant.

Black = suspicious = threat
White = safe = protection/protector

All these (short but long) years later, the racial logic remains the same. Black men are threatening. And murder is a proper response to that threat or at least an understandable one. Ida B. Wells could've told us that. And she did. But that soundtrack has been remixed to accompany us into a new era.

How does it feel to be White?

Whiteness, critical race theorist Cheryl Harris tells us, is a "form of property." In the classical sense, Whiteness, like property, confers "all those human rights, liberties, powers, and immunities that are important for human well-being, including freedom of expression, freedom of conscience, freedom from bodily harm, and free and equal opportunities to use personal faculties."

Does it feel like freedom? Whiteness. Well it certainly looks like justice. The kind of justice that we want for Trayvon.

But there is one problem. Trayvon is Black. And that matters when Whiteness is the *sine qua non* of the American legal system, when possession of White skin is the prerequisite for justice.

And it is precisely because of this deep-seated association of White skin with property that George Zimmerman felt he had the right to "patrol" his neighborhood for interlopers and outsiders.

It is not coincidental that Black men are routinely profiled for looking suspicious in nice neighborhoods because "they don't be-long there." The battle over who belongs in neighborhoods—even though Trayvon's stepmother lived there!—is just a modern site for a long-standing war over White racial entitlement to control land and everything that moves on that land.

So despite our cries of #Justice4Trayvon, we know that it is a toss-up as to whether Zimmerman will be charged with anything, that it takes a literal act of God for the system to work for us. That God is all we have when the system works against us.

We keep hoping that reason will take over, that the facts will be presented in just such a way that the crime committed here will become visible, *evident,* to the powers that be. Somehow, I don't believe that this is what President Obama meant by the "audacity of hope." And if he did, I hope he realizes that hope in the face of mounting injustice is an unreasonable thing to ask of us. We are the post–post civil rights generation, the hip hop generation. And we are tired of hope and dreams deferred.

The Western Gaze: On Photography in the Two-Thirds World[1]

Eesha Pandit

A young guy with a sandy-brown mop of hair, T-shirt, khakis, and sneakers crouched about ten feet from where I stood in Dilli Haat, an outdoor crafts market in New Delhi, and focused his telephoto lens. My eyes followed the direction he pointed his camera, and I saw it was aimed at one of the artisans who had come to sell his wooden handicrafts. About eighty, the artisan was wearing a crisp white sherwani amid bright pink and yellow sheets of fabric suspended from a stone tower in a pattern evocative of one of the hundreds of wedding tents one sees around Delhi during winter wedding season. His weathered and well-wrinkled face was serene, and he adjusted his skullcap as a coolish breeze came through the fabric around him. He had no idea this young White man was taking a photo of him.

It was a poetic scene, to be sure. Not unlike the hundreds of *National Geographic* photos we've all seen. The young man with the camera clicked about ten shots in a matter of seconds, ran his fingers through his now-ruffled hair, and walked away, camera still in hand, poised for the next shot.

This all transpired in perhaps thirty seconds, if that. I was uneasy for the rest of the afternoon because the scene surfaced many complicated emotions I've had throughout my few weeks here in India, specifically on the subject of taking photos. When I flipped through

---

1. This phrase refuses the first and third world categorical hierarchy and instead uses a demographic lens and acknowledges the "third world" as the part of the world where two-thirds of the global population resides. I could also have used "global South," but want to make the point about space, physical and psychic.

the photos on my phone I noticed that they were almost exclusively of inanimate objects, no Indian people in any shots. I'm not speaking of photos with friends, colleagues, or family—I have no compunction about those. Here, I refer specifically to photos of people I don't know or hardly know: people walking down the street pushing vegetable carts teeming with the reddest carrots you've ever seen in your life, children playing badminton without a net, women in saris of every hue, and yes, even those women from nearby towns and villages whom I met just once and for a few moments (through a local NGO that they work with), or the small children who smile a thousand watts and throw a peace sign when a foreigner with a camera passes by them (these latter two being willing subjects).

India is captivating. It is teeming with character and color, teeming with people. As a person born, but not raised, in India, I experience that beautiful confusion that many of us children of American immigrants feel when they visit their countries of origin: places where they do not have to hyphenate their identities. Here I'm just Indian, despite my Western privilege and some very conspicuous American habits. But, irrespective of residence or citizenship, I've never been seen by others as, nor felt myself, just "American." "No, but where are you *really from?*" people often ask if I happen to answer "New York" to the first question. And perhaps that is why I felt queasy and maybe even a little angry when I saw that guy literally objectify an Indian person.

Now what? What do I make of my unease? Do I stop taking photos of places I travel? Do I think others should as well? Not exactly. Am I asking questions to which there are singular and clear answers? Definitely not. Here, I think the tension between belonging and being foreign can offer something. I am not quite "from" here. Nor am I "from" the United States. I am not (for the most part) the documented, nor am I able to fully hold a Western gaze when looking at India. This liminal space offers me access to a certain intimacy and distance that might prove useful.

Some reflections:

1. On objectification: This is not a new concept in relation to images or photography. Feminists around the world are vigilant against the objectification of women. But what the question of objectification offers us in this context is a third

perspective, not just the relationship between objectifier and objectified, not just the intent of the photo, not even the impact on the objectified, but the question of the "gaze." This third element affords us nuance in the midst of asking who is taking whose photo and for what purpose, and pushes us to ask the question: How is the photographer *seeing* through their lens? Do they want to show the exotic locales to which they've traveled to their learned friends? Do they want to document the horrifying poverty, which they previously couldn't have imagined? Do they want to document the beauty of a particular scene for their own pleasure? Regardless of the responses to the questions of "why," when we raise the question of objectification we are forced to ask: *How?*

Evoking in me memories of Edward Said's description of orientalism as consumption of the East by the West without contributing to it, I can't know exactly how the young White guy saw the old Indian artisan in the sherwani at Dilli Haat. I can only speculate that he didn't care enough about the desires of the man himself to ask whether he might take a photo of him. Whether it's my political sensibilities or my Indianness or something else altogether, I'm unable to see the man as merely a subject for a photo. In *On Photography*, Susan Sontag asserted that "photographs really are experience captured, and the camera is the ideal arm of consciousness in its acquisitive mood. To photograph is to appropriate the thing photographed. It means putting oneself into a certain relation to the world that feels like knowledge—and, therefore, like power." The gaze in question confers power, and that is the essence of objectification.

2. The question of gaze is incomplete without a sociohistorical analysis, which places photography amidst the ever-present questions of imperialism, colonialism, and capitalism. It cannot be so easily forgotten that the West once sought to own every single part of India: the land, resources, labor, and property of each person, from the farmworkers to the kings. Depending on how one perceives current capitalist models, this is something that has not changed—previously it was imperial conquest by nation-states, today it is the same conquest but by multinational corporations, based

in Western countries. In this context, taking a photo is undoubtedly a political act.

3. On documentation: Memory is fragile—individual and political, both. The impulse to record is universal, as an aid
to memory, as a means of passing information through
generations, as a way to reflect and relive. This is an impulse I feel strongly, both on a personal level, having lost
my last living grandparent this year, and on a political
one, working for the past decade in a movement for social justice that sometimes spins its wheels and sometimes
forges great breakthroughs. All this, while the emergence of
social media reliant on photographs is at the center of many
of our worlds. There must be questions we can ask that
would help us illuminate the difference between documentation and objectification—but for the purpose of this piece,
I invite us to avoid jumping to these questions before we fully appreciate the value of our curiosity and documentation.

There is so much more to be said about India—its remarkable journey through colonialism, the rooted and powerful social movements
resisting the internal scourge of the caste system, and the neoliberal
development models that are ravaging the livelihoods of the poor.
There is a feminist fire ablaze here on questions of dowry, female
feticide and infanticide, and violence against women and girls. The
capital city just held elections that will undoubtedly shape the trajectory of the region for years to come.

The way that I see India has prevented me from feeling comfortable taking a picture of a person I don't know, and I certainly couldn't
abide such a photo being taken without the person's knowledge
and consent. Perhaps that is because the way I see India is also
about the way *I feel seen* when I am here. A part of who I am is visible
here in a way that it is not in other places in the world. Perhaps I
am hypervigilant because I know how it feels to be reduced to a
shade of your identity, to be tokenized, exoticized, and made other. Perhaps because the legacy of colonialism is so present in contemporary struggles faced by Indians. There is so much more to be
said about India, but I raise the question of photography as an entry
point into some of these conversations because the gaze is where our
understanding begins. Because the way we see is as important as
what we see.

Trayvon Martin and Prison Abolition

Chanel Craft Tanner

When I say I'm a prison abolitionist, people think that means I want to tear down the walls of the prison and free everyone today. But what it really means is that I want to work toward building a society that does not rely on prisons to address all of our injustices. As a prison abolitionist, I recognize that prisons treat the symptoms and not the root cause of social issues. I recognize that prisons have history. We did not always have them, and we can get to a place where we don't use them. (Hell, I see evidence of this already with the increasing use of house arrest to monitor people. Of course this is not better, and is in many ways far worse, but it does point to the possibility of a prisonless world).

And while I wholeheartedly believe in the possibility of a world free of prisons, I find myself struggling with this Trayvon Martin situation. How can I demand a criminal conviction for Zimmerman when I am opposed to prisons? This kind of struggle between my politics and my real life is not new. I often go through these "okay, now what do I think" moments when I am forced out of my activist bubbles filled with hope and promise. But when I walk into my home and my house has been robbed, or I turn on the news and a little girl has been raped and murdered, or I log on to Twitter and a young Black boy has been killed, that theory shit goes out the window and I find my non-prison-believing ass saying, "Lock his ass up!"

So how do I reconcile these things? I'm not sure yet. But what I do know is that this really is not about the prison but about a prison state that targets Black and Brown bodies in problematic ways. It's about a system of policing and surveillance, in which some bodies are always under the eye of the state. Be it police constantly circling their blocks, surveillance cameras in the project hallways, metal detectors in their schools, or overzealous neighborhood watchmen finding them "suspicious," Lil' Kim had it right in saying "police stay on us like tattoos." #WeAreAllTrayvon not just because we are Brown bodied in a state that recognizes us as inferior, but because we all live in a system that sees us as toxic and worthy of elimination—either by locking us up or killing us. Thus my call for no prisons is not really about ending the prisons but about ending a system that disciplines us for having the audacity to breathe.

But this does not mean I do not wish to hold Zimmerman account-able. A world without prisons does not mean less accountability, it means more. It would mean that Zimmerman would have to be held accountable to the communities he harmed and not just the state. It would also mean that the world that creates a Zimmerman would also be held accountable for fostering a culture that sees dark bodies as suspicious. It's about recognizing the structural and cultural con-ditions that make Trayvon's murder possible. So we must talk about policing in conversation with the ways in which Disney participates in this socialization by making all of the evil characters dark. (Scar was the darkest lion, Ursula was a black octopus, and Jafar wore a dark cape.)

So we can and *must* continue to demand accountability from Zimmerman, but we must also recognize the ways in which Zimmer-man is the product of a larger culture. We must recognize the ways in which our culture breeds individuals that perform such heinous acts, and ask who we hold accountable for that.

Working while Black: Ten Racial Microaggressions Experienced in the Workplace

Robin M. Boylorn

I grew up watching the women in my family go to work from sunup till sundown cleaning houses, dismembering chickens, doing cus-tomer service or janitorial work, bookkeeping, caregiving, and an-swering phones. I watched them get up early and come home late, smile when they were tired, and go to work when they were sick be-cause they understood that they constantly had something to prove on their job, places where they were always reminded they were disposable commodities.

These working women understood that showing their humanity jeopardized their jobs. They had to be superwomen, they had to compartmentalize their emotions, they had to separate the work they did from the people they were. I learned from them that my work does not define me. Even though my aunt cleaned other folks' houses, she was never a maid. Even though my grandmother kept other folks' children, she was never a mammy. Even though I was college-educated, I was never racially privileged. Working while Black, regardless of your circumstances, carries the weight of blatant or casual racism as a reminder that you must always do twice as much to get half as far.

Being Black and successful in the workplace is like being a so-called model minority. Model minorities know their place and don't stand out or shine. Model minorities grin and bear micro- and macroaggressions and call them coincidences.

I was not taught to be a model minority. Instead I was taught to have a strong work ethic, to do my work excellently and to the best of my ability, and to maintain my dignity and self-respect in the face of all forms of discrimination. I was taught that as a Black woman, oppression would be an inevitable part of my life but that I did not have to be defined by mistreatment. My mother and othermothers helped me understand that an acknowledgment of oppression is not acquiescence.

Working women in my community often complained about being treated badly on their jobs, but refused to react to the injustices they experienced out of fear of being fired. Instead, they woke up early enough to bathe, pull sponge rollers from their hair, apply makeup and lipstick to fatigued faces, and put on professionally laundered uniforms and comfortable shoes so that they could walk into their places of employment with their heads held high and their dignity in check. They refused to be shamed. They refused to be silenced. They refused to be stereotyped.

It didn't matter that they would never make more than ends meet. It didn't matter that they were talked to in harsh tones for making a mistake or showing any air of arrogance or self-respect, and threatened with sanction for missing work to care for sick children. They took pride in their work, even when the people they worked for, or with, worked against them.

They saw their jobs as necessary, but they rebelled against the discrimination by refusing to be defined by what they did for a living. Resistance cannot always be visible (working-class folk literally *need* their jobs to survive, and middle-class folk are generally one or two paychecks from poverty), and rejection is not always audible, but we can still resist and reject the harmful effects of workplace discrimination.

I have compiled a nonexhaustive list of racial microaggressions experienced in the workplace. Factors such as occupation, generation, education, income/social class, gender identity and performance, sex, sexuality, ability, and age impact how and to what degree these things are felt.

The list is presented in second person in an attempt to encourage the reader to "experience" the experience and consider its impact.

Ten Realities and Racial Microaggressions Black People Experience in the Workplace

1. You are expected to speak for and on behalf of people of color everywhere. You are sometimes expected to be the barometer of racism. If there is a conscience in the workplace, you are it. You carry the burden of calling out discrimination when you see/experience it with the risk of retaliation, which can be anything from being overlooked for a promotion to losing your job altogether for creating a "hostile" environment. If/when you don't call out racism, you experience emotional turmoil and guilt, feeling like a sellout for not standing up for yourself or others.

2. You are routinely accused of being hostile, aggressive, difficult, and/or angry. You are told that your colleagues/students/coworkers/customers are intimidated by you and are afraid to approach you. You are encouraged in evaluations to "smile more" and "be more friendly." You practice a fake-ass smile in the mirror on your way out the door and practice all the way to work. You fear that your resting face makes people think you are mean.

3. You are required to be the diversity on committees and in meetings because Black is the only diversity that matters. Your Blackness makes it easy to "see" that a diversity quota has been met.

4. You feel unappreciated, undercompensated, and overworked. You are afraid to ask for compensation, a promotion, praise, or affirmation. You have been socialized to be satisfied that you have a job. You feel guilty for not feeling grateful.

5. You are regularly nominated for or assigned extra tasks and responsibilities for things no one else wants to do (espe-

cially things involving other people of color). You are encouraged to work with other people of color, join people
of color groups, and attend people of color activities.

6. Your absence (at work, at meetings, at parties) stands out
with no regard to how exhausting it is to be the only Black
person in the room. You are encouraged to not think of yourself as Black when you are the only Black person in the
room.

7. You are often vilified and/or criticized for doing your work
(too early or on time, well or not good enough). You are
labeled as either an overachiever or a slacker, as too ambitious or lazy. You struggle to find the balance between these
things.

8. You feel that no matter what you do or how hard you work,
you need to do more (or sometimes less). Nothing is ever
(good) enough.

9. You feel the need to constantly prove yourself worthy of your
job or opportunity. You know that some people assume you
got your job, promotion, award, or special recognition, not
because you worked your ass off or deserve it, but because
you are Black. (There goes that damn Black privilege again,
'cause you know affirmative action causes folk to get jobs
they are unqualified for and shit. <Insert side-eye>)

10. You feel isolated, misunderstood, misrecognized, misrepre-
sented, and missing in action. You wonder how you can feel
invisible and hypervisible at the same time.

For Whites Who Consider Being Allies but Find It Much Too Tuff

Susana M. Morris

The following post is a CRUNK public service announcement for our own post most-racial times.

For the record, being a White ally means . . .
   Not expecting your friends/colleagues of color to do the heavy
lifting around your own privilege.

Not recentering the conversation back to yourself when difficult subjects come up.

Not asking people of color to be less angry so you can really listen. Child, please.

Not petulantly zeroing in on petty aspects of a person of color's argument or analysis because it makes you feel uncomfortable or illuminates holes in your thinking. It's really transparent.

Not bringing up the fact that your best friend/boo/adopted stepchild is Black/Brown/polka-dotted. Such "facts" are not get-out-of-jail-free cards for saying stupid shit or generally being racist. You can have intimate relationships with people of color and still have fucked-up race politics.

Not expecting/demanding cookies and milk because you are pursuing antiracist activism. While we may be happy to work with you, you are doing what you're supposed to do. Period. Point blank.

During conversations about race, the phrases "race card" and "oversensitive" don't even enter into your mind, much less escape your lips. It's *never* the right answer.

And, never forget, being a White ally means being less concerned with potentially being called racist and more concerned with actually perpetuating racism.

FAMILY AND COMMUNITY: CHOOSING FAMILY

Introduction

Family of origin. Beloved community. Fictive kin. Blood relations. Othermothers. Play cousins. Queer kin. Chosen family. There are perhaps as many ways to describe family and community as there are to describe people themselves, despite the fact that we've been sold the mythic ideal of family for decades: two adults (a man and a woman, of course), two-point-five kids, and a dog named Spot living behind a white picket fence. The reality is that the so-called perfect nuclear family is a bill of goods that is impossible to reach for most and far from perfect for all. Truth is, people of color survive and thrive with families and communities as diverse as we are. And so, over the years, the CFC has written about families and communities of color in ways that seek to honor all of the ways in which we connect with one another, and not just those that are socially approved.

We also recognize that, for so many people of color, family and community have been colored, influenced, and, in some cases, even haunted by legacies of imperialism and slavery. The recurring debates concerning Black families—for example, the claim that slavery permanently marred the nuclear Black family—underscore the complicated ways family units are understood. On the one hand, the Black family is recognized as a site of love, strength, and support, while at other times, in both popular discourse and in some academic scholarship as well, Black family life is shrouded in myths of pathology and identified as "broken" and "dysfunctional" when it is not led by a strong patriarch; ideally a cisgender, heterosexual man is the "head" of the household, literally and figuratively. "The Black family," then, is often a sad monolith that exists at the nexus of many often contradictory and competing meanings in popular culture and even some scholarship. It is a concept that is often the scourge that whips Black women's backs into submission. As crunk feminists, we reject narrow understandings of family and community that are simply longings for heteropatriarchal power dressed up in Black- or Brownface.

The CFC has its own origin story. In the beginning, there was the Collective. Before the CFC was a blog it was a community and a family. Back in the early 2000s, when Brittney Cooper, Susana Morris, and Crunkista were graduate students at Emory University, they and a group of friends began calling themselves "crunk feminists" as a way to describe their unique way of moving through the world and supporting each other in the face of racism, sexism, homophobia, and every other social ill. These newly dubbed crunk feminists were a crew, a squad that rolled deep. They took classes together, got crunk in the club, threw house parties, cooked for each other, talked politics, went to movies and talks, taking up an entire row. They laughed and cried together through everything from relationships to dissertations to deaths in the family. They were each other's lifelines, community, and close kin during the years they labored in what was often a very hostile White space.

The original CFC lasted several years, but when folks began to graduate and move away, the friendships remained while the more formal parts of the Collective faded away.

So when Brittney and Susana began talking about reviving the CFC and creating a blog, the idea that the CFC would be first and foremost a collective outside of the blog was key. Their idea was that the Collective would be a place to be in both conversation and community. During this time Brittney and Susana were living on the opposite ends of Alabama, working as junior professors in small Southern college towns. Feminist community was scarce and fun even scarcer. They realized they would have to build it themselves. They wondered, wouldn't it be great if we could gather a group of dope-ass feminists? We could be like a twenty-first-century Combahee River Collective—supporting each other, having fun, sharing our stories, and speaking truth to power.

But unlike before when the original CFC all lived in the same city, this newer version of the Collective was scattered across the East Coast. That meant that we, the new CFC, had to be more nimble and more intentional about building and sustaining our community. So we made use of lots of different types of technology—email, phone, the Internet, Google Hangouts—and arranged to meet one another at conferences and retreats to spend time together and connect. This new CFC became not unlike its predecessor. We were often each other's lifelines, community, and close kin.

We believe that the CFC has lasted as long as it has because we are more than a group of strangers coming together to write blog posts. We have supported each other through graduate school, relationships, job searches, job losses, births, deaths, and any number of other life changes. We have laughed, cried, argued with, and held each other down. The Collective itself has even gone through changes, good and bad, and weathered storms, emerging stronger and more unified. Building and maintaining community and family is far from easy, but it is gratifying, sustaining, and very necessary.

Because of our roots as a collective, it is probably no surprise that so much of our writing has been about family and community. Over the years we've covered the gamut on family and community issues, from praising the joy and resiliency that we see every day in our communities to calling out the soul-crushing practices that destroy love, trust, and solidarity. We also grapple with what it means to create and sustain family and community in a society where Black and Brown bodies are often under surveillance and harshly disciplined. Our work answers the call from our feminist foremothers and continues to call out patriarchal power structures for not being accountable to the most vulnerable members of our communities. We reject the secrets and lies that often dwell in families of origin, delving deep into the pain of family secrets and fragmented bonds. While it has often been difficult and certainly scary to be vulnerable about some of the most intimate parts of our lives, or to brazenly expose familial and cultural taboos such as abandonment, abuse, infertility, mental illness, homophobia, and violence, it has also been liberating. Our work at the CFC has meant actively rejecting the dissemblance that respectability politics requires. We have vowed through our writing not to be shamed or silenced because of our pasts or our truths.

Once we found our voices, it was easy to call out all we saw that was wrong. But digging deeper for our truths also asked us to lift up what was right. And so, to that end, we have also (re)imagined community through the lens of crunk feminism, celebrating all the ingenious ways people of color have etched our own spaces of love, caring, support, and just plain old fun. And because so many of us work in academia, a large part of our work highlights how we create feminist classroom communities built on respect and accountability. Being intentional about celebrating feminist family and community has been healing work and an act of resistance in a world that thrives on women of color burning ourselves out to care for others.

Whether or not the community is beloved or the family is chosen, it is clear that we need each other not only to survive but also to thrive.

Reflections on Coming Out and Family

Crunkista

As a queer Latina, I juggle intertwining, complex, and often competing identities. One of my most defining identities is that of daughter.
My mother is one of the most amazing women I know. Although she
would never refer to herself as the F-word, I firmly believe that I am
the independent, strong, determined, educated, and fierce feminist I
am thanks to her example. Growing up in a single-parent household
meant that for most of my life my mother was my best friend. That all
changed, however, when I came out to her.

Although realizing that I was queer meant finally figuring out another important part of my identity (and one that made me incredibly
happy), it was a part of me that my mother refused to accept and,
most of the time, even acknowledge. In her eyes I couldn't be both a
good daughter *and* gay. Inevitably, I lost my best friend and, in many
ways, a part of me.

The journey has been a painful one that I am still healing from. I
have had to distance myself from friends and family members who
could not accept *all* of me. Throughout this journey, however, I am
happy to say that I *have* been blessed. I found a community of crunk
feminist sisters who not only accept and love all of me but also
challenge me to learn, teach, grow, and forgive every day.

In an effort to find some humor in all of the sadness that oftentimes comes from coming out to family, I decided to compile a list
of some of the most memorable conversations between my mother
and myself. I shared this for the first time at a Queer Women of Color
and Friends (QWOC+) event titled "Queer Multiculturalism: A Discussion about Coming Out to Different Cultures and Communities
of Color." I share this again with the CFC community because you
showed me that although you can't choose your biological family,
you can always choose to have more than one.

Top Ten Interactions with My Mom after Coming Out

10. Why don't you have a boyfriend?
    *I'm the first to go away to college. Why don't you ever ask
    me about what I'm learning in college. And where the heck
    is my care package? My White friends get care packages
    every weekend!*
9. If you don't find a boyfriend soon, how will you ever get
   married?
   Mom, seriously, it's after midnight. I have a paper to write.
8. When are you going to have kids?
   *I don't know, Mom. I'm at a women's college. Might be
   tough.*
7. What do you mean you don't want to have kids?! You're
   already a graduate student! How much more do you need
   to study? What else is there to learn? Are there men in your
   classes?
   Mom, seriously, stop oppressing me.
6. Why is your friend's hair so short, and why is she always
   here?
   Yeah, about that . . . Mami, I'm gay.
5. How could you do this to me?
   *Mami, look at me. I'm glowing! I'm so happy! I've never
   felt this way about anyone else in my entire life! It took me
   twenty-two years to figure it out, but everything in my life
   finally makes sense now.*
4. I'd rather see you pregnant with a drug addict's baby than
   see you with a lesbian woman.
   *I was not expecting that one. None of the "coming out to
   your parents" books mentioned that as a possible reaction.*
3. Don't tell your younger sister or she'll think she is gay too.
   (Rolling my eyes) *Yeah, Mom, it's contagious. You better
   watch out.*
2. Your sister is gay and it's ALL your fault!
   That's impossible, she's gayer than I am.
1. You are my daughter and I love you, but why do you
   always have to bring up the fact that you're gay?
   Because you keep asking me about my boyfriend.

The Evidence of Things Not Seen:
Sex and Power in the Black Church

Brittney C. Cooper

After some trepidation, I watched the interview of Jamal Parris, one of four young men who has come forward accusing Reverend Eddie Long, of Atlanta megachurch New Birth Missionary Baptist Church, of sexual abuse and coercion. When the story of Long's alleged sexual abuse of these young men hit news outlets, I was shocked and initially reluctant to comment. You see, I'm a committed Christian, a weekly churchgoer, and the (step)daughter of a pastor. I attended grad school in Atlanta, where I also regularly attended a megachurch, led a ministry team, and heard Bishop Long preach on more than one occasion. He's my pastor's pastor. And my deeply spiritual and religious parents reared me to believe that we do NOT speak against pastors (God's anointed). All these things swirled in my head as this story broke. But alas, it's time to "put away childish things" and have some grown-folk discourse about sex and power in the church. Ironically, that verse appears at the end of Corinthians 13:1, the oft-quoted passage on love, because it is a reminder that real love is grown-folks' business. It cannot be undertaken and sustained by the childish, the immature, or the faint of heart.

If we are committed to a revolutionary love ethic, we have to be honest, even when it hurts. And what's honest is that there is something undeniably real when you listen to this young man's testimony. Given the parochial and limiting narratives of Black sexuality and Black masculinity propagated by the church and the unchecked power given to preachers, particularly at megachurch pulpits, this man has everything to lose and nothing to gain if his accusations are untrue. He admitted to a same-sex encounter with a married preacher. Because of our rampant homophobia and blind love for our pastors, this young man has been subject to much ridicule, I'm sure.

When I looked into Jamal's eyes, I was reminded of more than a few Black men I've come into contact with who have admitted being abused as children. Can we get real about the dirty little secret of sexual abuse in our communities? If we're honest, part of the reason that Tyler Perry and T. D. Jakes have been able to build the empires they have is because they actually will name this issue. The success of their films confirms that while much, very much, is to be desired, we at least have some kind of discourse about the abuse of Black girls and women. But we are virtually silent on the abuse of young men, even though it is too common to be uncommon. Because of our homophobia, insularity, and mentality of closing ranks, we'd rather not deal. And so we leave countless Jamal Parrises to be abused, with no outlet other than legal to address and redress their concerns. And just like we know that prior sexual abuse is a major cause of low self-esteem and other emotional ills among Black women, perhaps we should consider that much of the violent, self-hating behavior that we see among young Black men is due, at least in part, to un-named and unacknowledged sexual abuse.

But let's also be clear. What Long has been accused of doing isn't about sex. It's about power, as sexual abuse generally is. And we need to seriously rethink our stance on giving pastors all the power. At my church in Atlanta, a few years back, we voted as a congre-gation to take all voting power away from ourselves and to give virtually all decision-making power to the pastor. Back then, the de-cision made sense. I understood my pastor to be the one who heard from God about God's vision for our church, and I understood that that vision was not supposed to be left to the whim and fancy of the people. When I was confronted with the reality of these four young men, I realized the fallacy of that thinking. Everybody has to be accountable to somebody, and in a community of faith, if God gives the pastor a vision, surely God will confirm that vision with a substantial number of one's congregants. Otherwise it's suspect, no matter how good it sounds.

As I reflect back on that time, I am amazed at the degree to which I bought into all I was taught, the degree to which I was afraid to question, question though I did. The penalty for challeng-ing church authority is steep, and I've definitely paid some tolls on that highway. But my mode of challenging can't hold a candle to the courageous acts of these young men. So I know the price is inordinately high for them.

Yet, it amazes me that we can't speak about sex given that there is a book of erotica dropped right in the middle of the Bible. *Song of Solomon* is not just a Toni Morrison novel, in case you were won-dering. If the very preachers who continue to espouse this theology fail over and over again to live it out, perhaps the problem is not one of human frailty and sin as we are so wont to conclude. Perhaps our sexual theology needs revisiting and rethinking. And this for both straight and queer folks.

Later on, I watched the live coverage of New Birth's early service. Long is a powerful preacher, and his mini sermon on how to handle tough situations reflected the best of Black Baptist homiletic traditions. After mocking the crowd ("We're here every Sunday"), with raucous applause from the New Birth family, and standing ovations after every comment, Bishop Long got down to what everyone "came for." He said that though he was not "a perfect man," he "is not the man the television is portraying him to be." He indicated that he was "gonna fight this thing." And in a most arrogant twist, he put his accusers on notice, "I feel like David fighting Goliath. I've got five stones and I ain't thrown one yet."

On Sunday, I didn't see any Jesus in Eddie Long. He did not one time express concern for his accusers, and it stands to reason that if these are totally trumped-up charges, a pastor who admittedly claimed to love these boys would be troubled, would ask his congregation to pray for their well-being, would indicate his own hurt, bewilderment, and confusion at this situation. But no. None of that. Just an arrogant pronouncement that he was gonna come for (no pun intended) his accusers.

The question to be asked about this particular Sunday's shenanigans is a simple one: Where is the love?

> If I speak with the tongues of men and of angels, and have not love, I am a noisy gong or a clanging cymbal. And if I have prophetic powers . . . but I have not love I am nothing. If I give away all I have, and give up my body to be burned, but have not love, I gain nothing.
>
> 1 Corinthians 13:1

For all those folks who think Long's good works serve as an apologia for his abuse, they don't. You can't love someone and violate them, abuse their body, coerce them, emotionally manipulate them, and then lie on them, and subtly threaten them when they speak out against you. Abuse is not love.

If faith is the "evidence of things unseen," what is *evident* to me are four hurting young men, an arrogant preacher, and a Black Church largely unwilling or unable to get real about sex, even though there's a whole lot of it going on from the pulpit to the pews. With that much evidence, what more do you need to see?

Fish Dreams

Robin M. Boylorn

Fish dreams signal pregnancy in my family. The premonition, which was mostly my grandmother's or that of another maternal figure, has been consistent and accurate for as long as I can remember. Without fail, every time a woman dreams about water or fish, somebody's pregnant. When I was young, the dreams were frequent and urgent, causing concern and suspicion, especially toward girl children. The dreams would stir up fear and anger in our all woman and girl household, with watchful eyes watching for evidence of a missed period or overly eager appetite. I was never accused or asked outright, but the announcement of the dream served as notice that if I had, in fact, been doing the nasty, and I had, in fact, gotten myself pregnant, my burden-carrying ass would be a disappointment, an unwed, unemployed, unprepared mother-to-be.

When an older cousin or distant relative would finally announce they were expecting, I never anticipated an apology and never received one. Sighs of relief would replace the silent treatment, and we would return to our routines until the interruption of the next dream.

Menses meant I was to be watched, warned, and, if need be, threatened with the many ways teenage pregnancy would limit my options, embarrass my family, and guarantee me a life of struggle. A woman with fish dreams rarely had dreams of her own. When I got my first period, in lieu of a discussion about what was happening with my body, I was forbidden from playing with boys and told to keep my legs closed and my head in the books. I was led to believe that sex was to be saved and that any bodily pleasure was sinful and indecent. I was also conditioned to fear fish dreams, even when I had them myself.

Over the years, I learned the synchronicity of fate and the intentionality of not testing it by swallowing a tiny pill at the exact same time every single night, even during months, if not years, of celibacy, to fend off fish dreams. Fear and abstinence kept me from doing what I was perpetually warned not to do as a teenager: "come 'round here with no babies!"

For most of my life, not getting pregnant was a tremendous achievement. The hallmark of my success as a Blackgirl and my mother's greatest accomplishment as a parent was getting me through school without having a baby. My sister and I were the first of my grandmother's female grandchildren to make it out of high school without getting pregnant. But now, having never been pregnant sometimes feels like a failure. At family gatherings and reunions, while babies are being passed around and held too long, like collection plates, my family members question my life choices, wonder if my professional success was at the expense of motherhood and marriage (milestones they value more than my degrees and career), and suspect I took the warning about getting pregnant too soon too literally and waited too long. My unswollen belly holds all my unspoken dreams about my would-be child, even though I have only wanted him in transitory moments of silence or after good sex with a man I thought I loved.

No one expected me to still be childfree in my twenties and thirties, but I approached each year seeing a potential pregnancy as an unnecessary complication or distraction from my dreams. I poured my energy into my career and my maternal longings onto other people's children. I imagined that when I accomplished everything else I wanted to do in my life, I would plan a deliberate and well-orchestrated pregnancy with the man of my dreams. I would give birth to a son, with a biblical middle name, who would favor his father and my mother. His nickname would be Fish, because it would be a dream, not a pregnancy test, that confirmed his arrival. I would teach him how to be an intentional Black feminist, an intellectual artist, a progressive Christian, and a Carolina fan. My fantasy about being a mother usually ended there.

The reality is single, heterosexual, successful, professional women who desire biological children don't always have the luxury of waiting until the time is right. Timing is rarely right. Biological clocks start ticking when you reach the end of your twenties, and by the time you are in your midthirties they ring like an alarm signaling the urgency of being pregnant NOW, or potentially never being pregnant at all. I am utterly cognizant of the fact that with each passing year, I am less likely to ever be the source of a fish dream. The possibility of being a mother scares me, but the impossibility scares me more.

Still, in my twenties I decided I didn't want children. Like Sula, the main character of Toni Morrison's novel by the same name, "I [didn't] want to make somebody else, I want[ed] to make myself." News of my intention to be childfree passed quickly through my family, and soon church folk insisted I would change my mind "when I got my nose open." Even then I knew love doesn't make babies and babies don't make love. I was told I was selfish for not wanting a child. I was reminded that the Bible tells us to be fruitful and multiply. I was asked what I would do if I fell in love with a man who wanted babies.

I don't know if I ever really wanted a child, or if I believed the hype that suggests my life is meaningless without one. Sometimes I fantasize about my life as a mother, imagining the face of my butterscotch-Brown baby boy while detouring through the baby section of a department store or scrolling through the infant updates on my Facebook newsfeed. I don't linger long enough to feel baby blues for a loss that is only theoretical, an absence that is intangible. My ongoing ambivalence alongside the dwindling window of time to carry a baby in my body makes motherhood feel like somebody else's dream.

Inconceivable: Black Infertility

Aisha Durham

In her personal essay about motherhood, Robin Boylorn writes, "Fish dreams signal pregnancy in my family. The premonition, which was mostly my grandmother's or that of another maternal figure, has been consistent and accurate for as long as I can remember." In my family, there are no memories of fish dreams for me. Instead, there is a storkless, stark reality that in spite of my two-hour-long treks to an expensive specialist to be jacked open, probed, and drugged, in addition to my regimented record keeping of peek ovulation, period flow, body temperature, and patterned intercourse over the course of two years, the end result might still be the inconceivable: infertility.

As a child, I did not crave a Cabbage Patch Kid to cuddle when imagining a "play play" family with girlfriends. I used Barbie as a mannequin to model clothes made from remnants by my mother, who purchased my miniature sewing machine from a nearby Goodwill thrift store. I learned how to sew before I learned how to cook. My mother and my aunties indulged my creativity by asking to hear my latest poems or to see my latest designs from my so-called fashion portfolio. Most important, these womenfolk praised my elementary adoption of the closed-leg policy. I learned I could garner the spot-light and count on their unconditional support as long as I evaded the cardinal sin of Black girlhood: pregnancy.

Early pregnancy was a dream stealer. The praise I received as a child was always accompanied by a cautionary tale about a future swaddled and abandoned because of the immediate demands of motherhood. I became so terrified of teen pregnancy that I developed anxiety at the very anticipation of holding a baby as an adult. To this day, I can count on one hand the number of newborns that I have cradled in my lifetime.

In junior high school, I posed with my friend for our first year-book picture after we participated in an annual Halloween costume contest. She funked a full-length fur, a black headband, and hair feathers befitting a bluesy Ma Rainey. I donned a dookie rope, pur-ple hoodie, dolphin hoops, and a stonewashed-denim dress with a pillow stuffed underneath to become a hip hop baby mama. We were two make-believe mamas wearing wide smiles without won-dering why becoming an old woman or a young pregnant girl was hilarious and horrifying. Make-believe became real by the time we sat for our final junior high school pictures. She gave birth to a baby named Passion. I began to nurture my passion as a writer.

Twenty years later, I am sitting in the fertility clinic confronting my childhood fears and my grown-up fantasies about Black moth-erhood. I am facing the prevailing cultural myths about Black fe-male hyperfertility and hypersexuality—both of which suggest we are freakishly insatiable and therefore prone to pregnancy. I had escaped the social stigma surrounding urban teen pregnancy that befell my friend only to bump up against another one regarding Black female infertility at thirty. I was mother-less. Along with confronting myths, I had to face other factors influencing Black infertility. Obesity, uter-ine fibroids (or noncancerous tumors), endometriosis (characterized by tissue growing outside the uterus), and untreated sexually trans-mitted infections are medical conditions that adversely impact our reproductive health. The Centers for Disease Control estimates 6.7 million women aged fifteen to forty-four experience infertility, but Black women are less likely to receive an early diagnosis of infertility or seek medical treatment because of existing health conditions, the escalating costs, and powerful cultural myths.

Much of the public visibility and value ascribed to Black women is based on our perceived role as mothers. Whether the endearing mammy celebrated in early forms of popular culture or the "bad" Black mother (e.g., teen mother, crack mother, welfare queen) demonized in news media since the 1980s, she is still a mother. To add, our very theories of womanism and Black feminist thought use (other)mothering to describe how Black women engage with the world. In *Revolutionary Mothering: Love on the Front Lines,* for example, Alexis Pauline Gumbs posits the term "mother" is less of a gender identity as much as it is a "technology of transformation" we adopt to create, nurture, affirm, and support life. This is an important shift in how we discuss motherhood. Her framework provides a broader understanding of mothering as a radical, communal act. Yet with so much meaning attached to motherhood itself, the inability to conceive or carry a pregnancy to term remains a devastating and demoralizing experience for some Black women.

Infertility has been an emotionally debilitating experience for me personally and professionally. I have experienced shame, anxiety, and depression. I did not seek support because I believed I could grin and bear it. So said my inner strongblackwoman. For a moment, I believed my infertility was spawned by my inability to perform perfect would-be motherhood—window-shopping, name surfing, and publicly gooing over all things baby. For a moment, I convinced myself that my book—my professional baby—was undeliverable because of all of its imperfections. *I convinced myself that I was unproductive.* I contemplated aborting the book and academia altogether because putting a pen to paper seemed as fruitless as stabbing my stomach with hormones. Nothing was born of it. For a moment, I participated in the suffocating silence of infertility because I felt I had no permission to speak freely about my experiences—those tragic and triumphant. I spent months alone with my bare feet cuffed inside icy metal stirrups, staring at one-too-many ultrasound monitors because I still believed that *this time* would be *the time.* It was only a month ago that I allowed two years of tears to wash over me during an eight-hour cry-fest with a girlfriend. As I released the pressure bottled inside me, I experienced a baptism of sorts. That day, my sistahfriend lovingly sent me home with Yemoja, the divine mother of all life and the spiritual goddess to infertile women.

Most days I feel at peace on my path by creating new pictures of my future, my passion. I still dream about fish along the water, but when I write I am reminded that my mother has already given me life thrice—in her spirit, in my flesh, and in my first name that means life. This week, I will return to the cold white room with the monitor staring at me. This time, however, I will fold into myself to imagine my own rebirth.

What I Value Most

Rachel Raimist

> Such is the power of the photograph, of the image, that it can give back and take away, that it can bind.
> —bell hooks, "In Our Glory: Photography and Black Life"

October 11, 2010, would have been my mother's sixty-sixth birthday. She didn't make it to her fifty-fifth though; she died of ovarian cancer. The tumor was the size of a grapefruit when it was discovered, three weeks before my college graduation. The doctors said that she probably wouldn't live four months, but that was only because they didn't yet know her strength. She fought to live through surgery, chemo, a stem-cell bone-marrow transplant, and more chemo. She battled cancer for three years before she passed away.

When she died it wasn't the furniture or new cars my brothers and I argued over. It was the family photo albums. We each got a stack, mostly filled with snapshots from the time period we most treasure.

My favorite photograph, taken in 1979, shows me in my favorite white-and-yellow Bronx Zoo T-shirt. My back was to my father, who was behind the camera. This image shows me at age five, my face burrowed into my mother. She hated to be photographed but always beamed on command for Dad's snapshot. Her hair was bone straight naturally, but the picture captures her perm days, looking like Carla from *Cheers*. She carried a fifteen-pound purse, always in her left hand. In this image all you can really see are the straps, but I know what they held—lipstick, powder, wads of tissues, a small brown Coach change purse with a twenty-dollar bill stashed inside for safety, safety pins, a baggie of snacks like cashews or carrots, a baggie with Tylenol and Sudafed, and anything else anyone might ever need. This is a classic family photograph—Mom's big hair and big smile and me grumpy and frowning, hiding my face so that only Mom could see.

My other favorite photograph was taken in 1944, when my mom was just a baby. My grandmother, whom I most resemble, has a beautiful smile and the dark eyes I inherited and passed down to my own children. I have a baby picture of myself, hair sticking straight up, just like my mom's does in the portrait. The tacky gold "frame" was a specialty of my abuelo. Pepe loved loud, shiny things. I have photos of him wearing black-and-white striped Nuyorican versions of the zoot suit. He always wrapped the edges of photographs with gold foil.

My family hid tremendous secrets; I know now that most families do. They are like ghosts that hover invisibly but are always present, whether you understand them or not. For years, I asked my mother, who was Puerto Rican and nineteen years younger than my White, Jewish father, why she wore a wedding ring and my father did not. She replied, "We don't talk about those things in this house." When I asked her how she met my dad, she would say, "We don't talk about those things in this house." When I asked her why she loved my dad, she would stare silently and most often walk away. When I asked for help making a family tree for school, she only pointed to her few living relatives—her sister, brother, baby sister, and my cousins— and then swiftly moved on, probably to go clean something. When I asked her about her wedding, she would say quietly, "We don't talk about those things in this house."

Our house was full of pictures. Some were framed and on display while others were tucked away in the basement, out of sight.

In excavating family history and shuffling through secrets, I found stories in the old photographs. Stories, not truths. When it comes to the past, there is no truth, only half-truths, lies, and secrets made silent over time. The truth is not the point. The point for me is to see I have my grandmother's face, to see the fake smile my mother wore as armor, and to be reminded that I was too shy, as a child, to speak to strangers. What I value most is that my family photographs are an archive of our history, documentation to my memories, keeper of my mother's secrets.

God's Plan Ain't Black Mothers Dying Young

Sheri Davis-Faulkner

Yesterday I attended a funeral for a distant cousin, and I was angry throughout the entire service and for the rest of the day. I am still angry because we buried a forty-seven-year-old Black mother, and no one could tell me why. The family had to get an autopsy done to determine the cause of death.

The minister preached from Job 1:21, "The Lord gave, and the Lord hath taken away; blessed be the name of the Lord." Maybe it is because I did not know why she died at the young age of forty-seven, leaving four children to mourn her, but "the Lord has a plan" just wasn't doing it for me. Couple that with her White male employer stating that, "She put everyone's needs before her own," "She knew all of my family members by name," and "She was a loyal employee." I had real questions, like, "Who helped her raise her four children?" and "How many hours was she working a week?" and "What kind of health care did the major retail franchises she worked for all her life provide for her and her children?" And "God has a plan" just is not enough for me because I cannot imagine that God's plan is for Black mothers to work, work, and work some more and die young.

At the funeral for this amazing Black woman, all of the women involved in her life were made invisible by the scripture included in his sermon, for example Ecclesiastes 5:15: "[He] came forth naked from his mother's womb, so shall he return." This coming-forth idea perplexes me because last I checked, and I am a mother, women work really hard birthing children, and I know it must hurt like hell to have to bury them. These rhetorical and visual images of pregnant women with no bodies—missing breasts, head, face, or legs—are damaging. I'm fine with God being a "He" if that's how the church presents its God, but what I find disturbing is that at a funeral where the father of the deceased and the father of her four children are not present, but where the deceased and her mother are present, the sermon renders them both invisible. How can you be a present absence at your own funeral? And to end with, "Don't cry . . . *He* is not dead"? I'm sorry, but I'm crying because a hardworking Black mother is dead at forty-seven, and I'm crying because her mother is going to have to bury her.

To be clear, her death does not make me angry with God. I am angry because there is no fucking war cry. No call to stand up for and to support these hardworking mothers in our community, who we seem perfectly content to *let* take care of everyone else's needs before their own. We are too quiet when they are working themselves to death because there is no affordable housing or accessible health care, few sustainable jobs and no protection through unions, *and* no affordable free childcare. And when they die, all that can be said is, "God has a plan." That's not enough. What's the plan, and are we not the implementers of this plan? Isn't the preacher supposed to share the plan with us, inspire us to get moving, to help God help us? No, the message seems to be, do not question "the plan," but come worship at my church of four thousand and maybe I will let you in on a little secret.

I'm sick right now because Black women are dying unnaturally of EVERYTHING, and the supposed solution to all of our problems is getting a man. Get real. We need a community. We need burdens to be lifted in real ways now, not when we have "transitioned." We need people to tell us to slow down and to take care of us too, or else being an "angel" for others might get us buried at forty-seven. What we needed was a war cry.

The family did not need an autopsy to determine the cause of death because the answer was written in the obituary.

Mother Jones said, "Mourn the dead, but fight like hell for the living." It's time to fight like hell for hardworking Black mothers. Let's give them their accolades while they are living. And it would be nice if they could be addressed in the sermon at their own funeral as well.

After the Love Has Gone: Radical Community after the Election

Susana M. Morris

If you're like me, you're probably geeked when election season is finally over. I mean, now we can turn all of our attention back to important things like *Game of Thrones*, *Scandal*, and *The Real Housewives of Atlanta*. Finally!

Sure, I love a giddy Rachel Maddow gushing on MSNBC. Sure, I like the idea of chastened, sullen, defensive conservatives whining and licking their wounds, embarrassing themselves by saying increasingly stupid, pitiful, and asinine things, all the while revealing to anyone with good sense that their ideology and policies are out of touch, retrograde, wack, and shamtastic. (Their tears are delicious.) So, yes, I'm not above putting the shade back in schadenfreude.

Mostly though, I'm really ready to be done with the infighting among the radical Left. The radical Left is not a monolithic entity but rather a diverse set of communities that approach the realization of justice in a variety of ways. I'm not suggesting that we become more alike, but I am concerned that the way we talk about our differences is not only unproductive but oftentimes a violent distraction from our shared goals.

While some folks are still popping bottles and dropping it like it's hot to Jeezy's "My President Is Black" and looking forward to celebrating the first woman president in the White House, others are shaking their heads at the complicity of supposedly progressive folks with the imperialism of the state.

Between Obama's two terms and the dustups between Hillary Clinton and Bernie Sanders, progressive politics feels like a family reunion gone terribly wrong. Folks get drunk and start arguing, secrets get exposed, proverbial dirty laundry gets aired, people choose sides, and nothing gets solved. Then we do it all again in a couple of years. It's not that we don't love each other—we just got some major ish to work through. So let's work through it. What follows is not an exhaustive list, but a few ideas to the get the conversation started.

1. Let's reject binaries: good/bad, Democrat/Republican, liberal/conservative, revolutionary/Uncle Tom. I think we experience and engage politics on a spectrum and trying to take a snapshot of someone's beliefs from one action (e.g., voting and not voting) and then running around being like, "Ah-ha! You're not quite right because you believe in xyz!" is neither cute nor productive.

2. Along those lines, let's rebuke authenticity wars. I think the most recent fissures in the radical Left should invite us to consider the ways in which the organizing and ideology coming out of the liberation movements of the 1960s and 1970s challenge/inform/undermine our current work. I see some folks wanting to eschew the call to honor the legacy of the civil rights movement, finding such calls often mean shutting up about their concerns in order to appear legitimate. Other folks warn that if you completely abandon the ideology and action of what came before us, you are doing a disservice to history and not wanting to connect authen-

tically to the struggle. I don't think these conversations are completely at odds, but reducing the convo to one about legitimacy just doesn't serve us well.

3. Let's reject elitism and navel-gazing. We are a part of complex communities, and we don't deserve to be leaders simply because we have degrees or work at certain organizations. Yet some of us treat our family, friends, and neighbors with condescension and disdain, acting like we are radical evangelists among ignorant heathens. That's why sometimes the folks we work with and serve don't like and, more importantly, don't trust many of us.

4. Let's be nuanced in our discussion of respectability politics. I'm all about calling out investments in dominant notions of what is normal and acceptable as a way to harness power, especially in communities of color and among queer folk. But, sometimes the zeal in calling out respectability politics fails to recognize the complicated, ambivalent ways in which folks adhere to and/or reject what it means to be respectable. Also, see #3.

5. Let's recognize that pretty much all of us have some type of privilege and we should make pains to interrogate our ish and really listen to one another. Also, being an expert on racism, for example, doesn't mean you always get the nuances of, say, ableism. But, thankfully, you—we—can learn. Our brains are awesome like that.

6. Unless someone is being violent, let's passionately disagree with one another without eviscerating each other's humanity. For real.

Ultimately, my thoughts are that we need to have difficult dialogues without cannibalizing each other. Let's embrace our diversity in the movement and not call for a unity that steamrolls over dissension. We see how the Far Right is imploding, but the difference between us and them is that they have boatloads of cash and no scruples whatsoever and we have an abundance of ethical concerns, passion, and student loans we cannot ask our parents to pay for. They will rise again, but if we become too fractured it might be a different story for us. This is a call to keep our eyes on the prize—it's not just about being right, it's about working together for justice.

Mama's Baby, Papa's Maybe

Susana M. Morris

Father's Day has come and gone again. As someone who did not grow up with a father or father figures, this day has not traditionally been on my radar at all. These days, though, it's hard to forget Father's Day. Besides all the incessant commercials urging you to buy the fathers in your life any number of useless objects, there are all the obligatory posts and profile picture changes on social media that serve as poignant reminders. I often smile wryly when I see these public declarations regarding fatherhood. Some posts seem like wishes for what a father might have been. Others describe idyllic fathers who listened, laughed, and stayed around. I know the truth for most of these folks is somewhere in between because fathers, like mothers and everyone else, are wonderful, terrible, flawed, complicated, and messy.

It's been almost thirty years since I last saw my father. I was about five or six years old. My mom and I returned to Puerto Rico to visit folks after moving to New England the year before. I remember few things about the trip, but what I do remember has always stood out and is only now beginning to fade with the passage of time.

My mom and I stayed in a motel that had a chain lock, which I remember thinking was very fancy. My mom bought a package of Vienna Fingers and I remember lovingly eating every cookie I could get my little hands on. I can tear up a box of those things to this day. We went to a friend's house and I used the bathroom and this lady had a toilet-roll cozy that had a doll on top of it. I remember taking it out of the bathroom and telling my mother that this lady kept a doll in the bathroom. My mind was blown. My mother was embarrassed.

I remember seeing my father. He had a mustache and a five-o'clock shadow and looked a little bit like Tony Orlando.

I remember him being really tall and having a scratchy face. We went to a park, I think, and there were swings. He hugged and kissed me. It was a fun day. He said he would come visit me and that we would be together again soon.

Truth is, I never saw him again.

As a little girl, I used to wait for his call and used to pray that he'd send me letters and a plane ticket to see him. When my mom and I waited for the bus in the heat or the snow, I wished he'd come pick us up. My mom said he had two white cars, a Camaro and something else I can't remember now, and that he lived in a big house he owned himself. We lived in public housing. I wondered why he would leave me where I was while he lived in a nice big house all alone, one that didn't have a cute little Brown girl who liked to read and sing songs, and who loved him very much.

Things were tough with my mom and I think that, as much as she loved me, she was also really bitter that she had to raise me alone. If I ever asked questions about my father or his family, she'd get really upset. So I learned not to ask questions.

For a long time I felt really angry at my father. I felt abandoned and unwanted. It's taken me a long time to stop wishing that the past was different and to focus on creating and maintaining relationships that are reciprocal with folks who are emotionally available. That's a journey that I'm still on. And it is that lesson that I am left with this most recent Father's Day. I am happy to see so many of my friends and colleagues honoring the fathers in their lives who held or hold them close, and those who are making a way in their own lives as feminist fathers, godfathers, brothers, uncles, play cousins, mentors, and so on.

What Love Looks Like in Public

Robin M. Boylorn

I planned to write about the unconscionable, inconsolable injustice that is plaguing the Black community. I was going to write about how calling Black folk animals and savages for being treated like animals and savages is just that bullshit disguised as being deep, and how the protests in Baltimore following Freddie Gray's death and funeral, while still waiting for explicit details on why the hell he died, were just and justified. But when I searched for words they felt overly familiar. I have written that, said those words, made those arguments. The names are different, the circumstances are different, but the systemic and perpetual racism and disenfranchisement of Black and Brown folk who have the audacity to be poor and/or imperfect and/or disillusioned with the police is consistent. The failure of our (in)justice system, which creates and perpetuates injustices for Black folk but doesn't punish itself, is conveniently lost in the story line while the people on the frontlines are maligned. I don't want to explain that the media framing something as a riot doesn't make it one. I am tired of telling people that righteous rage is righteous, even if it makes folk uncomfortable, and that you can't keep telling people to "wait for justice" when it never comes. I can't conceive of why it is necessary to keep defending their frustration or my own. I am tired of spilling my tears at the altar of White supremacy.

That frustration and fear was put on full display in a video that circulated during the Baltimore protests of a Black mother confronting her son for participating. The footage captures Toya Graham slapping her son in the face and directing him away from the crowd. Michael Singleton, her child, her *Trayvon Martin*, her *Jordan Davis*, her *Tamir Rice*, her *Ezell Ford*, her *John Crawford*, her *Mike Brown*, her *Freddie Gray*, looked at his mother respectfully, if not indignantly, and led the way home.

We have seen the way Black mothers have been represented during the years-long move/ment for justice. Sybrina Fulton (Trayvon Martin's mother) was respectable. Lesley McSpadden (Michael Brown's mother) was not. Lucia McBath (Jordan Davis's mother) was respectable. Samaria Rice (Tamir Rice's mother) was not. The media portrays "respectable" mothers as compliant, quiet mourners who solemnly demand justice. Respectable mothers are constructed as married or marriable, God-fearing, well-dressed, and visibly middle class. Mothers who are young (or had their children young), single, or struggling, have multiple children or no father-figure present, are mad as hell about the death of their child, and refuse to be comforted or silent are considered disrespectful and rude and are blamed for the so-called "poor choices" of their children.

I find it fascinating that the same folk who police respectability and would condemn Toya Graham for putting her hands on her son in any other context celebrated her "parenting" because they assumed it was evidence that she was against the protests. She was heralded as a good mother (one who refuses to allow her son to organize) even though her personal presentation and background is similar to that of the supposed bad and disrespectful mothers. Because Graham was read as an "angry Black mother" whose anger served the purposes of conservatism, she was recognized as reasonable, her anger justifiable (because it was directed at her child and not the injustice system).

Ironically, I don't think Toya Graham's interference was a result of her anger, but rather her fear. A Black mother's fear might look like anger (or embarrassment) in public because it is a fully embodied expression. It might seem aggressive or abrasive or too much, but a Black mother's love is desperate and deep. I believe this woman wasn't just pleading with her son to go home, she was pleading with her son to live. In my opinion, she was trying to save her son's life, protect him from the possibilities of danger or recognizability that could put him in danger for being seen as an agitator or troublemaker. I don't believe her reaction was an attempt or intention to vilify the folk who were demonstrating. It was about protecting her son so that she doesn't have to know what it is like to stand in protest because something happened to her child.

The image of this mother, ignoring cameras and onlookers and directing her stare and concentration on her son, is a nuanced layeredness of loss, fear, sadness, rebellion, reaction, and love. The news station undoubtedly captured this mother loving on her son in public accidentally. She was not putting on a show or performing for the cameras. She was caught mothering her child the only way she knew how, of having that love looked at as something different, something political, something radical (though loving ourselves and each other, as Black folk, is always an act of rebellion and radicality), when all she was doing was what Black mothers do every day: protect and love.

Toya Graham, not unlike most Black mamas I know, is scared as hell that the presence of her child is dangerous because his Black-bodiedness and maleness and open defiance to authority could cost him his life at the hands of those who are supposed to protect and serve. I saw in her my mother and the mothers of sons who have died who wish they had had the opportunity to tell their sons to shut the hell up, to go the hell home, to turn the music off, to keep walking and not turn around, to not pick up the pellet gun in the store, to not play with a play gun in the park, to not run—because if it means pausing your protest so you can live, masking your masculinity so you can walk out alive, our lives are more important than our principles.

#CFCTaughtMe: Five Lessons on Life and Relationships on the Occasion of Our Fifth Anniversary

Brittney C. Cooper

This past weekend, I hung out with the Harvard Black Law Students Association at their annual conference. Megabrilliant, these young Black folk are poised to do great things, and I really enjoyed kicking it with them. I was on a "Black Media Matters" panel with Damon Young and Panama Jackson of *Very Smart Brothas* and Kimberly Foster of *For Harriet*, all fierce Black folk striving to making our lives matter in the realm of representation. It was a pleasure to panel with them.

So sitting in that room full of mega-intelligent, accomplished young Black folks, inevitably our panel turned to the question of "positive media representations." When I indicated that I wasn't particularly invested in seeing positive Black folks on screen, so much as complex and interesting Black folk, one young sister asked me all exasperated, "Why can't we just have Black women in *normal* relationships on TV?!"

It made me think back to that moment in my life, as a twenty-something, in grad school, whole world right out ahead. I wanted those same things too. A banging career, a good dude, a couple kids.

And before I knew it, I found myself being far more transparent than I had intended on being with her. Because I know how much (cisgender, straight) professional Black women's deep longing for certain kinds of partnerships and female friendships drives our engagement with visual representation, I asked her, "What happens if you do everything quote unquote 'right' and it still doesn't work out for you that way?"

These are the kinds of questions that being single in one's thirties and spending too many long, cold winter nights alone will have you asking.

I'm so glad that in the same moment I wanted all those things that this sister wanted, I was becoming a feminist. And because we are celebrating five years of doing this work together, I thought of five things CFC has taught me about life relationships that I would've shared with that sister if time had permitted.

1. Feminism will help you get free. Without feminism and the frameworks it has provided me, I don't know that I would have had the good sense to see all the things I see now in the way that I do. I think I would have thought my perpetually single self a failure at life and the things that matter if feminism hadn't taught me to see all the awesome things I do have. I couldn't have embraced my rage or made it productively political. I wouldn't believe we could change the world. I wouldn't have known I could simply throw off all the old ways of thinking that were holding me back.

2. For feminists, female friendships are not optional. If you can't point to at least one real, true, know-your-drawsize homegirl, you get the side-eye. Homegirls are necessary for survival. My homegirls both in the CFC and outside of it are heaven-sent. They are the answers to prayers I prayed a decade ago when my feelings had been hurt by one too many a sisterfriend that I had loved too hard only to have the effort, time, and care unreciprocated.

   Today, my homegirls show up and save my life regularly, whether that means keeping me from throwing my computer against the wall while I struggle to finish my book, reminding me why I'd lose all my cool points if I really did call and cuss out the last dude who did me wrong, or making me laugh raucously at least once a day. I have cultivated deep friendships with women because I need them to survive. Because they are family. Because without them there is no me. I invest time in those relationships in similar ways that I would invest in partnerships because my homegirls are family, even when we fight, even when they get the side-eye, even when they get on my nerves.

3. Singleness rocks. And self-love is the best love. My time is my own. My space is my own. My money is my own. I don't have to share, and since I'm an only child, I'm not much on sharing anyway. I have the freedom to craft the life I want without worrying about how it will impact someone else's life.

   My sex life is my own too. I have the freedom to go after the sex I really want, to move on if I'm not getting it, to try new things and new people, to draw boundaries between my intimate life and self, my career, and my homelife. Those kinds of possibilities are far more limited with marriage.

The other day I told some of my homies that I was assuredly on my way to becoming a church girl, but it turned out that I liked sex a little too much to achieve that single-and-celibate thing forever. But at the height of my church girl days, when the word "sin" and the practice of self-flagellation was always a priority, I remember thinking that the sin framework crowded out so much of the deliciousness of life.

As a literary scholar, I knew that the very best African American books were wonderful because they were filled with complex Black folks living life. I knew the church would call Sula walking sin. And Janie Mae Starks too. And Shug Avery. I reveled in those stories because they were messy and salacious and utterly human. And I realized that striving for Christian perfection felt not only unattainable but pretty boring too.

4. There are other things to want besides cisgender, heteronormative marriage. Knowing what I know now, I'm not even sure if marriage is the thing I really, really want. And I can only ask that question of myself because my twenty-four-year-old dreams didn't come true. Thank the Lorde. Now I know there are other things to want. Other things I can have. Other arrangements that may be more sustainable or more fulfilling or more enjoyable. (See for example: Mary Jane's "cutty buddy" on BET's *Being Mary Jane.*)

And I find myself wondering how the longing and waiting for a "normal" relationship has worked out for some of the women I knew back then. I know that I like my "new normal" much better. The sex alone is worth it. And I know the CFC freed me up to go after it.

The lie of winter is that it will have you believing that all the barrenness you see is all there really is. But if you look closely you'll see the signs of life all around. My girls are like those evergreen trees. They never go out of season. And my seasonal baes are like pops of color to give some pizzazz to the landscape.

5. Exceptional Black girls were never meant to live ordinary

lives. Too often ordinary Black girls settle for ordinariness. But I'm a big dreamer and I hope that every *Brown Girl Dreaming* experiences the extraordinary.

And here's one to grow on . . .

6. What you build matters infinitely more than what you tear down. Our work is the work of building, of making Black and Brown girls see possibility. This work of crafting a feminism that works for real sisters living messy, human lives has freed me up to make the life for myself that I really need. Crunk feminism, and this community, reminds me on the daily that all the things I want are possible, but sometimes I have to change my angle of vision.

GIRLS STUDIES:
BLACK GIRLS ARE MAGIC

Introduction

By the time the CFC was founded in 2010, two Black girls were living in the White House (Malia and Sasha Obama were alla ours), Beverly Bond had already declared that Black Girls Rock! (her partnership with BET was in the works), and Procter & Gamble's "My Black Is Beautiful" campaign, designed to celebrate the diverse beauty of Black women, was gaining momentum. Less than a decade later, Black girls and women continue to create and curate spaces for themselves to be seen, recognized, and celebrated. We are championing sports we were once excluded from (including gymnastics, tennis, and ballet), directing films that tell our stories, leading the #BlackLivesMatter movement, selling out Black dolls made in our likeness, winning awards for portraying complicated characters who are also Black women, demanding recognition from the federal government that acknowledges we are as at-risk because of racism and classism as Black men and boys, and appearing on the cover of a mainstream magazine heralding the headline, popularized by CaShawn Thompson, "Black Girls Are Magic."

And we are magic.

We live it. We breathe it. We make it. We believe (in) it. "A dollar out of fifteen cents"? Magic. Making a way out of no way? Magic. Little Blackgirls wearing cornrows with beads dangling daintily down their backs? Magic. Michelle Obama rocking a tangerine dream dress at her husband's last State of the Union. Magic. Taraji P. Henson caping for Viola Davis when she won an Emmy for Best Actress. Magic. Mikaila Ulmer, founder of Me & the Bees Lemonade, becoming an entrepreneur at the age of eleven. Magic. Black girls twerking to bounce music in booty shorts and high-tops way before it was a fad. Magic. We show up and we show out in ways that are mystical to outsiders.

Our magic is wrapped up in the fact that before anyone else would see or value us, we saw and valued ourselves. Our magic is in everything from sisters in matching yellow ruffle dresses standing in line to give an Easter speech to single mothers holding it down on little-to-no pay. It's best friends and play cousins, playing the mama and becoming each others' first sisterfriends, practicing our neck roll and hip sway. Black girl magic is stocking caps, greased scalps, and hand-me-downs. Adult slumber parties, ladies nights, and girl-talk.

Blackgirls are out here winning, but it is not without critique and misrecognition. Any time people of color cultivate and celebrate themselves and their culture, it is blatantly disrupted if not altogether co-opted. Black girl magic is nothing new, but because of social media and the curiosity of White folk, it is something that started catching on in the 2010s.

Our Black (girl) magic isn't voodoo that we do. Black girl magic speaks of resilience, resistance, and recognition. We are magic because of the purposeful and poignant ways we survive and succeed despite the odds rarely being in our favor. We are magic because we are at once individual and plural, Black girl and Black woman, me and us. We are magic because we are overcomers and overachievers. We are magic because, despite misogynoir and mythic lies about who we are, we see ourselves in each other, like mirrors, and we like what we see.

In an effort to capture the twoness of Blackgirlhood, Robin coined the term "Blackgirl" as one word, wherein she intentionally omits the space between "Black" and "girl" in an attempt to capture the connectedness of the lived experience. While White women and girls are not preoccupied with their race, and men and boys who are Black enjoy the favor of their gender, Blackgirls are consistently made aware of their race and sex simultaneously. There is not a pause, a break, a separation, a breather, a moment when their self-awareness as Black-bodied girls is not required in a racist, anti-Black, misogynist, and patriarchal culture.

Robin suggests that being a Black girl is being a *Blackgirl*, one word, no space.

Black girl magic is about our shared experiences, our shared oppressions, and our shared appreciation for the fierce, fantastic, and magical way we navigate a terrain that doesn't leave room for us at the table.

Michaela Angela Davis, the image activist, defined Black girl magic, saying, "We are shape-shifters, superheroes, styles-layers, soul scholars, truth seekers, sisters, healers, Holy Rollers, hotties, listeners, lovers, dreamers, divas, daredevils, doers of the damn thing—all at the same damn time."

Crunk feminism is based on a similar premise, creating a space to be our full "crunk" selves and celebrating one another in love and solidarity. Unfortunately, we did not always find those spaces in the academy. We view girls studies as a burgeoning academic enterprise that can standardize the lived experiences of Blackgirls and center their narratives. While there remains a dearth of research and literature that does not pathologize Blackgirls, hip hop feminist scholars like Ruth Nicole Brown and Bettina Love are creating a curriculum that celebrates, acknowledges, and centers Blackgirls. Their work envisions and builds a pedagogy of Blackgirlhood that provides a classroom and culture of visibility and encouragement rather than invisibility and relentless critique.

We believe that Black feminism captures the maturity of our experiences and crunk feminism speaks to our girlhood, our coming up and coming of age and our relationships with our homegirls, girlfriends, and sisterfriends. As crunk feminists we have an ethic of care around how we engage Black women and Blackgirls, choosing to celebrate rather than ridicule them. Our feminism questions what it might mean if Black girls were affirmed and praised. We recognize that sometimes, if not oftentimes, the incessant critique of Blackgirls comes from Black women. We learn from larger culture how to judge ourselves and each other against standards we are not meant to measure up to, policing everything from our sisters' romantic choices to hairstyles. And because Blackgirls are almost always read as "grown," they are not exempt from the community critique. As Jay Z said about Blue Ivy in "Picasso Baby," people "even talk about your baby crazy." When grown women go in on a toddler wearing pants, or the community discussion about a Blackgirl breaking barriers and records is about her hair and not her accomplishment, as was the case with Olympic gymnast Gabby Douglas in 2012, there needs to be a shift in how we perceive care for Blackgirls, and there needs to be an acknowledgment of what Black girl magic means in those moments when Black women believe the hype of cultural respectability more than they believe in magic.

The essays in this section include reflections of our own girlhoods and commentaries of Blackgirls growing up in a world where we are Blackgirl women, womanish from childhood in order to navigate spaces that don't allow us to stay innocent. We discuss the generational and patriarchal oppressions that Blackgirls inherit and imagine a world where Blackgirls are free.

Won't You Celebrate with Me?

Susana M. Morris

Warning: The following is a meditation on childhood abuse.

In April 2010 the family of Oscar-winning actress Mo'Nique went on Oprah to discuss an issue that has torn them apart. After years of denials, Gerald Imes, Mo'Nique's older brother, admitted to molesting his sister for several years. Though I suppose I shouldn't be surprised, what struck me the most about the interview was the family's defensive posture regarding the situation. Another of Mo'Nique's brothers was invested in maintaining that his brother "wasn't a monster" and that Mo'Nique seemed to have "gotten over" the abuse because she and Imes had a "great relationship" in the years after and are only recently estranged. <Side-eye>

Before I speak my peace, I'd like to start off with a feminist prayer, of sorts.

won't you celebrate with me

by Lucille Clifton (1936–2010)

won't you celebrate with me
what i have shaped into
a kind of life? i had no model.
born in babylon
both nonwhite and woman
what did i see to be except myself?
i made it up
here on this bridge between
starshine and clay,
my one hand holding tight
my other hand; come celebrate
with me that everyday
something has tried to kill me
and has failed.

I feel blessed every time I read this poem. While I love so much of Clifton's work, this is the one that speaks to me the most often, the one that I return to when I'm feeling low-down and sorry for myself. I think, I'm here, I'm a survivor. So much bullshit, and yet, I'm still standing.

Like an unfortunately large number of people, I was abused as a child. It's not something I talk about often or think about daily, but it's a part of my past that exists just below the surface of my consciousness, like a throbbing vein beneath my skin. When I was a little girl and we had just moved from the islands to the mainland, my mother and I lived in the basement "apartment" of some family friends. Our place was a very small room that, in retrospect, was probably a walk-in closet. We shared a twin bed and a small side table. We didn't have our own bathroom (we often used a chamber pot to relieve ourselves), and we alternated between freezing and boiling in the New England weather. Needless to say, these were conditions my mother wanted to get us out of. So, she got herself a couple of low-paying, menial jobs and left me in the company of the aforementioned family friends during the day while she worked.

Once left in the care of these people, I became easily frightened and I cried a lot. I became intensely afraid of my mother dying and being left with these people who treated me so badly in a whole host of ways. My mother was worried but was really focused on moving us out of there. My father was nowhere to be found (he'd abdicated his responsibility when my mother was pregnant with me), and the rest of my mother's people were a thousand miles away. So I learned to get through the days as best as I could. When my mother came home I fell into the tiny bed in deep exhaustion. I didn't say a word. This went on for two years. When I was seven, my mother lucked up and got a Section 8 apartment and we left that basement hovel and never looked back. Boy, wasn't no one as happy to see some projects as I was, I tell you what.

I was a fairly well-adjusted kid on the surface, though I suffered from nightmares and had intense crying spells. I loved to read and, after a couple of false starts, really began to excel in school, something my mom championed in me. She took me to the library and bought me books when she could. When I wrote up little stories and fairy tales, she told me they were great and that I would grow up to be a great writer and teacher. I really thank her for that because everywhere else I went I was getting the exact opposite treatment. I really was working against all the stuff I went through in that base-ment "apartment," and I can't tell you how many times folks—adults and children alike—told me how stupid, fat, ugly, not to mention how poor, I was.

Against all odds, I've been to college and graduate school. I'm gainfully employed, live in my own place, and drive my own car. I even have health insurance—the good kind that lets you go to the dentist and the eye doctor. I am surrounded by love from a whole host of folk who comprise a fiercely loyal chosen family. And I am very close to my mother, who is wonderful in all sorts of ways. All in all, I've turned out all right. Yet, mine is not a Horatio Alger story of triumph. Sure I worked hard, but I am here because I was able to tap into a feminist network of friends and create a loving family. The sup-port I get from these folks cannot erase the past, but it can engender a healthy present and a better future for me and perhaps others with similar experiences.

I'm not telling you this for your pity. Rather, I'm speaking out be-cause I'm in a safe space/place with feminist brothers and sisters who value my voice. There are many others who have gone through what I experienced (and even more) and who may have the desire to speak, but no safe space to do so. (I also recognize there are those who do not desire to speak about their abuse, and I respect that as well.) If we call ourselves progressives, radicals, and feminists of any sort, we need to take close, hard looks at the sort of communities we are born into and become a part of. What are we doing to make our commu-nities a safe space for children and the survivors of abuse? What are we doing to break the patriarchal patterns of control that promote exacting violence as a rite of passage? I do not have all the answers, but I am damn sure asking some questions, and no one's gonna shut me up for "airing dirty laundry."

Although I don't know all of Mo'Nique's story, I respect her need to disconnect and disassociate from her abusers. I, too, have had moments where I was expected to be cordial to the very people that violated my trust. Back in the day, I would've smiled and held down the bile, but now I refuse and will continue to do so.

Despite the fact that abuse comprises most of my earliest memo-ries, when I think of my past, I think of the last lines of Clifton's poem. And I think of my mother and grandmother and all the other women in my family who, like me, are survivors of abuse. Now, let's not get it twisted. I am not saying that abuse is a badge of honor. Far from it. What I am saying is that I went through the crucible and I'm still here. Sometimes I'm broken and bleeding, but I'm here, and that is something worth celebrating.

Meeting Girls Where They Are

Chanel Craft Tanner

One of the most fascinating things about feminism is the many roads to getting there. If you find yourself in a room full of feminists and ask each of them how they were introduced to the ideologies of feminism, the answers will be as varied as the women and men represented. My feminist sensibilities were sparked long before I had ever heard of the word; my introduction to feminism was through the lyrical and visual imaginaries of Lil' Kim.

As a hip hop head, I was often the lone girl on the stoop debating the flows of Biggie, Jay Z, and Nas. I could read lyrics and identify double entendres like no other. The words spoke to me, and I mastered the language of being able to speak about those words. But I was silenced when the conversations would center on sex (and as we were middle-school students, that's often where the conversations went). The music I loved articulated a very clear role for women. They were receptacles for penetration, unspeaking subjects who existed for the purpose of satisfying male sexual needs. I had no words to speak back.

That is until Lil' Kim came through, legs spread open, looking directly into a camera that functions for the male gaze. She was speaking back, with a little sass and a purpose. When Junior M.A.F.I.A. said, "Fuck bitches, get money," she responded with attitude: "Fuck niggas, get money." For me, Lil' Kim represented the ability to talk back. Screaming "fuck you" and "I can do it too" and "my body belongs to me," all at the same time, she was my introduction to an equality feminism of sorts, not much different from that strand of feminism represented in the mainstream.

And it is here where I feel like older feminists missed a key opportunity to engage with young girls by meeting us where we were. Me and my girls were from Brooklyn, from the same streets Lil' Kim walked, so we were protective of her. And even though we couldn't articulate then what she was doing for us, we were resistant to adults who wanted to critique her. We felt like they didn't understand her and, consequently, didn't understand us. What if they moved from a pedagogy of understanding? What if they had first paid attention to what it was we liked and then given us context for how this method of equality was problematic? Women's studies classrooms shouldn't be the only space where young women are asked if doing what men do is desirable. I didn't need to let go of Lil' Kim. I needed a context for understanding her.

As crunk feminists, we are now confronted with another opportunity to engage young women and girls where they are through the representations of Nicki Minaj. As we move into positions of elders, we must ask ourselves, what kind of elders do we want to be? One of the key skills that hip hop heads have developed over the years is the ability to listen. Hip hop has required a participatory listening audience from its inception. We must transform this ability to intently and purposefully listen into a pedagogy of hearing. If we listen to young women and girls, they will most definitely teach us something. We have to move beyond what makes us uncomfortable about Nicki and the way she is taken up by young girls and instead ask, why is she being taken up this way? We must ask, what is she doing for young girls and what can she do for feminism?

As a crunk feminist, I am always and forever dedicated to the disruptive voice, one that I hear through the rapping of Nicki Minaj. Listening to a Nicki Minaj song causes a disruption in your ear drums as she plays with her voice, both volume and accent, and causes one to pay attention. As the only mainstream femcee being represented, her voice is single-handedly disrupting the testosterone of the airwaves. Her performance disrupts the politics of normativity and respectability as she rocks her pink wig and Freddy Krueger gloves. And there is something remarkably different and refreshing about her linkage to other women in the game. In the midst of the representation of Black women in popular culture as being in competition with each other, she refuses to compete. Meanwhile, fans of Eve, Jean Grae, Lil' Kim, and other women beg their favorite emcees to battle Nicki, but they all refuse. They are not interested in the continual Foxy vs. Lil' Kim debacles that plague women in hip hop. There is a recognition that battle rap and competition that pits women against women isn't useful and instead they actively choose sisterhood.

All in all, Nicki gets crunk! And as crunk feminists, we are best equipped with the tools to engage with those aspects of Nicki Minaj that are not worth celebrating. Who, but us, can help young girls understand the false empowerment of Barbie and the way in which this image encourages women of color to drastically conform to White standards of beauty? Who, but us, can situate Nicki's sexuality in larger trajectories of materialism and the sex industry? Who, but us, can allow space for young girls to celebrate but also give them context to critique? And who, but us, can stand behind her and push through where she is able to make small cracks? (E.g., no one else could effectively read her verse in Usher's "Lil' Freak" alongside queer theory of color, I'm just saying.)

And to be behind her means we must watch around her. We have to watch for the times when she is crunk and "marching to the rhythm of her own heartbeat" and when someone else is choreographing her movements. We must watch when her movements are being made to uphold standards of domination and patriarchy. We must watch when her positionality as the lone female in the crew is serving as a stand-in for messed up gender norms of what it means to be a ride-or-die chick. We must push her forward when she's pushing in directions that disrupt all the bullshit, and gently push back when she goes astray. She needs to know that while she may feel like she's doing this alone, crunk feminists are behind her screaming, "Nicki!"

Baby Hair: For Gabby, Blue Ivy, Tiana, and Me

Robin M. Boylorn

I have always had a love-hate relationship with my hair
tucked in
stocking caps and shower caps
naturally curly when wet
but rarely on purpose
blue pomade melting in my mama's fingers
parting lines across my scalp
to scratch dandruff with a rat-tail comb
I'm called tender headed when it hurts

flaunting beads that hit against each other when I whip my head
    back and forth
sounding like baby bracelets
braided cornrows
twists
roller sets
ponytails
wrapped in rainbow colored plastic bows
barrettes
banana combs
rubber bands
ribbons on Sundays sometimes
picture day at school when I secretly took my hair loose so it
    would be "like the *White girls'*,"
my mama's disappointment and disdain when the pictures
    came back
my first grade hair "all over my head" from playing on the
    playground
sweating out Mama's Saturday sacrifice
of hot combed kinks pulled out for Sunday service
second grade revelations that hair mattered
all hair
wasn't good hair
and it was hard to love what people
called nappy, knotty, kinky, wooly, messy, saying,
Look at your hair!

Don Imus's "nappy-headed ho" remarks about the Rutgers women's basketball team in 2007 was a reminder that White folk don't understand Blackgirl hair, the way it grows up and out, or down and long, how it swells with sweat and shrinks in heat—our hair was not meant to be tame.

When Gabby Douglas won gold at the 2012 Olympics, the rants of Black folk more interested in talking about her hairstyle than her accomplishments was a reminder that some Black folk are ashamed of Blackgirl hair, the imperfection of edges that won't lie down without gel and hair clips, the propensity of uneven locks that refuse to fit neatly in a bun or barrette. Our hair has historically told a story of class and respectability.

middle school hair was damaged
box perms, split ends, receding edges, and curling irons
    held too tight for too long
high school hair fell out
temperamental growth and temporary alopecia
onset from stress, worry, and depression
fear of not fitting in
left me desperate for disguise
biweekly all-day hair appointments
updos, goddess braids, my first weave was glued in
I got compliments for days

In 2013 pictures of Blue Ivy Carter, then a toddler, surfaced on the Internet to vitriolic comments about her untangled baby hair, called unruly and reckless, without bows or braids. Beyoncé was blamed and shamed for allowing her child to be photographed with her hair uncombed, code word for not neat. Dissenters claimed that Beyoncé made too much money to have her daughter looking "like that"—like a Blackgirl.

Later that year, Tiana Parker was sent home from Deborah Brown Community School in Tulsa, Oklahoma, for having dreadlocks. The hairstyle, which was restricted alongside "afros and other faddish styles," was considered unacceptable and inappropriate, even unhygienic, according to a dress-code policy that was eventually changed. Tiana was punished and made to feel inferior for not conforming to a beauty standard. She was seven years old.

Internalized racism and internalized standards of beauty in Black communities lead to an obsession with Blackgirl hair that is tamed, in order, slicked down on the sides, wrapped around in braids, or covered in curls. We don't know what to do with Blackgirls whose hair is left to do what it will, with baby hairs flying with wild abandon and little afros sticking out every which-a-way. We want Black women and girls' hair to be "fixed" in the same way we want them to be "fixed" (whatever that means).

I hope the women basketball players at Rutgers did not internalize the hatred for Black hair when they listened to Imus's rude comments. I hope Gabby Douglas doesn't have a love-hate relationship with her hair because the public posted hateful comments about her hairstyle. I hope Blue Ivy will be taught to not be self-conscious about how her hair grows out of her head and not be concerned about what she looks like during playtime. I hope Tiana Parker continues to embrace her ethnic style and nappy roots regardless of how institutions try to police her appearance.

The politics of hair reaches back much further than I can tell it. Comparisons, confessions, and judgments lead to Blackgirl insecurities and deep-seated pain. All Blackgirls have a hair story. Measuring beauty and worth on the length, texture, and style of hair is one Blackgirl legacy we can stand to do without.

When Everything Hurts:
Black Pain, Silence, and Suicide Tries

Robin M. Boylorn

The first time I decided I wanted to die
my blues were so deep Billie Holiday couldn't climb out

The second time I collected prescription pills in a cloth
    pocketbook I hid underneath the bathroom sink behind
    Mama's sponge rollers and fingernail polish remover

The third time I pulled Grandma's gun from under her mattress
and stared at it for hours

The fourth time I wrote a note
confessing the names of people who made it worse by making
    me feel dead already

The fifth time I swallowed twenty-three pills and waited to die
when I woke up I felt like a failure

My wished-for death was a nightly prayer
whispered into tear-soaked pillows and dreams that didn't
    come true

This notion to die would stay with me most of my life
and the depression that inspired it would go largely unnoticed
    and undiagnosed

* * *

in my Black
girlhood
i was never told that
Black
girls
mattered
we don't see each other enough
to know we're not stronger than steel
that superwoman shit is made for TV
but made for real life
Blackgirls
break

we matter
but we don't hear ourselves enough
screams are muted by stereotypes and assumptions
that swallow and misunderstand our words
when they are not softly spoken
or standardized
making us feel foreign
in our own damn land

but we belong here
because we belong everywhere

we matter
but we are not present enough
forced, always, to think ahead
and defend ourselves
to think back
and protect ourselves
we are not always strong

being Black when the world sees you as all wrong
is like a degenerative disease
with an expensive-ass cure
we can't afford

Ntozake Shange's choreopoem, *for colored girls who have considered suicide / when the rainbow is enuf*, startled me. By the time I

held the paperback book in my hands, I had taught myself to see my suicide attempts as shameful acts that made my mother cry at the church altar. It was my family's secret and my burden. My heart hurt and everything about living exhausted me. No one understood why I tried to die so I kept my morbid manifestations to myself and pathologized my sadness the way my family did, the result of daddy issues, low self-esteem, and watching too much damn TV.

Shange's poems, narratives, and choreography spoke about episodes in my own life that I had been too afraid to say out loud. For a Black woman to admit that she had considered suicide was seemingly revolutionary. For a Black woman to admit that she was not impenetrable was remarkable. She put words to what hurt. Everything. She gave space for what was possible. Anything.

I had been told that my depression was all in my head and that there was essentially nothing Black Jesus, a good night's sleep, or good dick couldn't cure.

I pushed my pain into silence and my White woman therapist collected seventy-two dollars every two weeks for watching me cry and fantasize about jumping out her ten-story window.

for colored girls saved me. Woke me up from a dream I didn't know I was having. Taught me to look inside myself for the capacity to love myself and how to lay hands on myself, by myself, and for myself. I didn't stop thinking about dying, but I did start thinking about living.

> only recently i have learned how to resist the inevitable pull
>   of my blues
> how to live wide awake
> how to not want to die
>
> it meant not allowing other people to dictate my happiness
> or my sorrow
>
> it meant making my circle smaller and more discreet
> it meant learning to love myself on purpose and with full
>   consciousness
> it meant feeling all of my feelings
> and not doing the emotional labor of others
>
> it also meant paying attention to how people treat me
> and walking away before they can do damage to my soul

it meant never internalizing my insecurities
and honoring my frailties

it meant learning
i am worthy of respect, love, and security
and that everything about me is a gift
and if folk miss that
that's their loss to live with

it meant looking myself in the eye, in the mirror, every single day
and knowing that i am the shit
dreams are made of
alla that
and
all the times i have been overlooked, messed with, laughed at,
    ignored, dismissed, missed, passed by, fucked over, fucked
    with, lied to, left for dead
was an inexplicable misstep on the part of the other person

it was never about me

now when sadness comes
and it does come
like an unwelcome visitor
or lover i no longer desire
i sit with it awhile
and we talk about old times
while i collect my tears in open hands
laughing and crying at the same time
because there is no room
in my house
or my heart
for sadness to take off its shoes, get comfortable, or overstay
    its welcome
i won't let sadness move in
because i have moved on

I am oftentimes surprised when talking about my childhood fascination with dying does not inspire my grown-woman friends to call
me crazy. They don't ask me where it hurts. They know. They don't
wonder what the triggers are. They know. They don't wonder out loud
about my occasional morbidity or the days I am stingy with words

and attention. They recognize my introversion as a side effect of my depression. They understand. They know that being a Blackgirl in an anti-Black and misogynistic culture makes living without intermittent sadness a miracle. They know we are all each other's miracle.

Unbreakable, or The Problem with Praising Blackgirl Strength

Robin M. Boylorn

Amber Cole, a fourteen-year-old Blackgirl who was secretly recorded performing fellatio on a former boyfriend, was vilified in the media, accused of being fast-tailed and grown, and shown little to no empathy after being outed in 2011. Images and taunts spread quickly as the video went viral and commentary about Amber's agency, privacy, and sexuality sparked controversy across the Interwebs. There was slut shaming, blaming, and judgment (of Amber and her mother) with little mention of the three boys involved (the boy receiving oral sex, the boy recording it on his phone, and a third who watched in the background).

In my gender class we discussed Amber with empathy and understanding and attempted to make sense of the thoughtless and cowardly ways people were vilifying her, defending the boys implicated in the video, and seeking a scapegoat. It seemed inconceivable to consider Amber's vulnerability as an impressionable young Blackgirl. My class discussed how Amber's race (alongside her sex and age) colored her as anything but a victim, regardless of the laws of consent (for sexual engagement and being filmed). We opined that perhaps if Amber were White there would have been more sympathy, less visibility.

Misogynoir and stereotypes of Blackgirl hypersexuality made Amber fair game, and despite possible hurt feelings and embarrassment, folk assumed she would "get over it." She was Black so she was strong, right? The pseudoremedy for being bullied, shamed, and mocked in real time and online (to the extent of being included on Urban Dictionary) was a short-lived Twitter campaign and transferring to a new school. Not so much. Despite the inevitable emotional and psychological damage she experienced, folks did not defend

Amber. People were not inclined to protect or feel sorry for her. Instead, they blamed her for making a bad decision, bad-mouthed her mother for not raising her right, and assumed that as a Blackgirl she would be all right, eventually.

Three years after Amber Cole was bullied on the Internet, another Blackgirl was similarly hypersexualized and ridiculed online. Jada was a sixteen-year-old rape victim who was drugged and sexually assaulted at a party. Within days, graphic images of her before and after her assault went viral on social media with memes and videos being made mocking her unconscious body. In a brave and admirable response to being bullied, Jada, with the support and encouragement of her mother, used social media and television interviews to speak out against her attack, her alleged rapist (who continued to mock her online), and the countless cowards participating in attempts to demean her and her character. Jada stated, "There's no point in hiding. Everybody has already seen my face and my body, but that's not what I am and who I am." Jada is amazingly resilient, and initially I was impressed with how seemingly effortlessly she could recount her rape without emotion during interviews. But then I remembered she was sixteen.

While I support and celebrate Jada's bravery, I worry that being proud of her stoicism is an improper response to the trauma she experienced. Jada is sixteen years old, and not only was she raped but she was publicly exposed, outed, mocked, teased, and threatened. Perhaps instead of being proud of her for being strong, we should let her be visibly devastated, distraught, shocked, and inconsolable. Maybe instead of being impressed that Blackgirls can withstand so much suffering and become role models for strength, we should be concerned about their emotional wellness, their vulnerability, their humanity.

Truth is, Black folk feel implicated by other Black folk, and strength is something we feel we can be proud of. A lot of the backlash against Amber Cole by the Black community was shrouded in respectability politics and fear that her sexuality and participation in a public sex act might blemish an already-sullied and stereotypic image of Blackgirlness and Black womanhood. With Jada (and her mother), her strength and refusal to be shamed and silenced as a rape victim is seen as heroic and commendable (and don't get me wrong, it is, but I believe that part of the reason we "need" her to be strong is because it reflects the overall strength of Black women), but both of those girls were pushed into a spotlight they didn't design and became poster children for causes they did not seek out.

Society refuses to see Blackgirls as victims. We are made to believe that our feelings are dangerous, so we suppress them. We are told, repeatedly, even among ourselves, that we are not fragile, so we think we must live up to those expectations. When unthinkable and unspeakable things happen, we take a deep breath, hold back tears, and swallow our sadness. We perform strength like nobody's business.

The problem with Blackgirl strength is that it never lets up. Blackgirls don't have the luxury of a time-out or a break to breathe. The problem with Blackgirl strength is that our very lives are at stake, and if we don't learn to mask our pain we won't know how to survive. The problem with Blackgirl strength is that practice makes perfect, and after a while we have that strength, no pain, never-let-'em-see-you-sweat shit down pat. The problem with Blackgirl strength is that it doesn't offer protection. The problem with Blackgirl strength is it doesn't allow weakness or pain to push through. The problem with Blackgirl strength is that nobody ever tells us we don't have to be strong and we don't know how not to be.

Blackgirls become strongblackwomen, whether they want to or not.

That is a problem.

Anger is permissible as long as it is tempered with strength, but Black women cannot afford to be blue.

That is a problem.

No matter what happens to them, Blackgirls are taught they can "take it."

That is a problem.

Mistreatment, abuse, and misogyny are so commonplace it is common place.

That is a problem.

The incidents involving Amber and Jada reinforce the devaluation and hypersexualization of Blackgirls, but also the unspoken expectation that Blackgirls absorb all the sadness, insecurity, pain, and harshness thrown at them.

Blackgirls are not unbreakable. There has to be a way to protect our Jadas, our Ambers, and ourselves without shaming and silencing our visceral responses to trauma. There has to be a way to be okay without having to be so damn strong. We have to make room for Blackgirl emotional fluidity. We have to make room for sadness, for anger, for hysteria. We can raise a fist in the air with tears in our eyes and still be powerful.

Olympics Oppression? Gabby Douglas and Smile Politics

Brittney C. Cooper

I tune in to the Summer Olympics every four years primarily for one sport: women's gymnastics. I had the privilege of falling in love with gymnastics in the early 1990s, the golden era of Team USA. Coached by the great Béla Károlyi, the 1992 and 1996 teams featured the likes of Kim Zmeskal, Shannon Miller, Dominique Dawes, and Dominique Moceanu, just a few of my faves from back in the day. And my all time favorite moment was when Kerri Strug perfectly stuck that vault landing with an injured ankle at the '96 Olympics. I've never seen more heart. It simply doesn't get any better than that.

So I was mad excited to tune in to see the 2012 team of five girls, the favorite Jordyn Wieber, Aly Raisman, McKayla Maroney, Kyla Ross, and Gabby Douglas.

I cheered for all of them, but I had a soft spot for the girls of color on the team, including African American Gabby Douglas and Kyla Ross, who is of African American, Japanese, Puerto Rican, and Filipina descent. As with most sports coverage, though, every time a Black girl participates in a sport traditionally dominated by White women, you can count on the commentators showing their asses. And they did not disappoint.

Seventeen-year-old reigning world champion Jordyn Wieber failed to qualify to compete for the individual all-around finals. Instead, Jordyn's best friend and teammate Aly Raisman competed for gold along with Gabby Douglas. As shocking as it was—and it must be devastating to have your lifelong dream dashed before a watching world—Jordyn's understandable disappointment in no way justified the uneven and downright biased coverage that Gabby received for her performance.

First, during floor exercises, Gabby stepped out of bounds with both feet, resulting in a several tenths of a point deduction in her score. That's not an insignificant error for sure, but the rest of her routine was almost flawlessly executed.

But you wouldn't know it to listen to the sportscasters chomping at the bit, talking about how absolutely terrible it was, what a *huge* mistake she'd made, how low her score was going to be. And on. AND ON.

Never mind that Jordyn had a bad day. She gaffed on her balance-beam routine and almost fell, but the commentators focused on how she recovered and pulled it off by sheer strength of will. I'm not tossing any shade to Jordyn. It was a beautiful routine. But the sportscasters were *far* from impartial.

Both Aly and Gabby advanced to the all-arounds, and we saw coaches and teammates hug and congratulate Aly, and comfort and console Jordyn, but they did not say a word to Gabby. There were no high fives, no words of congratulations (not on any coverage I saw), no celebration at all. Just total disappointment on Jordyn's behalf, and the overwhelming sense, at least among the sportscasters who talked about Jordyn's dashed hopes and dreams, that Gabby didn't really deserve it, that she'd taken a spot that didn't belong to her.

Why celebrate Aly and not Gabby?

In the immediate interviews afterward, Aly got asked questions about how excited she was, how she felt about her friend, but ultimately what this meant for her (White girl) dreams. Gabby, on the other hand, got three questions about her shortcomings—her mistakes during the floor exercise, the belief among the coaching staff that she couldn't handle the pressure, and her feelings about coming in ahead of her teammate (who presumably deserved it more). The fourth and final question asked how she felt to be there, and like Black girls used to this kind of passive-aggressive White hostility are so deft at doing, she responded with an affirmation of confidence in herself. And then she gave a big beautiful smile, a smile that everyone focused on in their coverage of her.

A world in which Black girls smile, giddy from the joy of being able to pursue their dreams, is a world I want more of. But after having read Toni Morrison's analysis of Clarence Thomas's nomination hearings for the Supreme Court, and the copious amount of times that Congressmen referred to his great smile and jovial personality (rather than his record of legal scholarship and groundbreaking rulings), I am suspicious of these kinds of smile politics.

Perhaps focusing on her smile made Gabby seem nonthreatening. But make no mistake, she was in it to win it.

Gabby went on to lead the team to victory by capturing 33 percent, or one-third, of the total points the team received. The girl that the commentators repeatedly suggested was "unable to handle the pressure" was the only team member to compete in all four events—vault, bars, beam, and floor—and though she was only one-fifth of the team, she did 100 percent of the events and captured one-third of the points.

I took serious issue with the media's coverage of her accomplishments and the sense of White entitlement that permeated the sports coverage. The coverage magnified Jordyn's victories while minimizing Gabby's. And it wasn't right. Not to mention that it was classic passive-aggressive White racism. (Yeah, I said it.) The kind that injures, not by heaping insults, but by failing to grant recognition when it has the power to do so.

Gabby showed up for her team in each and every event, smiling graciously, and in Black vernacular, she showed out! But that reminds me of some more ol' school Black wisdom, too: "You have to be twice as good to get half as far." Every Black kid hears this at some point in their lifetime. It still rings true. And what our parents don't say is that even then, you still might be invisible. Invisible, that is, in your accomplishments. Your flaws won't be treated half as graciously.

What If We Were Free?
Riley Curry and Blackgirl Freedom

Robin M. Boylorn

While it is not uncommon for athletes to attend postgame interviews with their mini-mes in tow, Riley Curry, the adorable, precocious, and then-two-year-old daughter of 2015 NBA MVP Steph Curry, sparked some interesting controversy following her father's postgame interviews during the 2015 Western Conference Finals. Unlike her predecessors, who were seemingly trained to be muted and patient accessories for their fathers, Riley was fully herself and fully her own.

Riley's antics included talking over her father (and telling him to be quiet because he was talking too loud), playing hide-and-go-seek under the table, peeking from behind the curtains, yawning dramatically, talking into the microphone, and reciting lyrics from Big Sean's "Blessings" (*"waaaaay up I feel blessed"*). Riley demanded the attention of her famous father, whom she had likely not seen much due to the grueling practice and travel schedule of the play-offs. Steph calmly responded to questions from reporters while simultaneously appeasing his curious look-alike, but many reporters and fans complained, accusing Curry of being unprofessional for allowing his daughter to "act out."

On one hand, I get it. Reporters were frustrated because they were trying to do their job and the intermittent interruptions of a two-year-old was a distraction. I have certainly been that chick at the restaurant, in the mall, or on the airplane who has wanted nothing more than for a parent to "control" their energetic and restless child who was kicking my seat, talking too loud, whining or wailing, invading my personal space, or otherwise vying for attention. On the other hand, I have been around my fair share of two-year-olds (they don't call it the terrible twos for nothing), and find it unreasonable (and ridiculous) to expect a restless, bored, and rightfully self-centered toddler to be still or quiet.

Riley's presence made an otherwise run-of-the-mill presser entertaining. NBA players have routinely conducted interviews with their children at their sides, but Riley's perceived bad behavior suddenly made the practice controversial. It seemed that the daddy-daughter dynamic was less appealing to sports reporters than father-son.

Given the context of Black men and sports in 2015, there were several dynamics at play with this story: 1. an attempt to controversialize Black male athletes' relationship to media (e.g., Marshawn Lynch's refusal to engage reporters); 2. an opportunity to recalibrate how Black athletes have been characterized as fathers of small children (e.g., Adrian Peterson's child abuse charges); and 3. a policing of Blackgirls via politics of respectability. Folk don't know what to do with a Blackgirl who is free and a father who is fostering, rather than stifling, that freedom.

Politics of respectability requires a two-year-old to "act like a young lady." Society wants her to do what society expects all women (and evidently girl children) to do in public. They want her to sit down, be still, look pretty, be quiet, not take up too much space, not demand attention, not make a scene, and not talk (back). If Riley were a mute prop, her presence on the stage with her father would be welcome. If Riley were a boy child, her antics would be dismissed as biologically inherent peacocking. If she were White, we wouldn't be having this conversation.

Children are unpredictable, which is what makes them wonderful. They are expressive and creative and hopeful and forgiving, and, until they are taught to be otherwise, free. But Black children are not often allowed to be free. They can't afford to be free. Their parents have to teach them the rules of being a Black child, not for respectability, but for survival. So, for many Black children, their behavior is restricted from an early age. They are conditioned, especially in public, to be seen and not heard. They are warned, from parents and othermothers, that they cannot afford to be seen as disobedient and unruly. These lessons and warnings are missed on a toddler. Riley didn't understand that people were reading and scripting her through stereotypes (misogynoir for Blackgirls), and she was not concerned about the ways her ease and comfort made others uncomfortable. She was unabashedly and unapologetically free, and I, for one, celebrate her freedom. Her freedom acts as rebellion against those who don't want her to be as free as she is, perhaps as free as she'll ever (get to) be.

Come through, Ms. Riley. The world is watching!

POLITICS AND POLICY:
THE PERSONAL IS POLITICAL

Introduction

"Let me think it through out loud with you."

Halfway through her piece "My Brother's Keeper and the Co-optation of Intersectionality," Brittney Cooper pauses to demonstrate, with this line, that the CFC is a place for collective thinking and shared analysis. She is making her project plain—to think through a complex political moment in which a racial justice analysis was complicated by a feminist lens. When President Obama launched the My Brother's Keeper initiative, focusing on the perils faced by young Black men and boys around the country, the program did not include similar attention to Black women and girls.

The rallying cry of many feminist analyses of politics is, of course, "the personal is political." The Crunk Feminist Collective pushes the bounds of both that which is personal and that which is political. In particular, we locate ourselves in the South and anchor ourselves to the hip hop generation. These are markers of place and time that put us squarely outside feminism's mainstream, and so our personal is personal to our self-articulated time and place. Some of us are immigrants to the United States and are constantly negotiating the politics of place. Some were raised in the rural South, and others in big cities on the coasts. Our political is often bigger than the narrow definition that limits the scope of politics and policy exclusively to legislative advocacy.

We came to push these boundaries, together—to do it better and better in the face of a social and political climate in our home communities that, at its best, ignores our efforts, and, at its worst, actively dismantles them and causes irrevocable harm. In our pushing, we refuse to elide the intersections—race, place, class, gender, nationality, sexuality, and so many others—at which we live.

Despite the sometimes-frustrating or false picture of the South and its communities of color that the media can paint, we know that our communities are sites of brilliance and resistance. In fact, it is from the South that many of our most radical and effective strategies emerge. It is from besieged communities that the most creative thinking transpires.

A crunk feminist intervention on traditional ways of understanding and engaging political issues starts by asking the unasked questions about our laws and policies. Whose interests do they protect? Who do they target? Who do they benefit? Who do they harm? What about our families? Our communities? Our bodies? Where do we, and the people we love, fit in? We ask: Who are the women in the "war on women" that mainstream feminist organizations speak of? We ask: Where are the girls, the sisters, unmentioned in the national effort to support and advance the interests of young Black and Brown men? We ask: What has the politics of respectability done for us lately?

These questions illuminate a methodology—that of intersectional political analysis—that asks questions in light of the multiple social and political institutions that affect our lives. To begin by asking these questions is crunk feminist praxis. The questions pose normative challenges that open the door for a politics that includes us. Further, to name that which might otherwise go unseen. Or things that we deliberately render unseen.

A crunk politic includes, but is not limited to, making some invisible things, and people, seen. It is a generative and generous politic. It is collaborative and evolving. It can offer a new way of looking at an old problem. It can offer solutions. It can offer a new starting point. In one instance, instead of conceding that individual health is only a matter of individual responsibility, we interrogate the public health framework that ignores gender, poverty, and race in its understanding of a person's health.

These are normative demands for our epistemologies to reflect us, for our politicians to see us, and for our laws to reflect our needs. Cooper writes, "Juridical structures interpellate identities, which is a fancy way of saying that when the law recognizes your unique structural position, it sets a precedent for future forms of recognition." By telling the truth, by refusing invisibility and minimization, we make the personal political. We call for accountability. By telling the truth, we make crunk policy and politics possible. We render ourselves visible.

In addition to an intersectional analysis, what does a crunk politic entail? Crunk activism, of course. The CFC offers a space to move from analysis to action, to raise awareness about social justice issues, and to facilitate opportunities for our readers to act, to be crunk, in practice, and to directly and indirectly answer this question about making our work real, making our politics actionable, and living our values in our heads and hearts but also in the world.

There is plenty of space in a crunk politic for growth—as evidenced by many of the CFC members' own writings through both this anthology and the blog itself. We've grown in our feminisms, our stories of understanding race and class, and our anchoring in family. In this way, the CFC itself is a political project, anchored in Black feminist analysis and rooted in the South, that centers the stories our mothers and grandmothers told and didn't tell. Many of us have had conversations about politics and social justice issues with friends and family members around the country and the world. Our writing reflects the questions they asked, the challenges they made, the stories they told. Our political is personal, familial, national, and transnational. The CFC makes a space for this kind of political work—collective and collaborative.

The politics and policy we discuss in the CFC is never dispassionate. We don't aim to write objectively about political issues. This is the final cornerstone of a crunk political analysis: we center *our* stories and *our* communities and emphatically take back our subjectivity. We do this in conversation with each other and with our community of friends, allies, and readers. We invite you to join us in this endeavor.

Let us think it through out loud with you.

On the Pole for Freedom: Bree Newsome's Politics, Theory, and Theology of Resistance

Brittney C. Cooper

When Bree Newsome climbed a flagpole in Columbia, South Carolina, on June 27, 2015, and removed the Confederate flag, she became my shero. And my new favorite theorist and theologian of resistance. That flag, which I grew up seeing on the bumper stickers of pickup trucks, hanging from the flagpoles of residents of my town, and even being used as a curtain in a ramshackle house on a rural country road, felt even more offensive in the days after a vile and misguided millennial neo-Confederate named Dylann Roof walked into the sacred space of a Black church in Charleston, South Carolina, and murdered nine of our people.

Ten days before Bree Newsome's courageous stand, I woke to the news of the massacre of nine faithful souls at Mother Emanuel AME Church on a trip abroad for work and play. Startled and devastated, I lay in bed wondering whether to wake my homegirl sleeping next to me, because, like me, I knew she was tired of waking up each morning to structural devastation and systemic heartbreak. That's what these times of racial atrocity committed by police and vigilante citizens have felt like—like no time to catch one's breath between blows. Undone and outdone, I jostled her awake anyway, as the tears started to leak from the edges of my eyes.

I'm a church girl. My ardent feminism hasn't yet been able to overcome that. Believe me, I've tried. But I know that I am here today because of many a Wednesday night spent communing with God and the saints at Bible study and prayer meetings. This isn't so much my spiritual practice anymore, but it remains the practice of so many Christian folk I love. Dylann Storm Roof could have murdered any one of them. Any one of us.

In the aftermath of these killings, we've turned once again to debating the merits of the Confederate flag. I despise the stars and bars. I resent having grown up in a place where my classmates and their parents flew that flag freely, pasted it on car bumpers—with the disingenuous tag line, "It's heritage not hate"—and reveled in their nostalgia for rebellion. They expected Black folks to be silent and unoffended, expected us to ignore that the celebration of that flag essentially communicated the sentiment, "We wish y'all were still slaves."

Bree Newsome offered the holiest of "fuck thats" to such foolery and went up the pole and took that shit down.

My heart still swells for her courage. But I also think we would do well to see all the ways in which her act of resistance opens up space and possibility for us in the realms of faith and feminism.

As she took down the flag, she spoke to it: "You come against me with hatred and oppression and violence. I come against you in the name of God. This flag comes down today." On the way down, and as she was arrested, she recited the first verse of Psalm 27: "The Lord is my light and my salvation. Whom shall I fear? The Lord is the strength of my life. Of whom shall I be afraid?"

The clear Christian framing of her act of civil disobedience matters for a number of reasons. As the families of the nine slain offered their forgiveness to Roof for his heinous acts, I was incensed at what felt like a premature move to forgiveness. While I feel compelled to honor the right these families have to grieve and process this loss in the way that makes most sense for them—after all this is first and foremost *their* loss—I also wonder about whether churches have done a disservice in making Black people feel that forgiveness must show up on pretty much the same day as our grief and trauma and demand a hearing.

If God is indeed "Emanuel"—translated as "God with us"—then how could this God demand that we forgive and forgive and forgive again while we are being led like so many lambs to the slaughter? How about we leave the forgiving to Jesus and the grieving to human beings, assuming that Black people are in fact human and not superhuman? But here's the thing—this isn't a referendum on forgiveness. I'm clear that forgiveness does a particular kind of spiritual work, a work of healing, a work of freedom, that we need. My problem is that, however important forgiveness may be as a personal act, it does not make for sound and effective politics. Maybe I've finally found an area in my feminism that I want to remain personal and not political.

I don't forgive Dylann Roof. I don't forgive White supremacy. I don't forgive White supremacists. I don't forgive patriarchy. I don't forgive capitalism. I don't forgive these systems or their propagators (complicit though I am) because we have not reckoned with the magnitude of their devastations, deaths, and traumas. I don't forgive those who still have a knife at my throat. I'm not Jesus. Black women are not Jesus.

When Nat Turner, an enslaved Baptist preacher, led a slave rebellion in Southampton County, Virginia, in 1831, he rejected what his faith said about the primacy of forgiveness. He did not forgive his masters. The great antilynching crusader Ida B. Wells, a devout Christian, once argued that "a Winchester rifle should have a place of honor in every Black home, and it should be used for that protection which the law refuses to give." Wells did not advocate nonviolence, nor did she believe in forgiving White people for the atrocities they committed against people of color. She believed in accountability and change.

To be clear, I am not advocating violence. I am saying that Bree Newsome exists within a long history of Christian *resistance* to White supremacy—a resistance not predicated first and foremost on the offering of forgiveness to those who showed no remorse, nor on the demand for healing for those whose wounds are fresh and gaping. We have to stop talking about healing in communities that are forever ducking and dodging the bullets of White supremacy. And we have to stop acting like the presence of intraracial—"Black-on-Black"—crime excuses the wounds caused by those with White privilege and power.

So Bree Newsome was a reminder to me that forgiveness is not the only thing faith can look like in public. Faith in public can look like a demand—for justice, for recognition, for grace. Faith in public can look like calling White-supremacist evil exactly what it is and "coming against it." Faith can look like a Black girl climbing a pole. Faith can look like that Black girl looking into the face of power and telling those come to arrest her that she "ain't neva scared" in the name of God.

And because I'm me, and this is we, let me loop back to that penultimate line: "Faith can look like a Black girl climbing a pole."

We wouldn't be connoisseurs of crunk in these parts if we did not point you to the hilarity of those law enforcement officers yelling at Bree, "Ma'am. Ma'am. Come down off that pole."

Bree's nonviolent direct action against the state of South Carolina places her in the best traditions of the civil rights movement. There's no denying that.

But Black people have been staring at that rebel flag forever. What is new and important is that Black women, largely because of a heady mash-up of hip hop and Black feminism, now have a different relationship to the pole. I'm only being slightly flippant.

I mean, let's not trip: discourse about Black girls on poles is ubiquitous these days. Stripper culture made that flagpole a mere circumstance rather than an insurmountable obstacle. T-Pain fell in love with girls on the pole a few years back. Today Usher "don't mind." And despite how far we've come in prosex feminism, most bougie Black girls I know have as a goal the keeping of their daughters, if not themselves, off the pole.

So I'ma say that the pole here—flagpole though it were—still marks a liminal space of possibility for what Black resistance beyond respectability looks like. Bree Newsome's Black girl body climbed a pole, quoting scripture, to take down a flag that is emblematic of so much violence enacted on the Black body by the US nation-state. Her act exploded every simple discourse we are currently having about what faith demands, about what decorum dictates that we accept, and about what are acceptable forms of resistance for (cis) Black women's bodies.

Bree Newsome has challenged and enriched my faith and my feminism. She has reminded me that how Black girls move through space always changes the terms of engagement. She has reminded me that the only good use of scripture in public is to help us get free.

(If scripture got you spiritually and rhetorically beating the shit out of gay people, women, and Black folks rather than Bible thumping the shit out of capitalism, White supremacy, and heteropatriarchy, you're using it wrong. God ain't on your side and you might have the devil on your team.)

I still don't know where God was in that Charleston church on June 17, 2015. But I do believe God used a Black girl to serve notice on principalities and powers that be that a change is coming. That same day, the flag was placed back on the pole. A few days later, at the governor's behest, it was removed for good. Indelibly imprinted on my memory is Bree Newsome's body, fully in possession of the rebel flag, now untethered from its hinges. A Black girl with the trophy of White supremacy in her clutches is the only sermon on freedom I'll ever need.

The Wait of the Nation

Sheri Davis-Faulkner

Let's talk about the childhood-obesity epidemic. I'm thinking of this particularly in response to the four-part HBO documentary series *The Weight of the Nation*, which first aired in 2012. Having recently completed my dissertation on the framing of the childhood-obesity epidemic on television, I felt the need to respond after watching part three, "Children in Crisis." In many ways, the program provided precisely the type of argument and evidence lacking in typical mainstream narratives. Focusing attention on the difficulties parents have to contend with (such as the barrage of food marketing on multiple media platforms and availability of a variety of food products developed specifically for youth consumers) was good. However, in each family segment there was an "obesity clinic" at the center of the solution narrative.

I am not arguing that families may not need particular support regarding health and nutrition choices in their homes, but I do question the motives of the health-care industry, the second-largest industry in the nation, consistently conflating weight/size with health. Can we have a much-needed discussion about diabetes without making obesity the umbrella crisis? Can we recognize that the BMI categories are flawed, knowing they are consistently used out of the context of family medical and personal medical histories? Can we also acknowledge that a diversity of body sizes and shapes is biologically normal and that there are significant numbers of healthy "obese" and "overweight" people as well as unhealthy "normal weight" people? Can we address fatphobia, discrimination, and bullying as contributors to poor emotional health?

I am *waiting* for the nation to have a frank discussion about food production, labor, leisure, and human rights, but somehow the narrative is fixated on shaming parents into taking their children to the doctor and/or weight-loss programs to "fix" their bodies. I was *wait-*

ing for at least one explanation for why Tea, the eight-year-old Black girl, was bigger than her classmates and seemed to be developing early. I was *waiting* for a discussion about hormones in milk, eggs, and meat. I was *waiting* for some acknowledgment of genetically modified foods. I *waited*, but the solutions were framed narrowly within single-issue policy making for stronger regulations on marketing or food or for fitness programs. In the meantime, the solution is to visit obesity clinics and research centers, and don't forget your health-insurance card or your credit card because unless you have cold hard cash these industries stand to *gain* a lot in this weight crisis.

Never mind the fact that many youth regardless of their size are eating similar diets of high-fructose corn syrup, Yellow 5 or 6 Lake, Red 40 Lake, and salt. I, for one, am tired of doing workshops with kids where they cannot identify common fruits and vegetables, the components of a basic meal, or read the ingredients in the foods and beverages they consume daily. I am clear that this level of illiteracy does not happen by mistake on a national level. The undereducation and underdevelopment of this nation has been strategically deployed through marketing, which functions as our primary public pedagogy. We used to have cooks in school kitchens; now we have underpaid servers/contingent labor forces, typically women. We used to have cooking classes in school, and now we have well-paid advertising executives and recent college grad interns using all their creativity to market crap to my kid to pay their student-loan debts. If I am going to be called to fight this battle, I want to be clear that I am fighting to win peace for the nation. Peace means parenting that is not in competition with unaccountable and unregulated multinational industries. It means addressing widespread food and environmental illiteracy for people "at every size and every weight." We have had enough food-product (brand) literacy to last a millennium.

Peace means affordable after-school programming so that youth can be actively engaged in their communities with adult supervision at currently underutilized parks and recreation facilities. Peace means job security for mothers (of color)/parents broadly, and explicit recognition that leisure time (evenings, weekends, vacations) is a human right. I'm still *waiting* for my nation to roll out the peace and corporate accountability strategy for improving my community's health. For me this is the "wait" this nation can no longer afford.

Health-Care Reform, Politics, and Power: Is the Supreme Court Crunk?

Eesha Pandit

On June 28, 2012, at 10:07 a.m. (EST), the Supreme Court of the United States (SCOTUS) released its long-awaited decision on whether the Affordable Care Act (ACA), President Obama's major policy achievement during his first term, was constitutional. The ACA was Congress's first major effort at reforming our health-care system in many years, after many presidents tried and failed to make it happen.

Given the balance of the Supreme Court, there was lots of speculation in the hours before the decision that the ACA would be found unconstitutional and struck down. That did not happen. Chief Justice John Roberts, a staunch conservative, broke the tie by joining with the four more liberal members of the court to uphold the law.

Here's the breakdown of the ruling:

1. The individual mandate: The ACA's key provision is known as the "individual mandate," and it requires virtually all citizens to buy health insurance meeting minimum federal standards or to pay a fine if they refuse. Supporters of the mandate said it was necessary to ensure that not only sick people but also healthy folks would sign up for coverage, which is how we keep health insurance premiums affordable. (Note: the ACA offers subsidies to poorer and middle-class households, varying with their incomes. It also provides subsidies to some businesses for insuring their workers.) Twenty-six states opposing the law challenged the individual mandate and the Supreme Court was asked to rule on whether the mandate was constitutional. They found that it was indeed constitutional, but in the form of a tax.

2. Medicaid expansion: The ACA requires states to expand Medicaid coverage for poor and nearly poor households. About thirty million people were expected to gain insurance from the law, according to the Congressional Budget Office. Medicaid expansion was one path to making sure everyone had health-insurance coverage. The Supreme Court was tasked in determining whether it is constitutional for

the law to make states expand their Medicaid eligibility or risk losing federal funding for Medicaid. On that question, the Court held that the provision is constitutional as long as states would only lose new funds if they didn't comply with the new requirements, rather than losing all of their funding.

There was much more in the ruling itself, but these two issues were the major pivot points for the law's survival.
So, what did it mean?

1. The opponents of the ACA were fighting against the law as an unconstitutional use of the government's power, not to mention the horribly racialized imagery that accompanied the messaging around "Obamacare." Much of the opposition was hollering that the ACA was socialized medicine and a scourge that would best be eliminated. That is expressly not true: the ACA is anything but socialized medicine. In fact, some would argue (myself included) that the ACA is a love letter to insurance companies, who stand to gain millions of new customers with the implementation of the law.

    Also, please note this comment from *SCOTUSblog*: "The rejection of the Commerce Clause and Nec. and Proper Clause should be understood as a major blow to Congress's authority to pass social welfare laws. Using the tax code—especially in the current political environment—to promote social welfare is going to be a very chancy proposition."

    The only mitigating factor was that the ACA had many new and rather strong consumer protections, like making sure that insurance companies use almost all of the money they get from us on actually giving us health care, eliminating lifetime caps on the amount of health care they will cover, making sure they can't deny folks health care if they have a preexisting condition, making sure all kids are insured, and making sure insurance companies can't charge women more than men just because they're women. The bottom line is that this law is not socialized medicine, and it's also got some accountability measures to protect us from insurance companies. There were many passionate and dedicated advocates that fought for these protections during the passing of the law, and I'm proud to have stood with them to make sure they made it into the final version.

2. The narrow reading of the Medicaid provision is, in a word, unjust. By not requiring states to expand their Medicaid coverage, many poor folks will have no recourse for getting health care, aside from buying it from insurance companies. How will states ensure that it will be affordable? That remains unclear. States are going to have to do a lot more work to make sure that the poorest and most vulnerable get health-care coverage, and given that many states are facing extreme budget crunches, I have very little faith that the most marginalized among us will get what they need. There is a legitimate fear that many Southern states will opt out of the Medicaid expansion, and given that many of those states have disproportionately high poverty rates, it's a recipe for exclusion and further marginalization. The Medicaid expansion was my favorite part of the law, and it was significantly weakened.

3. The ACA was *never* a perfect bill. It was never really even close to that. The big problems with the bill remain. It's not a bill that provides us Medicare for all, which is the only real way that we can get equity across the board. Access to abortion and health-care coverage for immigrants were thrown under the bus in an effort to get the law passed. It's unclear, based on budget projections, whether and how the law will save the country money. And finally, the principle of using corporations as a means to achieve human rights has historically proven to be a hot mess. We still need to repeal the Hyde Amendment. We still need to challenge capitalism. And we still need grassroots organizing. Therein lies our hope for getting real, affordable, accessible health care for all.

So, is the Supreme Court crunk, you ask? On June 28, 2012, maybe just a little.

Reproductive Injustice and the "War on Women," or An Ode to the Intersections

Eesha Pandit

These days, it's hard to read something in regards to feminist activism without hearing the phrase "war on women." Despite important and sharp critiques regarding the limitations of the phrase, it continues to hold cachet as a means to characterize the depth and fortitude of the conservative legislative attack on women's reproductive rights. This attack—as characterized by many organizations that fight for reproductive rights—includes a full-on state-based legislative strategy to restrict access to abortion via attacks on Medicaid coverage, banning abortions earlier and earlier in pregnancy, mandatory ultrasounds, forced waiting periods, "fetal pain" bills, impossible physician and hospital requirements, mandatory parental involvement, and state-mandated counseling. Given all this, it's hard to ignore the fact that there is indeed a deluge: a river of reactionary regressive political actions, one after another, in swift succession, with the clear goal of making reproductive health care inaccessible.

In the summer of 2013 the Center for Investigative Reporting released a report revealing that, between 2006 and 2010, doctors under contract with the California Department of Corrections and Rehabilitation sterilized at least 148 female inmates, without the required state approvals. The report, informed by the brilliant advocacy work of Justice Now, found that coercive sterilizations occurred at both the California Institution for Women in Corona and Valley State Prison for Women in Chowchilla.

From the report:

> One former Valley State inmate who gave birth to a son in October 2006 said the institution's OB-GYN, Dr. James Heinrich, repeatedly pressured her to agree to a tubal ligation. "As soon as he found out that I had five kids, he suggested that I look into getting it done. The closer I got to my due date, the more he talked about it," said Christina Cordero, 34, who spent two years in prison for auto theft. "He made me feel like a bad mother if I didn't do it." Cordero, released in 2008 and now living in Upland, Calif., agreed, but she says, "Today, I wish I would have never had it done."

Let's pause here and take note of the eugenic history of the California Department of Corrections and Rehabilitation. In 2003 the California State Senate held hearings to discuss and shed light on the state's history of eugenic practices, which included the sterilization of about twenty thousand men and women between the years of 1909 and 1964. So significant and well known were these eugenic practices that Nazi Germany sought the advice of the state's eugenics leaders in the 1930s. Researchers documented these findings and presented them to California legislators in 2003, resulting in formal apologies issued by then Attorney General Bill Lockyer and Governor Gray Davis.

While it is certainly true that some of the women who received tubal ligations did so willingly, we must remember the structure and function of coercion, which relies on a distorted power dynamic in which women were often asked for "consent" while pregnant or in labor, not to mention the racist statements made, on the record, by many of the prison officials performing the sterilizations.

In June 2013, when Senator Wendy Davis stood on the floor of the Texas State Senate and filibustered for hours on end, my email inbox was flooded with requests for support and solidarity and fundraising. These requests were heartening. As a longtime abortion-fund volunteer, I know firsthand what happens when clinics close, when further restrictions are placed on women as they fight to get access to basic health care. Poor women, young women, women of color, queer and trans people, those who live in rural communities, people with disabilities, and numerous others who live at the margins of access to health care are all at the center of this fight. The fight that happened in Texas in 2013 was one in which the politics of intersectionality, the linking, overlapping, and diverging institutional oppressions, were in full force. The communities most affected by the regressive House Bill 2 live at many different intersections.

In solidarity with them (us), I give to the abortion funds in Texas. It is in solidarity with them (us) that I demand an intersectional analysis that names, accounts for, and addresses the multiple forms of oppression that so many of us face.

Clearly, if there is or was a war on women occurring in our country, it must include the kind of reproductive-rights violations that occurred and continue to occur in California's prisons. Coercive sterilizations surely must be counted among those egregious violations. The ability to control one's fertility, without coercion or constraint, is a central tenet of even the most mainstream reproductive-rights organizations. Where, then, are the action alerts from the reproductive-rights organizations? Where are the protests outside the California prisons? Where are the marches and the rallies and the email blasts asserting that these actions, sanctioned by the government, are a violation of women's human rights?

Who, we must ask, are the "women" in the war on women that so many feminist organizations were decrying? Are they the women forcibly sterilized at the hands of the state? Are they the trans women who face repeated acts of aggression in the form of hate crimes and at the hands of law-enforcement officials? Are they poor women of color, immigrant women, queer women, and native women navigating a foster system that makes the right to have a family a matter of demonstrating fitness to parent? Are they queer immigrant women fighting to keep their families together while navigating a punitive and racist immigration system? Who are those women? Am I one?

Courtney Hooks, campaigns and communications director at Justice Now, described the connection between the fight for rights for incarcerated people and the fight for reproductive justice:

> One of the key tenets of reproductive justice is for people to be able to have a child, not have a child, and parent the children they have. Whether through premature death due to overcrowding, violence, and severe medical neglect; being locked up throughout one's reproductive and family formation years; being cut off from one's children and loved ones via long distances, exorbitant phone fees, and visit denials; receiving abysmal baseline reproductive health care while inside that cuts one off from a full range of reproductive options and/ or results in de facto sterilization; or being sterilized via hysterectomy, oophorectomy (removal of ovaries), or tubal ligation in the inherently coercive prison environment—imprisonment interrupts the human right to family of communities of color and communities living in poverty targeted for lock up. Imprisonment and the sterilization abuse that happens behind bars—is a reproductive justice issue.

To ignore these women, these incarcerated bodies, seems more than a mere oversight. It is more than a political mistake, borne of limited resources and an onslaught of attacks. These limited resources are a reality, as are the political attacks on bodily autonomy. It is more than political expediency and the lowest-common-denominator politics to which we have become accustomed, from Right and Left alike.

Cynthia Chandler, cofounder of Justice Now, spoke to the CFC about the challenges they face in connecting this issue with other movements: "There has long been a tension between reproductive rights and reproductive justice movements on the issue of the right to have a family. Fundamentally, we at Justice Now believe that imprisonment is a form of reproductive oppression rendering some populations unable to reproduce." This belief has made it difficult, in Chandler's work, to build alliances with the reproductive rights movement specifically and across progressive movements more broadly. "Prison issues are often siloed," she said, naming the reliance on criminal justice solutions for many issues within the broader progressive community. "The progressive movement is very right wing when it comes to criminal justice issues, with a very limited lens on what we find deplorable in prisons, and in regards to the human rights violations of people in prison," she asserts. Per Chandler's assessment, this would be a perfect moment for the prisoners' rights and prison reform groups in the state and around the country to collaborate with their coalition to include a gender analysis in their advocacy.

The notable absence of this story in mainstream feminist conversations as well as in mainstream progressive and prison reform movements implied, and implies, that this might be an issue for a different movement. The agency, autonomy, and human rights of women in prison is not seen as a "mainstream" reproductive rights issue or a "mainstream" progressive social justice issue. That is a mistake. Because it is an incomplete, inaccurate, and heartbreaking representation of what could and should matter to feminist social justice activism. Also, because it fractures us, as a movement, at a time when we need more concerted efforts, more power sharing, and more collective strategy if we are to overcome the destructive political forces we are facing.

In more ways than one, an intersectional politic is a matter of survival.

My Brother's Keeper and the Co-optation of Intersectionality

Brittney C. Cooper

In the summer of 2014, while we lamented the SCOTUS decision to exempt Hobby Lobby and other corporations-cum-people from paying for birth control because it violates their religious freedom, I learned that thirty Black women released a signed letter offering their support for the president's My Brother's Keeper (MBK) initiative. This letter, from women like former Atlanta Mayor Shirley Franklin and Rev. Bernice King, daughter of Martin Luther King Jr., came on the heels of two major letters from the African American Policy Forum: one from a group of two hundred Black men asking for the inclusion of women and girls in My Brother's Keeper and one from over 1,400 women of color, including Alice Walker, Angela Davis, and Anita Hill, asking for the same.

In a moment when it was clear that the war on women was real, I wondered how Black women could accept analyses coming out of the White House, re: MBK, that marginalized Black women's struggle. I thought on it for weeks while I worked with the group of folks helping to organize a response to MBK. When I initially saw those sisters caping for the President, I thought of a favorite line from Project Pat: *"Don't save her . . . she don't wanna be saved."*

But I knew that was not productive. So let me think it through out loud with you.

Is our struggle invisible to us too? I don't believe that. Do we really believe that men have it worse than we do? I think many sisters do. I also think that while we have received and transmitted an incredibly sophisticated analysis of the nuances of racism and how it impacts our lives, we have been more reticent to think through the effects of patriarchy and sexism, primarily because it creates a rift between us and Black men. And at an affective level, we *feel* connected to Black men. Moreover, what so many sisters want, straight sisters who dominate the discourse on this, is a strong Black man, a knight-in-shining-armor type, to show up for us, save us, love us, care for us, ride for us, and provide for us. Hell, I want that too, but not at the cost of political invisibility. And even though most Black women know this program won't make that happen, we would support almost any program that makes it possible for us to have more Baracks for our many Michelles.

Also, when we dare to assert that our womanhood matters, that sexism is a racial concern, there is hell to pay. The charges of race traitor get thrown like so many grenades. As all the conflagrations pop off, brothers can't hear us when we say, *Yes, young Black men and boys are in crisis. And they need all the help they can get.* If that is all we were saying, they would hear that—but because we dare to say this, *Black girls need help too*, we get branded as race traitors.

There's a deep psychology to this that is disturbing. What will it take for us to become a both/and kind of people? What will it take for us to build racial freedom visions that include everyone? What will it take for Black men to stop telling the lie that our desire to be included is a call for Black men's exclusion? The opposite is far more true. When Black men call for their inclusion it is frequently predicated on our exclusion. Brothers feel very little political allegiance to Black women as Black women. Their political analyses make very little space for gender—other than their own.

At the heart of this, though, is a far more inconvenient truth. To deal with Black women's struggles would be to have to confront issues of male privilege, rampant sexism, and copious amounts of sexual and physical violence perpetrated on Black women at the hands of Black men. With us, it ain't just the system that beats us. Our brothers beat us, too. Not all brothers. Not even most brothers. But far too damn many. And no one wants to address those issues because it seems then like we are pathologizing Black men.

So instead, they say simply, *help the race*, and by helping the race, they mean Black men.

This is unacceptable.

It is unacceptable because we go to the same schools, live in the same unsafe communities, deal with the same systemic lack of access to resources that Black boys do.

It is unacceptable because, like Sandra Bland and like Ersula Ore, a professor at Arizona State University, Black women are frequently harassed and violently engaged by police, who have no problem using excessive force, even when it is clear that we pose no threat to anyone's safety.

But here's the thing: I'm not going to engage in attempts to prove that Black women and girls are doing worse than Black men.

For one thing, I don't have to prove that. I simply have to show that Black girls are doing badly and are in need of help. The idea that two severely sick people don't both need medical care is absurd. The measure by which we determine wellness is not whether you are as sick as another person but whether you are in fact *well*. And it would behoove us not to forget that.

So no intelligent person who responds to actual facts and studies can rightly conclude that Black women and girls en masse are doing well by any social measure.

This whole conversation isn't about facts. The facts are on the side of helping women and girls alongside men and boys.

This is about feelings. This is about the president's *feelings* about not having a father. This is about Black men's *feelings* of invisibility in a system that makes clear in so many ways that they are, first and foremost, a problem with which to be reckoned. This is about Black men's *feelings* of pride at having the leader of the free world, a Black man, stand up *finally* and say, "Black men matter." And this is also about Black men's deep and inexplicable *feelings* of hatred and resentment toward Black women, summed up the best by Chris Brown and Pastor Jamal Harrison Bryant: "These hoes ain't loyal."

And because most of those *feelings* are rooted in actual social realities (not including the disloyalty), it is seemingly impossible for brothers (and sisters) to see beyond their feelings and assimilate new facts into their frame.

So rather than engage facts, they use accusations: "You academics are elitist, out of touch, and you are letting feminism run amok."

To be clear, I grew up in a family where most of the men had had some level of interaction with the prison industrial complex. This shit is not theoretical for me. But I also grew up in a community where lots of young girls had babies before they had the resources to parent. My own father was taken out by gun violence, but he was a terrible domestic abuser and that meant that I had to deal with those things while going to school and trying to make excellent grades. Correcting his abuse would have helped, certainly. But resources to help my mom not struggle to make it would *also* have helped. Mainly, having governmental resources that not dictate what kind of family structure my mother should choose mattered most.

When I went to school I dealt with racist teachers who made me cry every day, teachers who saw my questions *and my right answers* as a challenge to their authority, teachers who tried in big and small ways to break my spirit. I made it, but so many of the other Black children—boys *and* girls—didn't. Again, this shit isn't theoretical.

Here are three prevailing responses to our advocacy for women and girls of color:

1. **Let the boys/men go first.** Well we've heard that one before.
2. **The Council on Women and Girls helps women and girls of color.** Oh, I thought our race was always supposed to matter first. Let us not forget the way the brothers tripped over Hillary in 2008. As one man said to me, the question is, "What matters more? Your Blackness or your womanhood?" To him I replied, "Find me the moment in which I'm not one of those at exactly the same moment that I am the other and I will answer your question."

   But now all of a sudden we are women first. And we need to lay our claims for resources that acknowledge the realities of both race and gender to the side.

   That is the most insidious and wrong-headed co-optation of intersectional discourse I've ever seen. As it goes, if it's not White women, then it's Black men, co-opting the project of intersectionality to narrow the parameters of our freedom vision rather than make them more expansive and inclusive.
3. **Women and girls of color are doing just fine.** To quote Clair Huxtable, "Let the record show" that that is complete and total bullshit.

   The frame that governs Black politics at large remains deeply patriarchal. That frame says a few things. First, slavery emasculated Black men and made it impossible for them to assume their rightful place at the head of Black families and communities. Second, Black men are targeted by racist policies in which they are killed, locked up, and otherwise disenfranchised by police. Third, even though Black women have also been harmed by slavery, Jim Crow, and modern day iterations, rape is a lesser crime than lynching. Moreover, if our men were able to lead families, they could protect "our" women from rape. So rape is first and foremost a disrespect to the Black man's right of sexual entitlement over his woman. Fourth, brothers are an en-

dangered species. Fifth, if we could just restore Black men
to the head of communities, all would be well.

President Obama may not subscribe to every idea listed above,
but he subscribes to and traffics in the father-lack narrative that binds
these ideas together, going around giving copious speeches about
how much he missed having a dad. A father-lack narrative is not the
basis of good social policy. Black feminist scholars have talked forever about how this idea of father lack, which also translates to the
larger idea of needing men to lead shit, functions to pathologize the
work of Black mothers and to minimize the leadership capacity of
Black women.

In this regard, the president has become Moynihan 2.0. And the
fact that he is progressive about women's issues more generally does
not mean he is progressive on the role that Black women play in
communities. More to the point, whatever he may know intellectually about the role Black women play, that knowledge is trumped by
the emotive force of his father-lack narrative. Long way to say, the
president remains all in his feelings about not having a daddy and
we are paying for it.

Let me also take this opportunity to respond to those critics who
say, "Why would we on the Left or Far Left actually expect or look to
the federal government to save Black people's lives?"

Good question. And valid point. At best, MBK is a neoliberal
framework that abdicates the federal government of actual monetary
responsibility to ameliorate the social conditions it created. It suggests that helping men and boys of color is a public good, but that the
actual machinery to lift them up is a private duty. It simply outsources
that private duty from communities of color to corporations.

And in a world where corporations are people (rich, White, male
people who can practice religion, apparently), outsourcing the fate of
Black boys to said corporations is dubious at best.

But here's the issue: MBK is the president's signature racial justice
initiative. I know it doesn't deserve that designation, but such as it is,
it is what we have. And what this initiative does at a discursive level
is make a powerful and unprecedented argument about the ways that
longstanding racial structures have systematically disadvantaged and
limited the pathways to success for men and boys of color, particularly Black men.

Thus the initiative suggests that when a group is structurally disadvantaged, the government has a prevailing responsibility to stand up and offer resources to ameliorate those conditions.

This is an important argument, despite the fact that I have serious reservations about its execution.

But when juridical structures interpellate identities, which is a fancy way of saying when the law recognizes your unique structural position, it sets a precedent for future forms of recognition.

What MBK does is remove Black women, very particularly, from this social equation. By arguing forthrightly for the legitimacy of excluding us, it suggests that we are not structurally disadvantaged by longstanding systems of racism. Or if we are, the refusal to commit resources to help us suggests that we have magical powers to overcome these systems.

Of course, neither of these things is true.

And while it is true that helping Black boys and men does help Black women, my question is, "Are we only worthy of trickle-down racial justice?"

Surely not.

When Kimberlé Crenshaw theorized intersectionality in 1989, she was offering a solution to a specific problem. Existing legal frameworks could not account for forms of employment discrimination that were unique to Black women. They could help if all Black people or all women were excluded but not if Black women as an intersecting category were excluded, for say, wearing braids.

A quarter century later, our first Black president, who enjoys the overwhelming support of Black women, is using the logic and social analyses pioneered by Black women to argue for our active exclusion. And some of our most powerful Black women are actively cosigning the madness.

Jesus wept.

Black women deserve better. Even the ones who don't know they do. And we won't stop fighting till we get it.

Reflections on Respectability

Susana M. Morris

Warning: Discussions of violence.

> Whitepeople believed that whatever the manners, under every dark skin was a jungle. Swift unnavigable waters, swinging screaming baboons, sleeping snakes, red gums ready for their sweet white blood. In a way, he thought, they were right. The more coloredpeople spent their strength trying to convince them how gentle they were, how clever and loving, how human, the more they used themselves up to persuade whites of something Negroes believed could not be questioned, the deeper and more tangled the jungle grew inside. But it wasn't the jungle blacks brought with them to this place from the other (livable) place. It was the jungle whitefolks planted in them. And it grew. It spread. In, through and after life, it spread, until it invaded the whites who had made it. Touched them every one. Changed and altered them. Made them bloody, silly, worse than even they wanted to be, so scared were they of the jungle they had made. The screaming baboon lived under their own white skin; the red gums were their own.

—Toni Morrison, *Beloved*

We hold these truths to be self-evident,
That Black and Brown people in America,
No matter our country of origin,
Are under surveillance by the police state,
Under attack by White supremacy, homophobia, and misogynoir,
And suffer under the threat of annihilation every day.
Respectability hasn't saved us.

You can get killed holding a sandwich,
Walking home from the corner store, for
Playing your music "too loud," or even while
Looking for help after crashing your car.
You can see your children swept away in the storm,
You can be gunned down in an aisle of a big-box store.
Respectability can't save us.

You can be assaulted at a traffic stop,
Be attacked while walking home with your friends,

Get shot forty-one times for reaching for your wallet,
Or be left to an ignoble death after second-rate health care.
It doesn't matter if you are heading to college
Or headed to the corner to slang rock,
Our pursuit of Life, Liberty, and Happiness is a Pipe Dream.
Respectability won't save us.

Don't think just showing your ID,
Speaking the King's English,
Letting go of saggy pants and gold fronts,
Is enough to stem the tide of all our spilled blood,
Is enough to prove that our lives matter.
Respectability was never meant to save us.

Only we can stem the tide
By showing up for one another,
Showing out for one another,
Loving on ourselves and each other,
Marching, agitating, organizing, and supporting each other.
We've always been here and
We are the ones we've been waiting for.

Citizenship and Silence:
Speaking the Stories Aloud

Eesha Pandit

I walk to the mailbox in a small town about an hour outside New York City. Slowly, I make my way down our cracked driveway. I marvel at the blades of grass; so soft and fragile yet they've managed to disrupt the concrete and find their sun. I fancy myself this strong when I observe the blades, my nine years of life have not taught me better, yet. In the mailbox is a letter. "To the Indians," it says on the front in a child's scrawl. No envelope, no return address. Just a hastily folded piece of wide-ruled notebook paper. Inside, a drawing in brown crayon of a teepee and stick-figures with feathers on their heads and spears in their hands. Underneath the drawing the words: "GO HOME."

More than a matter of simple enfranchisement, citizenship for the non-White immigrant is often a matter of existential importance, belonging, and security. Not that having papers inoculates Brown and Black bodies against unfair treatment. This complicated relationship to citizenship is particularly relevant in this moment when city streets and small-town squares are pulsing with marchers raging and staging die-ins. Protestors against police brutality are asserting that Black lives matter, but where do I locate my Brown body in the mix? My South Asian American community? What do we have at stake if we choose not to stand up in the face of institutionalized anti-Black racism?

Our very humanity is tied up in our ability to be seen as human beings, first and foremost. As we know, this is a country founded and sustained by the logic of slavery. This logic, infused in all American institutions from judicial to economic, creates a world in which Black people are seen as property, capitalism thrives, colonization is civilization, the prisons boom and teem with Black bodies at once disenfranchised and working for free. This logic allows us to create a racialized social structure in which Black people are dehumanized and treated like property, and the Native and First Nations people of North America are erased, facing an ongoing genocide. This logic foments a history that tells us that Europeans are the true owners of this land. Asserting that Black lives matter disrupts this logic. And for those of us non-Black people of color, asserting it out loud, in public spaces and in private ones, means that we must see our place in that structure and challenge it, consciously and willingly.

Also at stake here is our ability to be seen as human beings worthy of agency in the form of citizenship. This, of course, is a hot topic for a country in the throes of a demographic shift and a subsequent resurgence of White nationalism. For many of us, the lure of the model-minority myth is strong. But let's not forget the history of this myth: it arose as direct backlash to the civil rights movement, designed to isolate our communities from each other. As social programs and affirmative action policies made their way through Congress, many Asian Americans went from being depicted in the media as conniving foreigners to sparkling model minorities, the kind who didn't need government handouts to succeed. The myth is rooted in racist logic aimed at isolating Black people and allowing an attack on social programs that purportedly encourage them to stay dependent on the state, when facts show us a much more complicated picture about who uses social programs, why, and how often. To this day, conservatives cite this myth as a reason to dismantle security net structures, social programs for low-income people, and civil rights policies. See, if some people of color can "make it" in America, then the American Dream cannot be a lie.

The myth of the model minority is strong. It enraptures many of us with pats on the back, encourages us with social mobility, and seduces us with the promise of an unquestioned right to belong. It offers us a pathway to citizenship, literal and psychic. It makes these promises in secret, like a whisper, and if we believe them we can close our eyes for a moment and forget what it took to get here.

Just a few weeks before my senior year of college, I'm twenty-one and living in a hostel in New York, the summer after September 11. Working at the organization of my dreams, having landed the internship of my dreams, I pinch myself daily and muster quiet affirmations that yes, this really is my life. Having made, and remade, the case to my South Asian immigrant parents to allow me to live in the city alone, I have conquered the world to be here. One day, it's rush hour in Manhattan and I'm shuffling quickly, trying not to lose my balance in the crowd, still new to the pace of this particular borough. I turn on my heel and begin to descend onto the subway platform. I hear the train coming below, the precarious uptown 1. I hurry. I bump into a man with a thin blond ponytail. He looks at me and squints a bit. Grabbing the arm of the woman who is with him, he chortles and says, "Fucking terrorist."

In the wake of the ruling in Ferguson, Missouri, in which a White police officer was not indicted for killing a young, unarmed Black teen, and the subsequent Black Lives Matter protests across the country, we saw Latinx, Asian American, and Arab American organizations release statements of solidarity citing similar experiences with discriminatory law enforcement practices, and expressing an unmitigated urgency for finding collective solutions. Since those days, these statements have been coming in from all around the country. In Ferguson itself, in the wake of tear-gas canisters launched into peaceful protests, non-Black communities of color saw themselves reflected in this struggle, from the shopkeepers in town all the way to the people on the rubble-strewn streets of Palestine. The immovable center of the conversation: that Black lives matter.

Like African Americans, Latinxs, Arab Americans, and Asian/Pacific Islanders are disproportionately subject to police violence and racially profiled based on our skin color, religion/visible markers of faith, accent, language, and immigration status. Though I balk at a case made for human rights in which one group is asked to support the rights of another because of their own interest in the matter, since some are swayed by this kind of metric, here it is: in the matter of police brutality and racism there's no denying that all people of color might assert that Black lives matter, because their own are at stake as well.

The evidence mounts daily: Exacerbated after September 11, 2001, and conflated with issues of national security, Muslim, South Asian, and Arab American communities experience racial profiling and ongoing surveillance. Latinxs and African Americans are targeted by the New York Police Department's "stop-and-frisk" in staggeringly disproportionate numbers. As we move toward a country in which White Americans are no longer the majority, we find ourselves in a war on undocumented immigrants specifically and immigrants of color generally. We see unchecked profiling of Latinxs, South Asian, and Arab American communities by both federal and state law enforcement institutions. At the federal level we see programs such as the recently ended "Secure Communities" and the "show me your papers" (deportation) laws. In communities across the country this has meant an increase in stops and detentions of people based on their accents or skin color, and rooting and deepening fear of engaging with law enforcement by both documented and undocumented immigrants.

We must not forget that African Americans are the primary targets of racial profiling and police violence. We see this in painful clarity as we learn name after name of Black men and women, boys and girls gunned down by the police. Solidarity is standing beside and amplifying, not a sidling up and usurping. Non-Black people of color are inarguably impacted by these structural inequities and racist policies, but this is not ground for recentering the conversation around non-Black people of color. In fact, these data are meant to serve as a reminder about what we all have at stake in dismantling our harmful institutions, practices, policies, and beliefs. It is not license to change the conversation or dictate the terms of the movement righteously and rightfully led by Black folks and started by Black women. This information is just what we need to take this work back into our

homes and families to fight against the myth of the model minority
and uproot the anti-Black racism on which it thrives.

Now that we've explored it a bit, let's return for a moment to the
matter of the metric of self-interest. It is an anemic standard of solidarity to stand with and for the rights of Black people because you
yourself have a stake. Yes, if they come for you today and I say nothing, they will surely come for me tomorrow. But that's not why non-
Black people of color should challenge anti-Black racism in their
homes, communities, and workplaces. That's not why we should rise
up against our social structures rooted in an anti-Black ideology. It
might be a motivating factor for many, but a politic of self-interest
is not a politic of solidarity. We should challenge, rise up, and join
the Black Lives Matter movement because Black lives matter. Not
because we are also somewhere on a diffuse and damaging hierarchy of racism. Not because they matter in relation to other lives. But
because even if we had no self-interest in the matter, if our non-Black
communities of color had nothing at all to gain from asserting it,
Black lives still matter.

Take the self-interest argument and use it as you see fit, I say. We
must begin conversations where we can. Open up dialogues with
the argument, if we think it will spark. Tie our struggles to our shared
realities and experience of race and racism in America. But let us
not end there. Let us not elide an assertion of Black humanity. Let us
be sure to end with an affirmation rooted in unequivocal solidarity.
Black lives matter because they do.

*Just a few months over thirty-one, in a lovely dress at a dinner party
with social justice–minded friends of a friend: I'm visiting a new city
and so am along for the ride this evening, knowing only two other
people in the room of about twenty, at a small though well-appointed
apartment in a big city. It's been a hell of a year with a lot of change
and loss, but here I am, feeling, for the first time in months, a bit
more myself. The night before this party was the first night in months
I didn't wake up in tears after dreaming about the deaths of several
recently passed family and friends. I'm chatting with a new acquain-
tance about my work. She's standing in a doorway, in spindly heels.
She listens to me for a few moments, pauses, swills something, leans
a little too close and says, "Ah, it's so good that you do that work. Antiviolence stuff. I mean, especially given your background. You must
have had to deal with so much violence in the home. I mean, just*

from what I read, your culture can be so violent toward women. A real tragedy. Good for you, though."

There are so many stories of what it is like to be a suspect-class citizen in American. Some truly terrifying, having to do with experiences with law enforcement, torture, isolation, and a hundred state-sanctioned sufferings. But some of these stories are far more banal. For me to be suspect, all it often took was getting up and talking with someone new. I have so many stories like these, yet unspoken. Unwritten.

The violence perpetrated by the police secures the American racial order, protects and preserves White supremacy, and incites both resistance and silence. The resistance I've recounted a bit here, so far. The silence still lurks. Violence, is functional. Gender-based violence, racist violence, colonial violence, homophobic violence, transphobic violence are all the stalwarts of White supremacy and patriarchy. Some of us speak up and speak out, riot and rise. Others of us recoil, quiet our rage, and lower our heads and our eyes. This silence is also functional—our stories die in our throats.

When we join together to resist, to assert that Black lives matter. When we do not qualify or quantify the assertion with "because." When we name the women and girls, and host rallies, marches, and die-ins in their name. When we challenge our families with the same commitment with which we challenge people we've only just met. When we locate our silence, confront it, hold it close, and wrestle it with compassion and ferocity. That is when the silence slinks. That is how we make space for our stories. One at a time, all at once, unapologetic, and true.

Teachers Are Not Magical Negroes

Susana M. Morris

When I was in the seventh grade, I moved from Connecticut to South Florida. I was a nerdy kid who loved reading, science, and social studies and had been selected for the gifted and talented track at school. But when I got to Fort Lauderdale, I entered a middle school where we sat in class and watched *The Jerry Springer Show*, where we were being babysat rather than taught. I felt pretty bummed out about that and spent a lot of time in the library teaching myself. My mom worked twelve hours a day, six days a week, just to keep a roof above our heads, so although she cared she just wasn't that parent at the PTA meetings. By the time I was in eighth grade, I began skipping school and staying home to read, especially on Fridays. (I've been a fan of a three-day weekend since the early nineties.) I felt sort of hopeless about everything, living in a community where violence was rampant, facing street harassment whenever I left the house, and school had the nerve not to be a place of refuge.

Enter Ms. Bryant.

Even to my twelve-year-old mind, she seemed young, probably in her late twenties. I remember she wore her box braids in a short bob, which means she was killing the game in 1993. She taught math and was very no-nonsense. I was in her class for a few weeks, maybe a month, when she pulled me aside and told me that she was taking me out of her class and putting me in prealgebra—advanced math.

Say what?

I've been a good student most of my life, but math has always been a struggle. I'm not even sure I did particularly well in Ms. Bryant's class. I do know that I worked hard and didn't cause any trouble. I thank God every day for whatever it is that Ms. Bryant saw in me. I flourished in prealgebra with the tough but kind Mrs. Klevansky. In fact, that year was the first (and last) time I got As in math.

Curiously, this advanced math class had some interesting demographics. I went to a middle school that was at least 98 percent Black, yet the advanced courses were at least 98 percent White.

Hmm.

Only students in the advanced classes could attend workshops where you learned about the magnet high schools anyone could apply for. If I hadn't been in prealgebra, I would not have learned about the International Baccalaureate program that I would later attend and kick ass in.

Curiouser and curiouser.

So, in a school that was ostensibly all Black, pretty much only the White kids learned how to apply to the elite high schools in our county. That doesn't seem racist at all. No structural inequity here—nothing to see, folks.

Ms. Bryant, a person I haven't seen in over twenty years, is an absolutely integral part of my success. She stepped in and changed the course of my life. I was able to attend the college-prep high school of my dreams, get into and do well in college and graduate school, and then go on to become a professor. Ms. Bryant was one of several people who pulled me aside over the course of my academic life and said, "Take this path off to the side. You'll do better here."

When I talk to other women of color who grew up poor and working class, almost all of us have similar stories. There was a teacher in the second grade, or the fifth, or the ninth. Sometimes she is a Black woman. Sometimes he is a White man. Or someone else entirely. But this earth angel sees our humanity and nascent brilliance and not a little Black or Brown girl who needs to be quieted down, disciplined, erased.

But what about those who don't have a Ms. Bryant or a Mrs. Klevansky? What about them?

This is on my heart in the wake of the Atlanta Public School (APS) scandal, wherein several teachers and principals were convicted in a standardized-test cheating debacle. These educators, mostly Black women, were convicted of racketeering and faced up to twenty years in prison.

Yes. You read that right.

George Zimmerman and Darren Wilson can tootsie roll all across this nation, while these educators are now convicted felons. Where is the justice in that?

Let me be clear. I'm not condoning cheating. I'm an educator, and I think integrity is key in the classroom and when grading. But locking up these folks is like convicting the drug dealer on the corner and letting the kingpin run free. These folks are being made examples of, but trust and believe that the inequities at the heart of the APS remain and will remain until we pay attention to the structural issues that would push teachers and administrators to cheat in the first place.

What, you may ask, does this have to do with my clearly noble Ms. Bryant?

As much as I love and appreciate Ms. Bryant, I recognize that she was in an impossible position. I was not the only smart kid in her class. But there were limited spaces in advanced math. Without the proper resources to lift us all up and get us performing to where we needed to be, only one or two could be chosen. We treat smart Black kids and dedicated Black teachers like magical Negro unicorns that can individually save the world when the truth is that we need massive dedicated resources and structures to support us. We put students and teachers in impossible positions, berate them daily, and then wonder why our school systems are struggling. If we really believe that Black lives matter, they need to matter in the classroom and in the schoolhouse too.

Making Movement Mistakes: What to Do When You F@*k Up

Eesha Pandit

That moment: when some words have escaped your lips and you realize they were wrong/insensitive/politically incorrect/hurtful. Or the moment when you have made a decision in a coalition that has broken the "do no harm" principle of coalition work. When your actions have undermined someone's agenda. These moments can be big or small. These moments can consist of an interpersonal slight or they can be damaging to an entire political agenda. We all know these moments; we have witnessed them, experienced them, and committed them.

I am a professional activist. I've done work organizing and advocating for policy change at the local, state, national, and international level. And every single project I've ever worked on has had an element of coalition building and collaboration. That's how you know you're doing it right: If there are multiple stakeholders, with multiple goals. If we all, with our intersectional analyses and intersecting interests, can find a way to move our agendas forward, together. That also poses many challenges, as we who do this work understand. Intersectional work is hard, but of course, it's the only way.

I say all this because there are few constants in this kind of work, but if we do it right, if we work across our comfort zones and reach out to unlikely partners, and those with different goals but with a shared vision of the future, we will undoubtedly make mistakes. Here, I'm talking about mistakes made in good faith. Not malicious, calculated ones. I'm talking about the moments where we think we're doing right, but we mess up.

Why does this happen? Why is it inevitable? We make mistakes because we do not know better. We make mistakes because we don't understand another's truth, another's lived experience. Because we operate from some uninterrogated position of privilege, perhaps. We make mistakes because we don't think before we speak or just aren't sensitive to someone else's perspective. We make mistakes because we are human.

Here are some of my own strategies, things I've done myself, and things others have done that I've found useful. (Of course, all this depends on the offense, and these are generalizations.)

If you realize you've made a mistake:

1. Apologize. Sincerely. When doing this, think carefully about the best approach. It might not be in person, or it might be. It might need to be public. It might need to be done one-on-one. This depends on the nature of the mistake. But nothing else can happen until you acknowledge your mistake.
2. Don't conflate the mistake and your apology with anything else. The apology is not the time to try and fix the coalition or your relationship. It's not the time to make your broader political statement. It's a time to do just one thing. Recognize your mistake and apologize for it.
3. Ask what amends might be made, if that applies. Ask the person/team/group what might help. Ask without proscribing the answer. Wait. Listen. And then decide whether this is something you can or cannot do. Be honest about that.
4. Realize that trust is easier to break than rebuild. Your relationship/s might not ever be the same. And of course it might get even stronger. But you can't know that. You can't have an endgame in your apology. You have to say it, do what you can to fix it, and not expect more than that.
5. Keep doing the work as best as you can. Learn from it, and don't make the same mistake again.

If you're on the receiving end of a mistake, all I can say is: remember all the mistakes you've made. When I think of all the mistakes I've made, it's easier for me to identify with someone who's done something hurtful to me. I try not to hold it too close to my heart and, if at all possible, assume good faith. Sometimes things are fixed, sometimes they are not, but regardless I try not to carry around anger and resentment. That is, of course, easier said than done, but worth the effort.

HIP HOP GENERATION FEMINISM:
FEMINISM ALL THE WAY TURNED UP

Introduction

When Joan Morgan boldly put the terms "hip hop" and "feminist" together in her 1999 book *When Chickenheads Come Home to Roost*, she created a cultural and political revolution for a generation of Black girls raised up both on hip hop and in the aftermath of the Black feminist movement of the 1970s. Black feminism taught us to love ourselves, to fight for our revolution, and to prioritize our own freedom. Hip hop gave us something to bob our heads and shake our hips to. Both were essential parts of the constructions of our Blackgirl selves and lives, and we refused to give up either.

The insistence that we had the right to retain both our radical political heritage and maintain our stake in the greatest global youth arts movement the world has ever seen seemed at times impossible. How dare we come along and place crunk and feminism together? Southern booty-shake music seemed to traffic in some of the worst kinds of misogyny, sexism, and objectification of Black women's and girls' bodies. How dare we insist on keeping something that didn't seem particularly interested in keeping us?

The interesting thing about that question is that we could be asking it of hip hop or we could be asking it of 1970s-style Black feminism. Neither one seemed invested in keeping late twentieth-century Black women, Gen Xers, and millennials, on our own terms. Both seemed to try to dictate to us a future not of our own making.

And we weren't having it. When a group of us declared ourselves "crunk feminists" circa 2004, we gave ourselves permission to own the varied, competing, contradictory, and complementary parts of ourselves as Black women coming of age at the turn of the twenty-first century. When we undertook this project to theorize another iteration of Morgan's "hip hop feminism," we were attempting to make space for ourselves.

Remixing Joan, we added the word "generation" to our hip hop feminism because sometimes we don't love hip hop enough to declare unqualified allegiance to it. But still, we are children of hip hop. It has been the sound track to our childhoods, girlhoods, and adolescent years for multiple generations. So we wanted to locate our post-soul, Gen-X, and millennial selves, under the banner of the hip hop generation.

Crunk feminism, our particular brand of hip hop generation feminism (for we imagine there can be many) is, as we have said many times in many places, a percussive feminism that finds its way, its mode, its articulation in the spaces of noises, cacophony, and controversy. Ours is not an easily contrived feminism. Our feminism throws down best when it stands up to deal with hard shit.

The lives of women and femmes of color are summarily hard in these twenty-first-century streets. We need music, culture, art, and politics that speaks to all of it. And our Black mothers and Black feminist forebears taught us that the only thing standing between where we wanted to be and where we were was our willingness to make a way where none had existed before.

Crunk feminism is a kind of way-making.

Crunk feminism gives us the nerve to make our way off the dance floor, where we were shaking our asses just a moment ago, when a song comes on that dares to suggest that ass-shaking constitutes desire and consent. Ass-shaking is whatever we say it is, and our hip hop feminism means you will either respect that or you will learn today.

Crunk feminism has helped some of us to make our way through the tenure process in academe. It has reminded us that all that we are and all that we hope to be is not tethered to the university. Like hip hop, academe on our best day is a well-crafted hustle.

And crunk feminism is helping us all make a way through grief, stress, challenge, loss, and growth, in the healthiest way possible. Because we, the hip hop generation, helped build a global movement from two turntables and a microphone. We come from people who painted breathtaking murals from the contents of a spray can. We come from people who, in the bomb-ass way that they twerk, wine, and pop, lock, and drop it, recognize what is high and holy in the low art of grinding.

Crunk feminism helps us to see possibility in living out an unapologetic disrespectability politic. It takes pleasure in the dis, sees fleeting freedom in the rejection of decorum, and recognizes that Black women and Latinxs never quite get to occupy the space of American respectability.

Hip hop generation feminism does not justify bad behavior. It works from the proposition that Black women and girls get to be authors of their own lives, be they good, bad, or ugly. And hip hop feminism respects that authority, and the importance of being able to articulate and live one's life on one's own terms.

Because hip hop culture has fundamentally transformed even the way that Americans speak, we see it as a place that generates language and concepts that help us to fruitfully explain our lives under late capitalism and neoliberal state governance. Hip hop gifted us crunkness, ratchetness, the ability to dis and dismiss, the option to get buck, and the willingness to wreck shop when necessary.

This crunk, ratchet, profanely sacred posture of hip hop generation feminism insists on creatively reconstructing Black life each and every day from the ruins handed to us by the structural violence done to Black life under US neoliberal state formation. We might have to cuss somebody out every now and again so that we don't carry the weight of structural toxicity in our own bodies, letting it poison and kill us slowly.

Sometimes our hip hop feminism means we step to rappers, even the conscious ones, and tell them that they didn't love us right. Sometimes we have to call bullshit on homegirls who want feminist benefits but not the feminist title. And that isn't so much about being overly invested in labels as it is about calling a spade a spade. Is you is or is you ain't a feminist? Cuz that right there, what you just did, was some feminist shit. Own it.

Hip hop generation feminism does not mandate that we have it all together. Who does? But it does ask us to come correct in the way we do our scholarship, in the nuanced and complicated ways we approach the culture, in the level of self-reflexivity and criticality that we offer in the stories that we tell.

Hip hop reshapes the terrain of Black feminism, making it responsive to the political and cultural realities of women and girls born in the late twentieth century. And Black feminism reshapes the landscape of hip hop, pushing it to realize and elevate its political promise and possibility. So, with our oars of love, generosity, and respect for both these parts of ourselves, we row and wade our way through the choppy waters, knowing that we were made for this journey.

Ten Crunk Commandments for Reinvigorating Hip Hop Feminist Studies

Brittney C. Cooper, Aisha Durham, Susana M. Morris, and Rachel Raimist

The CFC attended the important Black and Brown Feminisms in Hip Hop Media conference at the University of Texas at San Antonio in March 2011. We had a great time and were reminded of all the wonderful possibilities in the field of hip hop (and) feminist studies, and we thought we would share a summary of our presentation and our thoughts on what can move the field forward.

1. **Know your history.** If you are going to engage in scholarship on hip hop and/or feminism, know and cite the authors who have helped to shape the field—Joan Morgan, Gwendolyn Pough, Mark Anthony Neal, Tricia Rose, and others are a few good folks to consider. In the rush to incorporate the sexy theorists of the moment, don't throw away important theorists like bell hooks, Patricia Hill Collins, Gloria Anzaldúa, Chela Sandoval, and others who have contributed to Black and Brown feminisms.

2. **Don't romanticize the past.** There is no hip hop Eden. Resist the urge to act as though there was a pure moment in hip hop when issues of misogyny, commercialism, and opportunism were not an issue.

3. **Positions. Know yours and take one.** Make sure that as you are doing this work you position yourself in relationship to the community. Recognize the need to acknowledge your race, gender, generational, and political positionalities. Be willing to take intellectual and creative risks to question accepted orthodoxy.

4. **Contextualize and situate.** Name the cultural, political, historical, and scholarly contexts of your work and your arguments. Make sure to articulate the key political and social issues that frame this moment. Other scholars pointed to

the seventies and eighties as the eras of deindustrialization, the defunding of arts programs in public schools, the war on drugs, etc. But this moment is very different. It is characterized by unparalleled conservative backlash, near-total deregulation of media and corporations, outsourcing, the economic and political dominance of transnational corporations, battles over the meaning of American citizenship, the War on Terror, the concretization of the prison industrial complex, and a massive economic downturn. These are the issues that have framed the creation of hip hop music and culture in the twenty-first century, and new analyses must be attuned to these issues specifically.

5. **Avoid the pitfalls of presentism.** You cannot have this moment for life. Do work that will last. Do not merely discuss those artists whose work is hot in the moment but will have no lasting value. Make sure that your line of inquiry ascertains the broader relevance of the subject matters you choose so that the formulations you offer will remain relevant even if the example you choose does not.

6. **Embrace ambivalence.** Reject false binaries. For instance, the line between mainstream and underground hip hop is at best blurry. Also reject formulations like the Madonna/whore split when evaluating the contributions of women in rap music.

7. **Envision the possibilities.** Rather than merely deconstructing, hip hop scholars and feminist scholars alike must ask: What kind of world are we creating? What do we want to create? We must also ask new questions. Questions about misogyny in hip hop are fairly uncreative at this point. Projects should begin to address hip hop films, hip hop literature, hip hop fashion, hip hop and the arts, and hip hop's epistemological relationships to other knowledge systems.

8. **Wield technology.** Technological literacy is critical for scholarship, creativity, and social movements. Open yourself to this world, and begin to ask questions about how the technological universe affects hip hop culture and feminist studies.

9. **Lived realities still matter.** Scholarship must be accountable to the people. Hip hop and feminist scholarship must still be connected to movements for social change. Also, remember

that theory does not flow in one direction (i.e., from the top down). In fact, in most cases, scholarship needs to catch up to the culture rather than the other way around.

10. **Recognize the power of the collective.** Collective organizing draws on the best creative, political, and scholarly traditions of both hip hop and feminism. Folks who actively move in these communities must remember and recenter the power of the collective in doing scholarly, political, and creative work.

Lensing the Culture: (Hip Hop) Women behind the Camera

Rachel Raimist

The Black Entertainment Network (BET) is primarily a cable space that aims to promote "Blackness" and Black culture but usually airs limited programming—lots of commercial rap videos that articulate a very narrow view of hip hop culture, have strict heteronormative codes of gender roles, and are often particularly troubling in their stereotypes of representations of race, class, and gender. Many scholars argue that BET has done tremendous damage to hip hop culture and community by promoting only limited and very specific representations of rap music, the larger cultural space, the elements of b-boy culture, and media messages that provide such a narrow box filled with stereotypes of all of the above. This is by design. This is a multi-billion-dollar industry built on research of target markets and demographics, and funded heavily by advertisers who see viewers only as potential product-buying consumers, as discussed in Beretta E. Smith-Shomade's *Pimpin' Ain't Easy: Selling Black Entertainment Television.*

So, perhaps it comes as no surprise that Nelson George, celebrated author, filmmaker, critic, and television producer for BET (among other venues), declared in his 2005 book *Hip Hop America* that "if none of these female artists had ever made a record, hip hop's development would have been no different."

In a sentence, George attempted to wipe out our contribution to the culture beyond tokenizing, marginalizing, and compartmentalizing, saying that we haven't had a real or significant impact on a culture that we have participated in as writers, rappers, artists, managers, publicists, filmmakers, supporters, journalists, photographers, b-girls, graf girls, and in every other capacity you could think of, since the beginning of hip hop. This passage gives us an easy target, but points to the notion carried by many folks in and around hip hop culture that simply is just not true. Battle rap would not be the same without Shanté and UTFO; videos wouldn't have inserted so much comedy without Missy and her black trash bag; Trina has brought agency to booty music; Lauryn has demonstrated that girls can write, sing, rap, play instruments, mother, and choose to participate or step away and come back. Anyone who attempts to discount, minimize, discredit, and ultimately erase our contributions is trying to (re)launch an attack that we hip hop feminists won't allow to happen.

That's why *My Mic Sounds Nice: The Truth about Women in Hip Hop* is so important. When BET first broadcast *My Mic Sounds Nice* in 2010, it was their first original music documentary. The hour-long documentary reminisces through women in rap history, celebrating legends including Roxanne Shanté, MC Lyte, and Lauryn Hill. It wasn't an exhaustive history and didn't include interviews with some of the key ladies: Queen Latifah, Lil' Kim, Foxy Brown, Da Brat, and so many others. I can imagine why some women didn't want to be interviewed—who wants to be asked about her sexuality in every interview, or confronted, questioned, or asked to be accountable for what they've said on records for a piece that BET may air over and over again in perpetuity? Cable outlets continually show limited and limiting positions for girls and young women, particularly as participants in hip hop culture.

Some women in the film reinforce ideas that if you have the right men around you, you can get produced as a girl group or maybe be the "one girl out the crew," like Rah Digga of the Flipmode Squad, Eve of Ruff Ryders, Foxy of the Firm, and so on, but it is likely that you'll get dropped or won't sell tons of records if and when your solo album is released. The story plays out that if a woman plays it all right and follows the label/handler's calls, she may be lucky enough to release a solo album and enter into the Foxy/Kim arena, or, of course, she can be a featured dancer in the crew's video, be an extra dancing in the club scene, or watch from home. There is nothing wrong with any of these options, but why are these the only options for young women? Can't women do more than be the plus one, or be more than fans who $upport, or be gyrating bodies without heads in the videos?

So, back to the good news: *My Mic Sounds Nice* by director Ava DuVernay (who first directed *This Is the Life*, about the legendary Project Blowed in Los Angeles) is an aesthetically beautiful film. The interviews with artists, journalists, and label folks are intimate and allow us to look each of these sisters in their eyes. Ava's choice of close-ups allows us to see the women rappers as we have never really seen them before—sitting, speaking clearly and articulately, and not intercut with images of them dancing, moving, grooving, or being hypersexualized (being portrayed as hyperfeminine or hypermasculine, as in most music video representations). Looking at women who are beautifully lit, with light reflected in their eyes, is a connective and very powerful experience for the viewer. The supporting cast of Joan Morgan and Kim Osorio, both key journalists, critical for their very different but important contributions, are framed in wider waist shots—they are important, but not (visually) at center stage.

The men interviewed in the documentary share their insights but aren't given the space to talk over the women. Questlove (The Roots), Jazze Pha, Chuck D (Public Enemy), and others are also framed in eye-level waist shots that don't give them any more visual power than the women rappers centered in the film. The framing, composition, and lighting (soft, beautiful key light) allow us to be close, intimate, and connected—and isn't that the point?

There are critiques of the film—too much Trina, not enough tough/"real" questions, failure to include key women, and treating Lauryn like she died after *Unplugged*—but *My Mic Sounds Nice* is not an exhaustive history. The film is critically important to our story and includes Invincible, Eternia, Jean Grae, Tiye Phoenix, Medusa, and other non-major-label rap women in an ending montage, showing women that BET doesn't usually show. Overall, the film offers beauty, insight, celebration, struggle, and history and shows us as women who (yes, Nelson George) have impacted rap music and hip hop culture.

If you loved *My Mic Sounds Nice*, check these other films by and about women in hip hop:

- *Say My Name* (2009), directed by Nirit Peled. In a hip hop and R&B world dominated by men and noted for misogyny, the unstoppable female lyricists of *Say My Name* speak candidly about class, race, and gender in pursuing their passions as female emcees.

- *All the Ladies Say* (2010), directed by Ana "Rokafella" Garcia, is a film that highlights the lives of six iconic female street dancers from San Jose, Atlanta, Miami, and Chicago, who have carved a niche in the physically challenging, male-dominated break-dance world.

- *The Revival* (2009) is a tour documentary by rapper Invincible that gives a candid glimpse into the first meeting of legendary hip hop pioneer Roxanne Shanté and veteran Philly emcee Bahamadia as they trade stories of their struggles and triumphs in the industry over their long careers.

- *Scene Not Heard* (2005), directed by Maori Karmael Holmes, features interviews with some of the originators of hip hop such as Lady B, Schoolly D, Monie Love, and Rennie Harris, with vanguards chiming in, including Bahamadia and Ursula Rucker.

- *Counting Headz: South Afrika's Sistaz in Hip Hop* (2007), directed by Vusi Magubane, reveals the struggles and victories of South Africa's women from the perspectives of women in South Africa's hip hop scene, including MC Chi, DJ Sistamatic, and graf artist Smirk.

- *Nobody Knows My Name* (1999), directed by Rachel Raimist, tells the story of women who are connected by their love for hip hop music. Despite the fact that these talented female artists exist within a culture that revolves around self-expression, the subjects of Raimist's documentary must struggle to be heard.

- *Soundz of Spirit* (2003), directed by Joslyn Rose Lyons, draws the connections between the creative freedom and the spiritual outlet that hip hop culture provides for the current generation, featuring KRS-One, André 3000 (Outkast), Common, CeeLo, Nappy Roots, Talib Kweli, Blackalicious, Jurassic 5, Dilated Peoples, The Last Poets, and many others.

- *Anne B. Real* (2003), a feature film written and directed by Lisa France, is a coming-of-age story about a young female rapper who finds her inspiration by reading *The Diary of Anne Frank*.

- *Miss M.C. Presents: Queens of Hip Hop* (2003), directed by Danila Perkins, claims that although the rap scene has been ruled by men for twenty years, women are making big moves in the industry. Featuring interviews with Salt-N-Pepa, Lady Luck, Rah Digga, and Charli Baltimore.

* *Estilo Hip Hop* (2009), directed by Loira Limbal (aka DJ Laylo) and Vee Bravo, is a feature documentary that chronicles the lives of three hip hop enthusiasts from Brazil, Chile, and Cuba who firmly believe that hip hop can change the world.

Sticks, Stones, and Microphones:
A Melody of Misogyny

Aisha Durham

I can still hear a whisper (song). Arms oval. Neck curled. Hips sway to the familiar Southern bass from a Black (male) speaker rapping to me on the dance floor. Before I can face the voice coaxing me to move, he drops his hook—a line about a violent sexual fantasy, a common come-on echoed in hip hop club culture. Still. Arms raised, I am arrested by his lyrics likening sex to a beating. He wants to *"blow my back out."*

His lines are in step with other rap courters recounting sexual conquests by the penetrative acts of cutting, bussing, stabbing, screwing, hitting, pounding, smashing, thrashing, tapping, or slicing my body (into parts). The hearty bass thump with the choreographed slow-motion flutter from the strobe light stages a sensual seduction, or what he describes as "making love" in the club. But love in this space is an illusion. It is a manufactured special effect similar to the one simulated by the strobe light. It is this conversation between the flashing light and darkness, between bodies and sound, where I am swayed by a melody of misogyny.

Over the years, I have developed coping strategies to "manage misogyny." In the past, I have defiantly put an "X" in the air while walking off the dance floor, or persuaded the DJ to play more woman-friendly songs, or created other words to replace the ones I could not bear to hear. Each year, I emotionally prepare myself to watch the BET or MTV awards. As a new crop of crooners emerge, I begin listening to more R&B than rap, to no avail. *The love songs don't even love me.* These days, I find myself storming out of clothing stores and restaurants, feeling accosted by the background sound taking over the physical and psychic space. I cannot turn off or tune out all of the car stereos, metro ads, or highway billboards where these images and words have become commonplace. Just how much hate can one woman tolerate?

October is Domestic Violence Awareness Month, and I want to take time to reconsider the matter of words. I want to think about the weight they carry in the everyday lives of Black women. More than a discussion about our love-hate relationship with popular culture, I want to take seriously the way misogyny impacts our relationships with menfolk and ourselves. "Managing misogyny" has become an unwanted, collective experience for women and girls of color from the hip hop generation(s). Language that humiliates, demonizes, objectifies, and threatens is a form of violence. It is verbal and emotional abuse accelerated and intensified by mass-media technologies that make it so pervasive and systematic it is virtually inescapable.

We know how language impacts our lives. We are witnessing how the state deploys labels such as terrorists, insurgents, or enemy combatants to dehumanize (and kill without accountability). What about the words echoed by the Black (male) speaker and transmitted by state-regulated media to dehumanize Black women and girls? How does the language of hip hop sustain an environment conducive to our continued sexual and gender exploitation? Rap misogyny is verbal abuse. Let's name it. Let's call it what it is because we've spent too many years feeling silenced by it.

Words hurt.

Confessions of a Backslider

Chanel Craft Tanner

I've been backsliding, y'all. I mean really backsliding. I act like I forgot how feminism saved me, way back when. The way it taught me how to listen more closely to the music that moved me. The way it stopped me from saying things like, "I don't really hang out with girls because they're too catty" and helped me to appreciate sisterhood. The way it showed me the intersections of my Black face, my gendered body, and my poor status. The way it beautifully awakened my consciousness. I forgot about my feminist rebirth.

In the beginning, my "born-again" identity caused me to scream it from the rooftops. I was suggesting that everyone I ran across read Angela Davis's autobiography and Patricia Hill Collins's *Black Feminist Thought*. Studying the good books was everything to me. I was alive and engaged during discussions. Eager to hear the testimonies of others who had been saved and excited by the potential of a world on fire with a feminist politic. I was that feminist. Yes, the one that pointed to the sexism in every single rap song and music video. The one people hated to go to the movies with because I was going to destroy all the fun. The one that wanted to live in a totally feminist world and wouldn't stop preaching the glories of the mothers!

I became a feminist scholar so I could continue to learn more and do more. I worked with nonprofit organizations on a tangible, on-the-ground feminism that blended theory and practice. I'll never forget the excitement I felt participating in the first US Social Forum in Atlanta. I was beyond hyped. This is what it was all about. Saving the unsaved!

There was even a point where I would completely write off anti-feminists as ignorant patriarchy worshippers. I didn't even have the desire to save their minds. Why, when I could just surround myself with like-minded people and just be in complete feminist circles? (That's super easy in Atlanta.) And those days were amazing! Sitting over wine and spaghetti talking about sexism in hip hop and constructing conference panels. I was on it!

And then things happened in my personal life where I had to be around the heathens more often. And at first, while difficult, I enjoyed the challenge of imparting feminist knowledge into their conversations about phat asses and the difference between a good woman and a slut (you know the whole Jay Z "Sisters vs. Bitches" thing). I enjoyed the opportunity to be around a small male child on a consistent basis and balance his male socialization with feminist contradictions that allowed him to play more with his identity.

But somewhere in between dealing with reading feminist theories that didn't look like the foremothers I knew, being situated in the academy that was never designed for my Black female self, constantly being around sexist voices, and mothering a child I didn't birth, I got tired of fighting feminist fights. So I stopped and let a few things slide. Then a few more things slid by. Then before you know it I was finding more problems with feminism than with the world. And I was critiquing the uptight feminists of yesteryear. And I became quite skilled at theorizing why certain behavior can actually be read as feminist if you looked at it in a different light.

Then I caught myself laughing at something that would have pissed me the fuck off before and in the middle of my laughter something didn't feel quite right. And I realized I liked my life better when feminism was more present. It had more meaning and I had more purpose and was much more hopeful. And for some reason I forgot that.

But I'm back! And I'm coming down the aisle today ready to get crunk for the Lorde once again! I'm excited to spread the word in my intro course this fall and ready to renew my faith in feminism. I have *Borderlands* open and ready to read. I have my notes from *Methodology of the Oppressed* pulled up and color-coded. And I have Erykah Badu on repeat. I am slowly coming back and looking forward to some intentional feminist fellowship soon and reminding myself of the power of feminism for my personal and political life. Pray for me!

Disrespectability Politics: On Jay Z's Bitch, Beyoncé's "Fly" Ass, and Black Girl Blue

Brittney C. Cooper

The birth of baby girl Blue Ivy Carter to parents Jay Z and Beyoncé earlier this month has cemented their status as the First Family of Hip Hop. Seriously, they have become the Obamas of the hip hop generation, a comparison that is no less compelling given President Obama's public admission of Jay Z fandom, Jay Z's claims that the multiracial fan base of hip hop made an Obama presidency possible, Beyoncé's performance at the first inaugural ball, and her partnership with Michelle Obama's childhood obesity campaign.

But within the context of hip hop culture itself, this couple represents the possibilities of hip hop all grown-up, in love, married, and pushing the proverbial baby carriage. In fact, based on age alone, they are the blending of the first generation of hip hop heads Jay's age who came of age in the eighties and hip hop's second generation (the middle children, I like to call us), folks Bey's age who came of age in the nineties.

So the conversations—both doting and derisive—that have surrounded the newly nuclear Carter family in the last few weeks offer a pretty interesting gauge for how hip hop's multiple generations are thinking about family, beauty politics, gender issues, and the potential of hip hop. The ways in which these two perform couplehood and parenthood have become a marker (alongside the Obamas) for both the possibilities and limitations of the traditional family narrative among a generation most known for popularizing the terms "baby mama" and "baby daddy."

Over at *Very Smart Brothas*, Champ rightfully called foul against those women who were ready to let Jay off the collective Black girl hook and rebrand him as a role model after doing two decades worth of dirt. I think that rush to see Jay as an upstanding father and family man is summed up thricely:

1. Black women are too damn forgiving (which is ironic considering how bitter everyone says we are).
2. Nothing can get the panties wet like a reformed bad boy: a bonafide alpha male, who in a questionably feminist (but nonetheless desirable) Black masculinity narrative has the potential to sex you senseless, ~~beat the shit out of somebody for~~ . . . protect you, cuddle you, and listen to you, depending on your needs at the time.
3. Hip hop generation Black folks still have a deep love affair with respectability politics, or this notion that obtaining/creating a traditional nuclear family makes us grown-up, middle class, and "fit" to participate in the larger body politic, American dream and all.

Just a couple of days after Blue was born, Jay dropped a touching tribute to her called "Glory (feat. B.I.C.)" While the current ur-text of hip hop masculinity showed his soft fatherly side serenading the "most beautifullest thing in the world / daddy's little girl," Blue made her debut via gurgles and cries not only to the world but also onto the Billboard charts, becoming the youngest person ever to do so. While Jay was content to let Blue speak herself into existence amidst his loving words, his audience looked askance, wondering whether other Black girls will have such luxuries and pleasures of voice in the discursive world that Jay Z has helped to create.

A world in which bitch trumps beautiful, ho trumps human, and gold-digger trumps golden. #EveryDamnTime

A world, incidentally, in which Beyoncé's ass provides the inspiration for a group of Australian scientists looking to name a new species of insect with a golden posterior. They call it the "Beyoncé Fly."

I ain't blaming Jay for that. But suffice it to say, Beyoncé's "flyness" is forever memorialized in insect form. The legacy of Saartjie Baartman lives. In this world, the global desirability of a Black girl's ass excuses her allegedly less desirable dark complexion, full lips, and kinky hair. Somehow, I think this will be a sorry consolation prize for Black girl Blue, whose beauty (or potential lack thereof) is already fodder for Internet renditions of internalized Black self-hatred.

This is a world where disrespectability politics reign, a world where Black women's bodies and lives become the load-bearing wall in the house that race built, a world where the tacit disrespect of Black womanhood is as American as apple pie, as global as Nike. (Just do it. Everybody else is.) In this world, Black women have moved from "fly girls to bitches and hoes" and back again to just, well, flies. Insects. Pests.

But getting back to bitches . . .

Right on cue (and a little too conveniently), reports surfaced that Jay Z was relinquishing his use of the B-word, and it seemed that Blue had already begun to work her magic. Like others, I was skeptical but intrigued. I mean, if you weren't already convinced, read Jay's (and dream hampton's) book *Decoded*, and there's no denying that he's a highly intelligent brotha, one who is no stranger to defending his word choice. Even Oprah, who took him to task for using the N-word, respects him enough, finds him worthy of an OWN *Master Class*.

Turns out that the whole thing was a hoax, a story hatched with a halfway-believable poem, by an Internet writer hoping to create buzz served up with a side of consciousness. Annoying as such tomfoolery is, I can't knock a Black girl for wishing that a man's relationship to the women in his life would lessen rather than heighten his investments in patriarchy and misogynoir. As much as I didn't believe the story, I thought the strategy ingenious. I mean, what self-respecting new father, what respectable man, would actually issue a statement reasserting his right and intention to the use the B-word copiously?

But fellow Sagittarian Jay Z is nothing if not principled, so that's exactly what he did, letting it be known throughout his camp that all B-words—bitch, Beyoncé, and baby Blue—remain in his lexicon. It was a respectful "fuck you" to doing the respectable thing and a straight up dis to respectability itself. Hip hop aesthetics at their finest.

And herein lies the conundrum. Black feminists have long pointed to the limitations of respectability politics, steeped as they are in elitist, heteronormative, and sexually repressive ideas about proper Black womanhood. When disrespect becomes where we enter, we confront a reality that is pretty dismal for Black womanhood. But when we enter at respectability, there we confront limitations, too. I mean, Michelle Obama, the country's leading lady, can't even get no respect. It is time to face the fact that the more-than-century-long project of respectability politics has been an utter failure, particularly since it hasn't convinced Black men to treat us any better either.

Our recognition beckons new strategies, even as we confront the terrible realities of the challenges that give rise to them. If you'll permit me to put on my professor Kangol and theorize for a moment, I think we must consider the potential in the space between the dis and the respect—the potential (and the danger) of what it means to dis(card) respectability altogether. This space between the disses we get and the respect we seek is the space in which Black women live our lives. It is the crunk place, the percussive place, the place that makes noise (and music), the place that moves us, the place that offers possibility in the midst of two impossible extremes. And frankly, that is what I would wish for baby Blue anyway, the ability to make her own way in the midst of two largely unattainable extremes of Black woman- and manhood represented in her mommy and daddy. I hope that, in having access to their humanity, she can draw from who they actually are, rather than who we make them out to be. And I hope she will know that she, like every other Black girl, is the most beautifullest thing in this world, simply because she is.

For the rest of us, we might have to accept that this magical, Edenic place when and where Black women "can enter in the quiet undisputed dignity of [our] womanhood" is not forthcoming. We're gonna have to fight for the dignity that's rightfully ours. So, um, #NoDisrespect, but excuse me while I #TakeOffMyEarrings.

LOVE, SEX, AND RELATIONSHIPS: BLACK FEMINIST SEX IS . . . THE BEST SEX EVER

Introduction

We seem to need feminism most in our intimate lives. Despite stereotypes of feminists being antisex, we know feminists put it down in the bedroom. And we proclaim, as our friend Alexis Pauline Gumbs once did in the comments section of one of our dating posts, that Black feminist sex is the best sex ever! Fuck what you heard.

But giving ourselves permission to ask for what we need, be creative in the building of our intimate lives, and be unapologetic about the work of centering our own pleasure is not nearly as glamorous or orgiastic as it sounds. Sometimes feminism can mess up your sex life, because sometimes, as Crunktastic points out, your partner can say sexist-ass shit. And if there is not agreement unequivocally that violence against women is wrong, then letting the dissenting party get the draws is kind of hard to do.

Being a prosex Black feminist in a world where Black women's asses are automatically taken as the world's playground is hard-ass work. Negotiating the narratives of exoticism that attach to Latinx and Asian sexuality isn't easy either.

So since beginning this work together, we have insisted on writing about the reality of what happens not only in the streets but also between the sheets. All kinds of characters show up between the sheets of the CFs—knucklehead dudes, chicks who wind up breaking your heart, literal cuddle buddies who are there for a good spooning session, and the old trusty reliable partners of the battery-operated variety, who've never met a clit they didn't know how to handle.

If sex matters to you, then a good sex life is essential. But good sex lives are incredibly difficult to come by, it turns out. Often, for those of us who came up in the church, conservative theology tells us that sex is reserved for marriage. But since most of us are ambivalent about marriage as an institution, given how much even the best marriages tend to end up looking patriarchal in some guise, then saving sex for the person who puts a ring on it is kind of not what we're into. We are, however, into imagining partnership and intimacy in as many healthy ways as possible.

Love isn't necessary to have good sex. But care very frequently is. Good feminist sex requires care, beyond simple protection against pregnancy and disease, and beyond the acquiring of consent. Good sexual partners need to care about your pleasure; they need to care about what turns you on, care about what gets you off, and take care of you for the length of the interaction.

Good feminist sex is rooted in an ethic of care. That doesn't mean the fucking has to be gentle or that the sex can't be carefree. It means that you should be clear that the other person took care with/of you during the interaction.

And that's sometimes why it's easier to forego sex with other people altogether and get out the Hitachi magic wand and go to work. Cuz people be trippin'.

The problem is that nothing beats skin-to-skin contact and the intimacy of human connection and physical touch. When it's healthy and consensual, and the communication is right, that is. It's powerful stuff.

So powerful that sometimes, as Robin Boylorn reminds us, you can't pull off the "no strings attached" situation despite your best efforts. Feminists aren't invested in attaching strings to sex. But sometimes they get attached anyway. And surely we are feminist enough to say that, too. To say that our hearts and our feelings show up at inopportune moments and that we need to write poems about it or crowdsource methods for dealing with a breakup from our homegirls and our feminist community.

If feminists are going to theorize the sex lives of grown women, then we gotta be able to talk about all of it.

We are long overdue for a Black feminist theory of touch, one that acknowledges how the tactile dimensions of intimacy are necessary, sensual, and political; one that acknowledges, as affect theorists (who are all the hotness right now) might say, the affective impact of the energy that passes between us. Black women's and Black people's bodies have been the victims of unwanted, nonconsensual, nonloving touch since our arrival on the varied national shores of the American empire. Even in the nineteenth century, though, Black women were obsessed with what they called "impressions," ways of touching that could transmit messages to Black children about how they were loved, how they were powerful, how they could achieve anything they set their minds to. Touch has always been political.

But in a world where many sisters don't always have access to the intimate agency they want, and can't always find the partners they would like, being touched like you want to be touched is not always an easy thing to find. Being touched when you don't want to be is violent. Remaining untouched for years or decades isn't healthy either.

Brittney Cooper says that sex and intimacy are forms of epistemology, ways of knowing the world. That's a truth that should undergird how feminists think their way through sex and sexual politics and the politics of touch. The terms of our intimacies affect and shape the terms of our knowing—about ourselves, about the world, and about each other.

It isn't just sex, though. Feminism also demands parity and equity and partnership in our intimate relationships. Whether you are monogamous or polyamorous, given to a singular partner or a bench with a few different players, feminism insists that you know that your needs matter. We insist that you advocate for the intimate life you want. We insist, as Brittney has said, that "there is no justice without pleasure."

Being givers and servants and caretakers is rarely a problem for women. We are socialized to be everything to everyone from the earliest days of doll play. That our partners, whatever their sex or gender, would show up for us with the same level of magnanimity is a harder proposition.

These essays highlight what good partnerships might look like and what they certainly shouldn't look like.

How we build family, secure partnership, and undertake intimacy are always huge areas for concern. And the work would be entirely unbearable without a little humor.

We insist on centering pleasure and humor in the midst of our laments about the tomfoolery we encounter, because hip hop generation feminist sex is not conceived of solely in terms of historic trauma, coercion, and rape. At the CFC, we often say that what we build is infinitely more important than what we tear down.

Sex is one of our most powerful creative forces. Sex must certainly give a hat tip to the power and importance of feminism. But feminism also gotta respect what sex is bringing to the table. In a world where far too many people still insist on respectability, still engage in slut shaming, still stereotype Black women as hypersexual and unrapeable, we insist that good sex—sex which brings pleasure, honors the mind, body, and spirit, and is consensual for all parties—is liberatory.

Single, Saved, and Sexin':
The Gospel of Gettin' Your Freak On

Brittney C. Cooper

Like most conservative Christian folks, I grew up believing that sex was reserved for marriage. For years, my sexual experiences were laden with guilt. I routinely went years at a time with no sexual contact, until I would finally, in a fit of weakness, give in to my urges. I was caught in a continual cycle of self-denial, self-indulgence, guilt, confession, rinse, and repeat, topped off by five years of celibacy. I was treating sex as if it were a bad habit that I desperately needed to break.

All of that is a prelude to a confession: I'm single. I'm saved (as in born-again Christian). And I have sex. Unapologetically.

At my former church, I spent at least one Friday a month hanging with the dynamic, beautiful, thoughtful, educated sisters of faith who did ministry work. These women were not stuffy; they were totally real: about how lonely it is without someone, about how they never saw themselves at thirty-five or forty still being alone with no prospects, about how frustrating the prospect of perpetual celibacy is. But I respect these women because they decided that "doing it God's way is best," even if that means an indefinite period of celibacy. And so inevitably there would be the roll call of who had been celibate the longest. Five years, ten years, etc. . . . And because these women believed strongly in the Bible as a rule book, no extramarital expressions of sexuality are permitted, not even masturbation.

I, however, have had a long-standing off-again/on-again relationship with more than one B.O.B. (battery-operated boyfriend), and I simply don't believe that someone else should get to touch my clitoris when I don't.

So while I love these women and while I believe we love the same God, I do not love their sexual ethics. I do not think one can live and thrive in them. For me, Christianity is too much about grace, too much about freedom, to engender the continual guilt, frustration, and anxiety that I confronted merely for expressing my sexual self-hood. Surely there must be a better way.

But when it comes to the sex life of the single Christian, it's hard to take the Bible as the gospel truth, because for us, there ain't no good news in it. Song of Solomon's erotic imagery notwithstanding, no scriptural loopholes permitting me to get my much-needed freak on presented themselves.

But a loophole is not what I needed. I needed a bigger view of God.

For so many women, the biggest faith struggle of their life has been "believing God for a mate." Year after year, these women serve, pray, and live chaste, believing that God just requires more faith, or alternatively, that God is still working on them. And the Black Church, in its refusal to consider the impact of overincarceration, poor education, underemployent, violence, and AIDS on Black families and heterosexual Black marriages, only makes it worse by reinforcing Black women's feelings of personal and relational inadequacy. The Church's parochial sexual politics and double standards have made it even harder for Black women to find the kinds of relationships they so desperately seek. My sisterfriends want dudes who are in church often, "know the Word," love God, and are willing to court them for as long as it takes with little to no physical contact. Most preachers don't adhere to that standard, and while there are some men who would, there are many, many, legitimately good brothers who won't. Our churches rarely even preach celibacy to men. <Side-eye>

So when I recognized the way social conditions and religious guilt shaped my options for partnering, I began to ask different questions about my relationship to God, to the Bible, and to faith. Because my friends were following the rules, to a T, and yet the rewards elude(d) them.

I don't want the good stuff, sexual or otherwise, to elude me while I'm over here dutifully following the rules, so I've actively and painfully gone in search of a better way, filled with life-affirming principles and enough grace to let me enjoy my life and some good sex, too. 'Cause frankly, now that I'm over thirty, getting some, getting it good, and getting it on a regular basis is nonnegotiable.

I refuse to live a fear-driven life any longer, based upon a set of rules that mete out punishment and reward based on how well I perform. I think Jesus came to free us from performance-driven living. As women, we are no stranger to performance-driven lives, which often leave us empty and unfulfilled as we try to be all things to all people. And then we turn around and try to do this same thing in our faith, and it isn't working. For Black women who are already forced to be superhuman in every other aspect of the world, our faith space, personal and communal, can only be liberatory when it permits us to be fully human, sexuality and all.

If we choose to be honest and intentional, we can build life-affirming intimate relationships, both inside and outside of marriage. But our conservatism has stripped women of the right to be intentional about engaging and enjoying their sexuality, even causing some women to avoid condoms and birth control so they don't have to acknowledge their choices. AIDS is real, fam.

Sex is a form of creative power. And it is in the literal fact of its creative aspects that we feel alive, fully human, and connected. I think God wants nothing less than this for us, and that requires regular, intimate connections of bodies, or at the very least a very regular, intentional, and unapologetic intimate connection with our own bodies.

So sex is back on the table for me in an emotionally safe, intimate connection with another person. Because marriage or no, I am clear about this one thing: celibacy is not for me. I need connection. I need intimacy. I need sex. Period.

That's why I'm unapologetically single, saved, and sexin'.

She Got a Big Ego?
Thoughts on Dating with a Doctorate

Brittney C. Cooper

Recently, my romantic interest accused me of throwing my PhD in his face. Most Black women with PhDs will know exactly how egregious an accusation that is, especially since we are hypersensitive and overly vigilant about making sure never to "throw our degrees" in the face of less accomplished potential boos or family members.

During a casual phone convo about our respective college experiences, Dude, who is a high school math teacher with a couple of advanced degrees in math fields, remarked to me that he found most humanities/social science majors, including English and political science—my undergrad majors—"illegitimate." Now, given that all of my degrees are in humanities fields, I was majorly incensed.

And although I'm used to—and normally unfazed by—these inanely conceived verbal-jousting matches that dudes engage highly educated women in as a way to see if we are really as smart as our degrees seem to indicate, this time I was pissed. It's college administrators and other knuckleheads who think like him that make my job so hard in the first place. Thinking like this explains, partially anyway, why my students can't write for shit and why my salary is a comically paltry percentage of the student loans I owe.

When I questioned his logic, he got defensive. When I further exposed the flaws in his arguments (skills gleaned courtesy of my humanities education), he explained that he would not "back down" or "give in," even though he could admit that his opinion "wasn't well thought out," because he knew that this is what I was used to men doing: "backing down to stroke my ego." Projection, anyone?

What I'm actually used to men doing is attacking me once they start intellectual fights they can't finish. I'm used to men putting me in the friend zone because they find my smarts intriguing but not sexy. I'm used to men straight-up belittling and insulting me—calling me stupid, unattractive, or using "feminist" like an expletive—in order to get the upper hand when they feel intellectually outmatched.

Yep. So I went off. Reiterated the illogic of his arguments. Told him my feelings were hurt. Explained that it is important to me that folks who are close to me value what I do, as it is a part of who I am.

His reply: "Well, I think it's cool that you're a teacher. And people should teach subjects they are passionate about." *Subjects that he doesn't respect, mind you.* "I don't just teach; I also conduct research and write books and articles," I told him, trying to get him to understand that his remark was patronizing at best.

What did I say *"just"* for? To that came his snarky reply, "I don't *just teach* either, and just because I don't have three little letters behind my name, doesn't make what I do any less valuable." I'll spare you the sordid details; let's just say it's was already a thin line and he crossed it.

But the situation reminded me of all the ways that patriarchy conspires against our ability to build loving connections with men.

1. Patriarchy makes men competitive. It makes them see women with more education as competition rather than as folks who would make good partners.
2. Patriarchy conditions men to use emotional extortion and passive aggressive behaviors—saying hurtful things and then claiming them as innocuous opinions; shutting down after deliberately saying something provocative and offensive and then accusing the woman of picking fights or being emotional; demanding your silence in the face of offensive behaviors in exchange for love and affection—as a way to gain control over women who intimidate them.
3. Patriarchy makes straight men feel justified in domesticating smart women. In the case of Black men, with whom I'm most familiar, they largely measure success by their ability to create traditional families. By contrast, many accomplished straight Black women have become that way largely by jettisoning their investment in traditional gender roles. I get it at a historical level. The civil rights movement for Black men was as much about manhood as about race. Black men wanted to be able to perform the traditional roles that they'd seen White men performing for their families. And they built concepts of masculinity around such outcomes. Black men want women who are impressed and content if they stay, provide, and lead. For Black women, there were different outcomes, courtesy of civil rights and Black feminism. These sisters imagine men who champion their careers and are willing to actively coparent—men who partner, support, and communicate.
4. Male privilege allows Black men not to interrogate these relational preferences but rather to see them as natural and innate. Hence, they never have to explain why it feels emotionally safer and more comfortable to date, conquer, and domesticate a high-achieving sister. Black women have not had such luxuries. Many of us have had to relinquish our supposed natural desires for a traditional heteropatriarchal setup and entertain/embrace other possibilities for partnership. But if dudes can't or won't get on board with that, then, largely, we are shit out of luck. And the reality is that most Black men don't have to get on board with it; with 70 percent of highly educated Black women having never been

married, our choice not to submit to traditional expectations will not cost Black men anything in the way of finding a partner.

And perhaps it was that realization, that Dude could just pick up and move on to the next one in a way that my lack of options has not seemed to allow thus far, that made me stay when I knew to go. But perpetual romantic droughts can make one's principles ("You're the best thing I never had," "There's a good in goodbye," etc., etc.) seem like the most unconsoling of consolation prizes.

But I never have the Beyoncé "sucks to be you" moment, y'all! Will I never be vindicated?

Being Single: On Mary Jane, Gabrielle Union, and Those of Us Who Are Imperfect

Robin M. Boylorn

On January 7, 2014, Mara Brock-Akil unveiled her BET brainchild, *Being Mary Jane*. The series, which was prefaced by a made-for-TV movie pilot the previous summer, introduced us to Mary Jane Paul, a gorgeous and successful journalist negotiating conflicting and often-times competing roles on and off screen. Unlucky in love, Mary Jane flourished in her career while combating strongblackwoman legacies and loneliness in her personal life. The character was equally praised and criticized for the portrayal of professional, single Black women. Mary Jane was just what we needed within a context of misinterpreted statistics claiming Black women were disproportionately unmarried (read: unmarriable or undesired) and unattractive (*Psychology Today* ran an article claiming Black women were biologically ugly, a topic that was discussed in the first season of the series).

Mary Jane came after Olivia Pope (*Scandal* premiered April 5, 2012) and before Annalise Keating (*How to Get Away with Murder* premiered September 25, 2014), but Mary Jane is a peculiar prototype of the progressive, thoughtful, educated, and every-now-and-then ratchet Black woman professional. Mary Jane offered a representation that Black women, like myself, could relate to. Usually images of well-off Black women on television are unremarkable and unbeliev-able. Our skepticism of the characterizations is linked to our inability to directly relate to them, our suspicion of their cultural authenticity, and the present absence of race-specific situations and/or microag-gressions that are inevitable realities in real Black women's lives, es-pecially affluent Black women. *Being Mary Jane* makes visible issues, concerns, and realities that are familiar and specific to Black women. The show tackles topics oftentimes limited to our interior and inti-mate thoughts.

I see Mary Jane as a new representation of twenty-first-century Black womanhood. Her imperfection and humanity and her person-al life choices (or lack thereof) mimic the lives of many professional Black women who want "it all." We see Mary Jane struggle, in the first season, with discerning whether her desire(s) for marriage and children are truly hers or Blackgirl brainwashing. In season two, she proactively pursues love and pregnancy (via an unsuccessful attempt to freeze her viable eggs) and, when those attempts fail, shifts her focus to her career. In season three, she reimagines herself and her dating life, taking responsibility and control of her career and shifting her goals after an unimaginable loss.

Mary Jane is an extension of the Black lady stereotype. Like Pope and Keating, she is successful, hardworking, overachieving, finan-cially independent, childfree, and (eventually) single. Further, the new age performance of the Black lady is nuanced because it ab-sorbs the stigma associated with the Jezebel stereotype (both because of unapologetic sexuality and problematic and adulterous relation-ships with married men) while expanding the notions of matriarchy through caregiving and caretaking for biological and chosen family members. Mary Jane (alongside Pope and Keating) is a fixer, but her ability to fix things stops at her own front door.

Another point of distinction for Mary Jane is her consciousness and awareness of what it means to be a Black woman. Gabrielle Union's performance is authentic, believable, vulnerable, and Blackedy-Black. There are moments when it is hard to distinguish Gabrielle from Mary Jane. Perhaps that is why, when Gabrielle found herself with Mary Jane problems toward the start of the first season, onlookers judged her personal life and choices with the same rigor they criticized the character she portrays.

In many ways Union's real life (as herself) imitated her art while she was being and becoming Mary Jane. During the first season of the show her engagement to longtime beau and NBA star Dwyane Wade was mired in controversy due to a sexual indiscretion that resulted in the birth of Wade's third child. Union, who is ten years older than Wade and childless, not unlike Mary Jane, was at a point in her life and career where her options around starting over (in a new relationship) and/or hoping to have a biological child were immediate considerations with real consequences. People harshly judge Union for forgiving her now-husband, but the reality is that even (perhaps especially) beautiful and successful Black women struggle with finding a mate in their forties. Gabrielle was in love with Dwyane, had been coparenting his children for four years, and was invested in the life they were creating together. Whether Gabrielle accepted Wade's proposal because of love, lingering feelings, good sex, insecurity, fear and/or/of loneliness, or all of the above, her decision, to me, was the same decision Mary Jane would probably make, and it was a decision that at least half of the Black women I know, myself included, would wrestle with.

I appreciate that *Being Mary Jane* is about being a Black woman hustling to make it, but it is also about the choices that are not really choices, the struggle for Black women to find and sustain love, and what it looks like when a Black woman tries to cultivate a livable life in the midst of less-than-ideal circumstances. For some women, like Mary Jane, that means making unpopular choices in their love lives, but given the dearth of possibilities Black women post-thirty have for love, it is important that we honor and respect their choices, even if we don't agree with them.

Like other fans of *Being Mary Jane*, I watched "The Wade Union," a wedding video released on the one-year anniversary of Union and Wade's marriage. The ceremony and reception were opulent, lavish, over the top, Blackedy-Black (they gave each other dap after the kiss), and not unlike what I imagine the fictional Mary Jane's wedding to a millionaire might look like. I relished in the romance of it all, the gorgeousness of Black love, and the fact that despite the literal heartache, Mary Jane got her man! Not unlike the show, the video made me hopeful that lasting love is possible for all of us Mary Janes, even, and especially, those of us who are imperfect.

On the Glorification of the Side Chick

Robin M. Boylorn

Side chicks, or women who knowingly and willingly entertain some-body else's man, ain't nothing new. In 2013 *Bossip* published a list of mistress music over the decades that included everything from Shirley Murdock's "As We Lay," to Mary J. Blige and Lil' Kim's "I Can Love You (Better than She Can)." So, clearly, side chicks existed long before millennials, reality TV, BET, and tabloids, but the popu-larity of reality shows like *Love and Hip Hop*, fictional dramas like *Scandal* and *Being Mary Jane*, and side chick anthems like "V.S.O.P." brought attention and seeming glorification to the side chick in the early 2010s.

Popular culture's fascination with and justification for side chicks and cheating men in a decade where ratchetness was on the rise makes room for a critique of how Black women, in particular, are implicated. A race and class analysis of the perception of side chicks disrupts the slut-shaming narrative often attached to Black women who (knowingly and/or unknowingly) share a man, while exposing the racist insinuations of the term.

Language and naming practices are used to punish, disgrace, and denigrate Black women who find themselves in love with men who are in relationships with other women. There is no sympathy for ed-ucated and professional heterosexual Black women who, in a dwin-dling dating economy, are more likely to be perpetually single than ever married. This same mechanism of shame and judgment relates to how working-class women of color have always been treated, par-ticularly in relation to (unconventional) love relationships. If/when the "other woman" is middle to upper class or White, the framing is more generous and empathic.

Soap operas, for example, have long glamorized the side chicks of powerful White men, making them seem more exciting, loving, and desirable than their housewives. It seemed that as long as a man could "afford" two women, his choice to be unfaithful was his prerogative and not worthy of attention or appraisal. Working-class Black men and the women they juggle (baby mamas, friends with bennies, main chicks), however, have always been seen as cultur-al taboos and degenerates with no self-esteem or shame. Further, upper-class Black men (like Sean Combs, for example) are excused from harsh judgment because of their ability to financially support multiple women and children.

While the so-called side chick phenomenon is nothing new, the language/slang repackages infidelity as something Black folk invented, therefore making it more tawdry and scandalous. White women who have affairs with married men are called mistresses. Women of color who have sex with men in relationships (regardless of their financial situation) are called side chicks. Mistresses are taken care of, taken out, splurged on, and at times prioritized above the wife. Side chicks are secrets, limited to booty calls and late-night texts, and are expected to play their position (never interfering with a man's "real" relationship). Further, there is usually one mistress, but a side chick is generally one of several. These race- and class-based distinctions contribute to ongoing slights toward Black women. Mistresses are assumed to be White and upper-class and are therefore redeemable. Side chicks are assumed to be poor and of color and are therefore viewed as thirsty, grimy, low-down, gold-digging whores who actively pursue somebody else's man and deserve their heartache and humiliation.

The commentary is telling. We call women who are involved with men in multiple relationships a "jump off," "side chick," "side piece," or "thot." We call the main woman a "ride-or-die" (because she is willing to tolerate infidelity), a "main chick" (because she was there first), "wifey" (because she is either married to him, has a child with him, or is holding out for either of the two), or "bae"—but what do we call a man who has a side chick?

I'll wait.

Because men have no accountability or consequences for these relationships, there has been a tendency to credit and/or blame Black women for the existence and/or popularity of the side chick. Part of the cultural fascination with and glorification of side chicks is attached to our complicated viewing relationship with shows like *Being Mary Jane*, *Scandal*, and *Love and Hip Hop* (created and/or produced by powerful Black women), where we watch Black women fight over unfaithful men like they are going out of style. It is telling, I believe, to think about the stories and story lines these shows pursue about the naïveté and poor choices women of color sometimes make in their love lives. It is not a glorification of the side chick, but rather an observation on Black love relationships and the plight Black women often find themselves in when trying to establish, maintain, or end relationships with Black men.

What's Up with Dudes Not Being Able to Give Compliments?

Brittney C. Cooper

I tend to roll with a crew of badass bawse women in addition to being one myself. (It's 2015 and time's out for lack of self-confidence.) And because I'm grown and love myself, I no longer date asshole dudes.

But I do date dudes who love badass bawse women. In theory at least. But in practice, I've noticed that many brothers (of the cis-het persuasion) really do have issues with smart, attractive, assertive, high-achieving women. It doesn't show up in overt forms of disrespect, but in the more subtle, passive-aggressive form of diminishing or ig-noring a sister's accomplishments through lukewarm compliments, withholding of affection or praise, or refusal to be accommodating.

So here's an example.

You call or text your boo to share a major accomplishment or award, something that only enhances your current bawse status.

In reply, your boo says something wack like, "Kudos!" or "That's great!" or "Congratulations!"

That's all.

No elaboration.

Now, your homegirls are all, "You da best, you da bomb, so bril-liant, magnificent, I'm *proud* of you!" #TurnUP #PourUP #Drank

But your dude is still stuck on "kudos!" And somehow you might find that in the next few minutes you are back to talking about his challenges or his accomplishments.

Welcome to my world.

What's up with that? Now, maybe you are simply dating some-one who isn't good with words. I'm not particularly into express-ing feelings, but since we're grown and grown people know how to "use their words," for the sake of having productive relationships, I've learned.

Even if words aren't your bae's thing, you'll sense their support in other concrete, recognizable ways.

But this ain't that. This is about brothers being far more intimidated and bothered by the accomplishments of successful women than Steve Harvey would ever care to admit. I've experienced countless times the struggles of a brother to be genuinely excited and happy to see me doing well and being at the top of my game.

By contrast, I cheer on the brothers I date, offer generous affirmation, and give pep talks even if it means stopping in the middle of an always hectic and busy life to do so. I call this modeling loving treatment, or rather, treating dude with the same care, respect, and thoughtfulness with which I want him to treat me.

Now, before you tell me that I simply date crappy dudes, please don't. (Cuz I will ignore you. I'm not here for armchair therapy about what I need to do differently. I'm quite clear that it's the dudes who need to change.) And anyway, I'm talking about good, thoughtful, funny, interesting, well-read, successful brothers who have a lot going for themselves. They aren't disrespectful or mean-spirited.

But they are often competitive. Not always explicitly. But quietly, they want to be better than you in the relationship. (If you ain't this dude, great! One of your boys probably is, though.)

In my experience, these brothers want to date the baddest chicks, but they don't want you to be in any respect better than them. They want you to be smart enough to entertain them, make them look good to their boys and their coworkers, and smart enough to raise them some smart babies. But if they perceive that you are potentially on your game at a level comparable to or above them, they can't deal.

While they may brag to their boys about you, in private, you never hear it. Instead, you are awash in noncompliments or compliments by virtue of technicality only. If you bring this up, you are made to seem unhinged, told you are "picking a fight," while your partner points to the technicality of his words, without ever having to be responsible for the spirit of what he said.

Dudes are deeply emotionally dishonest about the ways they are socialized within patriarchy to compete, to be the best, and to dominate women and each other. While many men have done the outward work of wanting to be with a certain kind of feminist, progressive, overachieving woman, many have not done the emotional work required to be with her.

And there are no societal or cultural structures of accountability that require dudes to acknowledge this, be honest about it, or fix it.

The refusal of these kind of men to affirm us, our talents and gifts, is one of the intimate ways that patriarchy works to put women "in their place." The unspoken sentiment is "you may have accomplished x, y, and z, but you ain't that great."

Here's another subtle example. I have fifty million jobs and a ridiculously busy schedule. I mean, who doesn't? But I've dated multiple men who can never bring themselves to say, "When can I see you?" or "When do you have some free time?" They always say, "I'm free this day or this day or this day," or "I have this or that to do, but then I can see you." Now if that syncs up with my schedule, then cool. I'll usually accommodate. But notice that statements like, "I'm free this day or this day" don't even require an acknowledgment of the other person's schedule. It's a way to center the dude's time, his tasks, and his priorities. I've found these kinds of dudes to be often inflexible about availability. Yes, they'll make time to see you, but only on their terms. They also never have to acknowledge that when you agree to see them, it isn't that you simply *have* all this time, but that you, too, are *making* time.

Assuming they aren't cheating (and I'm pretty sure in my case they weren't), I maintain that this refusal to acknowledge that your busy life might mean they are the ones who need to accommodate you, at least some of the time, and not the converse, is just one more way that dudes who are in some respects less busy or less high profile maintain power. It's almost as if that simple acknowledgment is too large a concession of power.

Here's the larger point. Part of what it means to date as an overachieving feminist chick is dealing with these subtle power struggles and denials of affirmation in relationships with otherwise good dudes.

I don't have any solutions. I mean, is asking to be with a dude that is genuinely, earnestly, proud of you, in public *and private*, too much to ask for?

Usually, I tell the offending dudes about themselves, give them a few opportunities to clean it up, and then remove them from the long-term partner prospect list (and maybe even from my life) if they can't get it together.

But surely this is not a long-term strategy for finding bae.

204 Love, Sex, and Relationships: Black Feminist Sex Is . . . the Best Sex Ever

How Chris Brown Is Effing Up My Sex Life

Brittney C. Cooper

For the last month or so I have been entertaining a new Friend. This brother is cute, sensitive, ambitious, educated, knowledgeable, adventurous, and funny. For these reasons and others, he could most definitely get it.

Sounds great, right? Yes. And then Chris Brown happened. The day after the shamtabulousness occurred in 2011, in which Breezy threw a chair through a window at ABC Studios after Robin Roberts questioned him about Rihanna, I told Friend of my intention to discuss the whole ridiculous incident with students who are taking my hip hop class.

Here's a brief excerpt from our text conversation:

ME: *I'm supposed to be preparing a lecture on Hip Hop: The Modern Era, Part I: 1992–1994. But in light of the C Breezy shenanigans I'm gonna lecture on gender politics instead.*
HIM: *Breezy bad now*
ME: *He needs a therapist like yesterday!*
HIM: *In his defense . . . ppl fuckin with him for no good reason*

What?! (Red flags waving)

ME: *Nobody fucked with him. Robin Roberts asked very reasonable questions and she cleared them with his team first. Asking about the past is not the same thing as dwelling on it.*
HIM: *Hey . . . I'm just thinking stop mentioning it . . . he's suffered enough tho*
ME: *This is not about suffering. He beat that girl senselessly. He is nobody's victim.*
HIM: *Look. No one knows what happened in that car.*
HIM: *Furthermore, it's no one's business. Yeah he shouldn't have beat her . . . but that was years ago now.*
HIM: *It's over . . . talk about the man's album not past transgressions.*
ME: *Domestic violence is our business. And clearly the past isn't the past if dude destroys shit at the slightest provocation [. . .]*
HIM: *Let's talk about Lindsay Lohan and how she can't seem to*

*put the bottle down. Or Charlie Sheen who can't seem to put
the pipe down.*
ME: *Re: Sheen and Lohan all that you say is true. And yet racism
is still not an excuse for bad behavior. That argument is the
equivalent of blaming the man. Again it's some bullshit.*

Much more was said. But y'all get the gist. Given that Friend and I
have had conversations of this ilk before, I wasn't entirely shocked
that he would take this tack. But I am wondering what this means in
terms of my own gender politics and my own acute understanding of
the personal as political.

The necessity of that question was driven home the next day as I
broached the subject with my students. Disturbingly, all of my Black
women students said almost exactly the same thing as Friend—that
the past was the past, that Robin Roberts goaded and pushed Chris,
that we didn't "know the whole story" with Rihanna.

I was/am livid, sad, and afraid for them. These same students
who were visibly disturbed at many of the misogynistic lyrics we'd
listened to in class failed to see how their own belief that a Black
woman could ever do something worthy of violence was a complete
contradiction. Frankly, being mad that someone calls you a bitch or a
ho, but not being mad that a dude beats a woman's ass, seems to be
an exercise in missing the point.

How do we change this thinking in our communities that a
woman's behavior is responsible for pushing a man over the
edge? That she can ever do something to deserve to be beaten to a
pulp? That a man has a right to a violent response simply because
he doesn't like the way he's being talked to or treated? That violence is a legitimate response to being mistreated? That any policy
other than nonviolence (on all sides) is good for relationships? That
men are out-of-control beings around whom we must tread on
eggshells?

And if I ask my students to question their assumptions and to
demand better treatment in their relationships, then what kinds of
things must I demand in mine? And does that standard apply to all
relationships, romantic and platonic?

Can you be a good feminist if you have intimate engagements
with partners who have diametrically opposed gender politics?

In an earlier post, I lamented the fact that I was meeting men
who were rarely physically interested in me and who were always

and only intrigued by my mind. Now I've met someone worthy of genuine interest, and my brain and my politics are getting in the way again. But while last time I was concerned that my brain occupied too much space in my romantic encounters, this time around I'm afraid to check it at the door.

And that is exactly what I would have to do to share my intimate space with someone who doesn't get the politics of intimate partner violence.

Can I share intimate space with someone who thinks that asking questions about questionable actions is antagonistic?

If you think opinionated women are threatening, will you use intimate space to dominate and tame them?

To what extent is and should my sex life be political?

I mean *should* I withhold sex from dudes with sexist attitudes as an act of solidarity with my sisters?

It wouldn't be the first time that Black women withheld sex from Black men in service of larger racial interests. After the Civil War, Black men (but not Black women) could vote for a few brief years. Back then, most Black folks voted Republican as they were the more liberal party at the time and the party of Abraham Lincoln. But there were times when some Black men voted Democrat so they wouldn't be the target of White racial backlash. In addition to accompanying their men to the polls to monitor their votes, Black women banded together and encouraged each other to withhold sex from any man who voted against the community's interests. These sisters knew how personal the political was long before White women said it. They knew that when it comes to Black women's quality of life, there is nothing more political or personal than the person we're sleeping with.

In a culture where sisters are dying in alarming numbers from domestic violence, what responsibility do I have to them and to myself to choose intimate partners whose thinking and actions are sound on these matters?

Doesn't the fact that Friend and I had a civil and honest dialogue that ended amicably count for something? And if so, what does it count for? Honest dialogues are feminist, right?

And since we're being honest, I have some more questions:

How can I get next to you if I can't get next to your politics?

How can I let you touch me if I wouldn't touch your politics with a ten-foot pole?

Can I feel safe in the softness of your touch if you don't feel led to question a culture where other men routinely touch other women violently?

Can we really cuddle if you have the option to not care about women and violence?

Isn't that choice, the choice to not care about how the world affects the woman you're spending time with, a violent one?

How can I trust you to hold me when your beliefs hold me down?

Damn. Who knew politics were so intimate?

POP CULTURE:
THE RISE OF THE RATCHET

Introduction

Popular culture is a powerful shared language. Informed by mass media and consumerism, popular culture reflects and influences people's everyday lives and includes everything from movies, music, and TV to sports, politics, and technology. It represents the entirety of mainstream vernacular, is recognizable by most consumers, and is rooted in lived experience.

Until the twenty-first century, there was no writ-large Black feminist pop culture icon who was recognizable to the larger public. Even though we grew up knowing Hattie McDaniel's name, watching old flicks of Pam Grier's Foxy Brown kick ass and take names, hearing Aretha Franklin demand R-E-S-P-E-C-T, and learning the legacies of Black women artists like Billie Holiday, these women did not call themselves feminists. They did dope shit and made important contributions to how we would later articulate our feminisms—but without the label.

When we think about feminism in its most basic sense—as a call for equal rights for women—everyday, nonfamous Black women doing any damn thing could have easily been mistaken for feminists. Women we knew in our own families—who struggled as single mothers, maids, and matriarchs—embodied our first understandings of women's power and value, but may never have understood themselves to be feminists. Fictional women on sitcoms like *Good Times* (Florida Evans and Willona Woods) and *The Cosby Show* (Clair Huxtable) were strong, but that didn't make them real, and that didn't make them feminist. We desire and deserve a representation of Black feminism, in public, that looks like *more* than struggling and barely getting by. We deserve representations of Black feminism that push past the image of a Black woman holding down her man and/or standing up for/by herself. We deserve nuanced characterizations that are not caricatures, that pay homage to where we have come from and point to where we are going.

As we were coming of age in the 1990s, our heartbeats were connected to the lyrics of our own generation of fly-ass Black women. We rocked out to the likes of Queen Latifah, MC Lyte, Mia X, Gangsta Boo, Lauryn Hill, Lady of Rage, Da Brat, Lil' Kim, and Foxy Brown, but none of them were checking for or claiming feminism. Many of us were called to this movement from our roots and found feminism in the academy, but we would never have had access to Patricia Hill Collins, bell hooks, Barbara Smith, Joan Morgan, Kimberlé Crenshaw, Alice Walker, and others if we didn't read about them in graduate school. These women were not on our television screens or playing on the radio. Similarly, for many of our homegrown and hometown homegirls, their only exposure to feminism will be through the feminist cultural artifacts they are exposed to in mainstream popular culture, and very few of them offer representations of feminism that are inclusive, accessible, or Black.

Enter ratchet feminism.

Like crunk feminism, ratchet feminism combines terms that are seemingly incompatible to represent a new reality and possibility. Brittney Cooper defines ratchet feminism as critiques of sexism and patriarchy that happen in otherwise "ratchet" spaces and/or the female-focused friendship that can exist between Black women (whose performances of race and class are read as lowbrow or low-class), despite the complicated and messy relationships we have with men, and oftentimes with each other. This iteration, inspired by women on *Love and Hip Hop*, suggests that regardless of how ratchet or reckless we may act, sisters have each other's back when it counts, and we hold men accountable for their sexism and double standards. Brittney, like all of us, used the images and conversations happening in popular culture to create language that can help everyday Black women—including those who self-identify as ratchet, thots, baby mamas, gold-diggers, money-makers, bawse bitches, and haters—discuss experiences of sexism in their lives.

Ratchetness in popular culture didn't come out of nowhere. It is the second or third cousin of the terms "ghetto" and "hood" that preceded it, has similar meanings, and it has been embedded in popular culture as long as Black culture itself. Black communities have used the term "ratchet" since the late 1990s, predating its popularity among White celebrities in the early 2010s. Despite its co-optation by upper-class White folk, the term was consistently connected to the realities and behavior of poor people of color.

When we think about the rise of ratchet culture, we associate it with the sudden visibility of people of color, Black women in particular, in the popular imagination. This new moment (not wave) in feminism represents the feminism of Sapphire's belligerent daughter smacking gum and rocking bamboo earrings, cherry-red lipstick, a Black Girls Rock! T-shirt, and some Js, while listening to Beyoncé's "Flawless" on her iPod.

Ratchet culture, accessorized with gold-plated grillz, spinner rims, and twerk tutorials, is the antithesis of respectability.

While ratchetness is generally framed negatively, some scholars have argued that ratchetness offers Black women opportunity for resistance. Brittney Cooper argues that ratchetness can be seen as a dismissal of respectability—a rejection of (rather than a failure to embody) propriety—what she calls "disrespectability politics." According to Brittney, disrespectability politics are an act of transgression that Black women can use to push back against too-rigid expectations of acceptable womanhood.

Disrespectability politics, a play off of both the terms "disrespect" and "respectability politics," urge Black women to have more agency in their race and gender performances while offering a critique of Whitewashed identity politics. This stance is particularly relevant because of the harsh critiques Black women receive for not "living up to" conservative and upper-class Black elitist expectations for femininity. Similarly, Professor Heidi Renee Lewis resists the assumption that respectability and ratchetness are incompatible categories. Lewis believes respectability and ratchetness are capable of coexisting in the same woman at the same time.

Ratchet respectability engages Brittney's and Heidi's arguments by advocating for a rereading of women of color as complex characters with inevitable influences from their cultural and social standpoints. Robin Boylorn coined the term as a framework for understanding how Black women are characterized on reality TV. She states that ratchet respectability allows women to coalesce ratchet behavior (often linked to race and class) and politics of respectability (often linked to race and gender), claiming that you can be both ratchet and respectable at the same time.

In the same way that crunkness is not clearly thought of within the context of feminism, popular culture is not a decidedly progressive and inclusive space. As critical consumers of popular culture, we use the tools we have available to us as feminists to better understand and/or deconstruct the representations, images, and narratives that feature people who look like us. We look for opportunities within popular culture to make feminist interventions, but we also look for possibilities for feminist interpretations when they are not always apparent.

This embrace of ratchetness, in our viewing and listening practices, as well as in our cultural consumption and academic output, inspired many of the essays in this section.

As did Beyoncé.

Nicki's World

Aisha Durham

When BET aired its documentary about women and hip hop in 2010, I found my thirty-plus, old-school-feminist self working hard to gear up to get down with the over-the-top, lyrically layered, brand-savvy rapper that is Nicki Minaj.

The self-described Barbie is inescapable. She works every rap and R&B hook and changes her look to fashion what could be categorized as camp, cultural appropriation, or classic sexual objectification. Until Minaj, I managed to safely maneuver around mainstream new-millennium starlets because they offered no more than a cookie-cutter replica of the unique hip hop dynamism I remembered. Likened to Lady Gaga for her eye-catching performances, this former theater student is adept at staging media spectacles, such as autographing breasts, adopting different voices, and orchestrating a coming-out tweet to squash rumors about her bisexuality for those who might have misread the Remy Ma viral video confession from Roman, her masculine persona, as Nicki Minaj. You can call the latter a cop-out or a capitulation to a commercial model that demands all women perform hyperfemininity period. When I enter Nicki's world (slowly and with caution), I am not only considering the ways she uses her body, but I am thinking of three ways her performances of race, gender, and sexuality instigate a feminist engagement with the popular.

Beauty and Postfeminism

Postfeminism advertises the sexy, smart, economically successful, self-absorbed it-girl from a postpatriarchal world where politics are defined by "style wars" rather than issues of gender inequity. Here, beauty and postfeminism seem to be disconnected from critiques of consumerism, gendered labor, or political citizenship. On the one hand, the look-good-feel-fine empowerment that Minaj offers feels as lifeless as the dolls she suggests every girl wants to be—you know, the nonspeaking, decorative plastic bodies to be handled and watched. Then again, I can imagine her Barbie thang as her way of injecting a sense of beauty and wonderment for homegirls, like herself, who've had to create other worlds to escape the ugly one they lived every day. In either case, Minaj has managed to capture the attention of young women—hook, line, and stiletto.

The Lady and the Freak

In what could be described as a post–"Tip Drill" moment where folks are "manning" the line to distinguish the ladies from the freaks, Nicki Minaj is not the only one who is creating personas to perform otherness. As Roman Zolanski she can express desire for another woman, and as Harajuku Barbie she can perform a sexualized Asian girlhood without damaging her central "brand" or image. Beyoncé is another celebrity with a freak persona. In big hair and tall heels, Sasha Fierce does Beyoncé's "dirty work." Both entertainers talk about a sense of freedom—which is almost always connected to sexual freedom. Celebrity aside, ordinary young women, on and off screen, are crafting "real" and alternate/virtual identities as a response to the increased policing of their bodies through this hip hop binary. Rather than marking public/private bodies, young women like Minaj are now describing their "real" good bodies and their fake freakish ones. In our sincere efforts to "free the girls," it is possible we might have caged our "real" sexual selves.

Camp, Celebration, or Cultural Appropriation

From her anime-inspired June/July 2010 *Vibe* magazine cover, her Harajuku Barbie persona, to her music video "Your Love," where she plays a geisha girl (among others), Minaj reprises dated stereotypes about Asian women that suggest desirability comes in part from submissiveness or obedience. Costuming conceals and reveals her body and both frame her as the exotic; the hand gestures she does in separate scenes either to seduce her lover or to fight her foe are grafted from other forms of popular culture depicting Asianness. I can remember the debut of the Harajuku Girls shadowing Gwen Stefani at a music awards show. Then, folks flipped about a White woman co-opting Asian culture and parading other women (as objects of her imagination). Yet, as Minaj mines the visual landscape to reinvent herself, her Afro-Asian encounters—whether camp, celebration, or cultural appropriation—remain unchallenged.

Nicki Minaj is a hip hop icon whose performances provide us with an opportunity to consider the possibilities and limitations of feminism in popular culture. She offers up consumable sex expected of all women, but she does so with a sense of wonderment, levity, and camp that defies how we are used to seeing Black women in commercial media. The Trinidadian-born, New York–based artist looks like a Black woman who is free. For this alone, I want to live in Nicki's world.

(Un)Clutching My Mother's Pearls, or Ratchetness and the Residue of Respectability

Brittney C. Cooper

News in 2012 that Atlanta rapper Shawty Lo (of "Laffy Taffy" fame) may have been the potential star of a new reality show featuring him, his eleven children, and his ten baby mamas had this feminist searching for somebody's pearls to clutch, seeing as how even the First Lady's love of pearls has not inspired me to cop a strand of my own.

I watched the trailer for the latest train wreck out of Atlanta in mild disgust and mega internal conflict. On the one hand, I felt compelled to embrace this potential portrayal of what one friend called an "alternative family." I mean, my family—composed of my single mom, my only-child self, my cousins who were stand-ins for big brothers, and more recently my stepfamily—is certainly "alternative." At least I felt that way as a kid when I was asked to fill out those old-school ditto sheets with the members of my family, which curiously left off slots for cousins and aunties and grandparents.

And when I see the "rabid" nature of respectability politics that makes grown-ass women feel justified in referring to other sisters hustling trying to make it as "brood mares," I am reminded that I don't ever wanna be down with the myopia and pathology of the respectability racket either! It is so absolutely clear that this respectability shit IS. NOT. WORKING.—no matter how we remix it. The refusal to see that requires what I like to call indignant ignorance, and frankly, ain't nobody got time for that!

On the other hand, the Shawty Lo biznass is utterly ratchet! And ratchetness gives me pause, every single time. It's meant to. Ratchet acts are meant to be so over-the-top and outrageous that they catch your attention and exceed the bounds of the acceptable.

This is the manner and mode of ratchetness that Beyoncé invokes, but while Bey's ratchetness is about flamboyance, about doing the most, and "Bey-ing the most," Shawty Lo's brand is "ghetto" "hood" ish on steroids. In this regard, his show was certainly poised to succeed even though it never aired.

My initial thought was: When there's a show about a woman and her ten baby daddies then we can have a discussion about alternative families. Until then, this just sounds like women with few options capitulating to Black male patriarchy.

By and large, I believe this is true. There is something fundamentally off-putting about a brother with eleven kids by ten different women, even though it appears that he supports them all, claims them all, and works to have some level of relationship with their moms. I'm tired of brothers not having to be emotionally accountable for their relational choices. I'm tired of the way patriarchy's love affair with capitalism sets men up to think that manhood and fatherhood are tied to one's bank account.

Patriarchy exempts men from having to emotionally grow the fuck up.

I mean, it's great that Shawty Lo knows and claims all his children. But, um, when did that become a high standard?

Men don't want superficial relationships, but they have little motivation to cultivate the habits of character—emotional generosity and maturity, selflessness, self-confidence (not ego)—that are necessary for good relationships. Intuitively, most men reject women who want them only for what they have, and rightfully so. But these same men are rarely challenged to cultivate the kind of emotional consideration they seek in others. They want these things from women, benefit from the time we spend cultivating these attributes in our friendships with other women, but are ill-equipped to provide them themselves.

Even still, in the crevices of my wrinkled forehead were the residues of my own respectability politics, my ambivalence about the limits of our alter(n)ations, and our excessive celebrations of alterity. Even as our generation works hard to stop clutching the pearls and with it the respectability that we think is held intact by the thin tie that binds, we are confronted with the challenges that led our foremothers to embrace respectability in the first place. We might not be striving for Respectability, but we are all over respectability.

Why?

Well, "Ask me what I do and who I do it for." For the future kids, for my mama, my grandmama, my aunties, all those people, for whom I am the embodiment of hope.

When I was growing up, watching way too many girls become mothers before they had the resources to make sustainable lives for themselves, and watching my mother hustling to make ends meet, I caught the cautionary tale real quick. Whatever you do, *don't do this*.

Not justifying. More like confessing. And inviting us—respectable, super-educated Brown girls, the ones who "did it the right way," whatever the hell that is—to tell the truth about our continued investments in respectability, and about all the ways that our love for all things ratchet is as much about getting free as it is about reminding ourselves of all the reasons why we made the choices we made. *So we wouldn't end up like that. Like them.* I mean it could be good ol' fashioned "chickenhead envy" on my part. Cuz damn. It definitely feels like "hoes be winning."

But are they really? Are any of us winning in a scenario where respectable and ratchet are the only two options?

Yes, the alternative family that Shawty Lo and the baby moms have built may be subversive, transgressive, and even admirable in its insistence on creating meaningful kinship bonds despite the dictates of respectability. Alternative families are incredibly difficult to create and structurally discouraged at every turn. And in some ways our affective lives (our emotional selves) have not caught up to the space, time, and resource demands of this neoliberal moment. Ratchetness emerges under these conditions as a kind of habitus through which (some) working-class folks and folks with working-class roots interact with every aspect of their lives, from entertainment to family to government.

More and more though, I am coming to understand that subversive and transgressive politics do not a revolution make. I mean, how exactly does the subversion and transgression represented here undercut patriarchy?

Just because it's alternative and nonnormative—and thus even potentially queer—should I, as a feminist, embrace it?

From what I see, this radical reimagining of family works primarily to balance the public portrayals of Black men as oversexed deadbeats against the reality that "as long as he takes care of his kids" we can't really have anything to say, because ultimately "he ain't that bad." What do we do with a man that sleeps around unprotected with all these women, given the alarming rates of HIV infection in Atlanta? (And how many people will read this and remind me that the women also chose to have unprotected sex with him?)

As I watch the mothers of Shawty Lo's children form strategic alliances all in the name of parenting their children and getting what they need from this *one* man, I think about the continued imbalance of power that Black men have over Black women despite all the ways White-supremacist, capitalist patriarchy conspires to keep Black men locked into a form of subordinate masculinity.

I knew that if the show became a full-fledged series, everyone would focus on the mamas, on how stupid they all were to take up with dude, who has a reputation for foolishness. Their maturity and the wisdom of their choices would have surely been discussed. His? Not so much.

As I've said before, reality (television) frequently makes Black women the victims of persistent acts of disrespectability.

So even as I unhand my (mother's) pearls, I think Shawty Lo's pilot, and the numerous reality shows featuring Black women, invite us to consider Black women's deployment of ratchetness as part of a kind of disrespectability politics.

Or in Bey's case, as a kind of joy and celebration that the rush to respectability simply doesn't allow.

I have written about ratchet feminism primarily as a kind of female friendship forged in the midst of complicated relationships among men, their mothers, and their many women. The possibility of the "baby mama" show resurrects this concept, as it demands we think about all of the creative ways women negotiate patriarchy.

At the same time, we have to think about how the embrace of ratchetness is simultaneously a dismissal of respectability, a kind of intuitive understanding of all the ways that respectability as a political project has failed Black women, and continues to disallow the access that we have been taught to think it will give.

We must ask what ratchetness itself makes possible, even as the gratuitous and exploitative display of it attempts to foreclose possibility. What does ratchetness do for the ratchet and nonratchet (and sometimes ratchet) alike? Are Black women not always already perceived as ratchet anyway? As over-the-top, excessive, doing the most and achieving the least, unable to be contained, except through wholly insufficient discourses like ghetto and hood and ratchet. *And* respectable. Are Black men ratchet? Can White women be ratchet? Is this ratchet?

I don't have the answers. The best I can do is own my contradictions and then let go of these damn pearls, because despite my desire to hold on, this ain't our mothers' feminism.

Girl, Bye: Why This Moment Is Bigger than Paula Deen

Susana M. Morris

Unless you were living under a rock during the summer of 2013, you probably heard about the kerfuffle with Our Fair Lady of Butter, Paula Deen. The quick and dirty of it all was that Deen and her brother, Bubba Hiers, were facing a discrimination suit from a former employee, Lisa Jackson, who accused the two restaurateurs of creating a hostile work environment that included racist business practices and sexual harassment. As a result of the suit, Deen answered questions in a deposition regarding the accusations, and it was there that Paula Deen showed her entire ass.

The following is an excerpt from a June 19, 2013, piece by Hunter Walker in *Talking Points Memo*:

> According to the complaint . . . as evidence that Deen "holds such racist views herself," the complaint details an incident that occurred when Jackson was in charge of "food and serving arrangements" at Hier's wedding in 2007. The complaint includes a comment Deen allegedly made when asked by Jackson what type of uniforms the servers should wear at the wedding. "Well what I would really like is a bunch of little niggers to wear long-sleeve white shirts, black shorts, and black bow ties, you know in the Shirley Temple days, they

used to tap dance around," the lawsuit claims Deen said. "Now that would be a true Southern wedding, wouldn't it? But we can't do that because the media would be on me about that."

In her deposition, which was given last month, Deen denied many of the allegations against Hiers and addressed the alleged comment about his wedding. Deen said she remembered telling Jackson and another employee about a restaurant she went to with an exclusively African American waitstaff that she wanted to emulate, but was worried about the potential reaction. Though Deen admitted to using the phrase "really Southern plantation wedding," she denied having said the N word.

Of course Miss Paula not only got roundly denounced in the media, she got dragged within an inch of her life on the Internets. Awesomely Luvvie and Kid Fury and Crissle of *The Read* had me rolling, but let me tell you about the hearty guffaws I experienced reading Twitter (on Juneteenth, no less!). Between #PaulasBestDishes, #PaulaWontCookIt, and #PaulaDeenTVShows, I died and then was resurrected several times. I got my entire life. I mean "Nat Turnip Greens" and "We Shall Over Crumb Cake"?! If Black Twitter is wrong, I don't want to be right. Remember what sister Zora said about Black people and the "adornment of language"? This is it!

Then your girl PD went on damage control and issued a series of rambling apologies that expressed how truly sorry she was.

Chile, please. As Jamilah Lemieux writes, she can keep her deep-fried apology.

Of course there has been the inevitable backlash by Deen's supporters, folks who think she should have gotten her contract renewed, and the usual suspects who think that "Black folks are too sensitive" and are "hypocritical" because "we use the N-word too."

I did not feel at all guilty for laughing this woman to scorn, especially considering the millions of dollars she made and is yet to make. Yes, yet to make. The uproar eventually died down, and she was back to selling deep-fried butter in no time.

What I did feel was missing from a lot of the conversations around Paula Deen, though, was what was really at the heart of the matter: the discrimination suit and what it alleges about Deen's workplace practices. See, several more folks came forward accusing Deen and Hiers of discrimination.

Fran Jeffries and Wayne Washington wrote in the *Atlanta Journal-Constitution*:

Deen "preferred white and light-skinned blacks to work with customers" and that darker-skinned blacks were relegated to "back-of-
the-house operations." . . . Employees have been reluctant to talk . . .
about their experience with Deen because they fear retaliation.

Understanding how institutionalized oppression works and having
worked in a few hostile work environments myself, I know how scary
it can be to call out the powers that be and stand up for oneself.
There's a lot to lose. So, it is no small thing that folks came forward
and exposed what seems to have been a workplace shit show.

The fall of Paula Deen had the potential to be a productive moment to have a conversation about race, class, gender, sexuality, and
accessibility at work; to discuss fair labor practices; and to support
organizations in the trenches advocating for workers' rights. Also,
rather than being reactionary about being called racist (I'm talking
to you, Miss Paula), folks could try not being racist. A pipe dream,
I know. Bottom line, then and now: we must keep our eyes on the
prize and not forget the systemic issues that make Deen's alleged
behaviors not only possible, but also endemic.

The Unending Heartbreak of Great Expectations: Why I Can't Watch *The Mindy Project* Anymore

Eesha Pandit

Mindy Kaling is a boss. Widely regarded by her coworkers and critics
alike as the best writer for the popular sitcom *The Office*, she starred
in, wrote, produced, and directed her own prime-time TV show, *The
Mindy Project*, which aired on Fox for three seasons, and was picked
up by Hulu for a fourth season in 2015 and a fifth season in 2016.
The Mindy Project is the first TV sitcom starring an Indian American:
definitely a historic achievement. Importantly, just a few days into
the start of the first season, trolls, in the form of TV-critics-who-write-
under-cover-of-Internet lost their collective minds and began harping
on Mindy Kaling's smug and self-satisfied nature. In a twist of what
amounts to the most ironic of ironies, that bastion of independent
thinking and critical analysis, *Gawker*, called Mindy the "human
equivalent of a retweeted compliment."

Writer Nisha Chittal broke down the root causes of this tedious and predictable resistance to Mindy's success, comparing it to the kind of response given to young White women in leading roles:

> When Lena Dunham launched *Girls*, Dunham was praised for creating and portraying a character not typically seen on TV screens: a young, post-college, average-looking, single woman with romantic woes, whose flaws and insecurities are on display. Kaling portrays a similarly flawed character, but has not received the same praise. Bloggers and critics hailed Dunham's characters as relatable, real women. But I haven't seen one critic yet say "I can see myself in Mindy's character," the way many described the appeal of Dunham's *Girls*.

Now, I have never watched *Girls*, largely because I cannot see myself in the characters and their lives are not particularly interesting to me. I reference it as a way to illuminate the racism and misogyny that Mindy Kaling continues to face, despite her talent and obvious work ethic.

So, there are a lot of reasons I watched the entire first season of *The Mindy Project*. First, the almost immediate emotional sigh of relief to see an Indian American woman on TV, being beautiful and funny. Being beautiful, funny, and not playing a deranged sex kitten or terrorist (or both, simultaneously). Being beautiful, funny, and not tokenized as the sassy best friend or tragically comic officemate. That kind of existential relief can only be felt in contrast to the otherwise ubiquitous feeling of never seeing someone that looks like you or your family on TV, save for the times you can count on one hand.

Then there's the boss factor. Both Mindy Kaling and Mindy Lahiri (her character on the show) are confident badasses—a characteristic I love and relate to. Women who clearly love their jobs and their friends, and are unapologetic feminists, are the stuff of my dreams. Note that I haven't yet said anything about Mindy's body, though it is oft discussed as something revolutionary about the show, which is a commentary on Hollywood and its inability to think of "leading ladies" outside a very oppressive and narrow set of body parameters. Mindy Kaling is not unusual looking. She's strikingly beautiful and rather small, actually. There's not much more to it than that. But I will say that she is unusually fly, and some of those outfits are the absolute freshest.

So I took a deep breath, thanked goodness for Mindy, plugged in, and began to watch the show. It did not take long before I laughed. She's lovable, and a little nutty. It was also not long before I cringed. In the first episode of the season, Mindy (Lahiri) made a disgusting "joke" about women in burqas (nevermind that the woman was not actually wearing a burqa, but a headscarf). Now what? Well, actually, I stopped watching the show. It wasn't until several months later that I returned to the series on Hulu and made my way through the next several episodes in one sitting.

I watched the season like that, in a couple of sittings, a few episodes at a time, and pretty quickly realized that the show had an uncomfortable and painful-to-experience relationship with race. Mindy Kaling has said that she finds the racial tensions between different minority groups to be fertile joke ground. I disagree, both because I don't find lowbrow, race-based jokes funny, generally speaking (humorless feminist alert), but also because I don't find the show's execution of those jokes to be successful.

I acquiesce to the limitations of this analysis, however, knowing that Mindy Kaling's job is not to represent me, or any or all other Desi women. It has, regardless, become clear to me that Mindy (Lahiri)'s feminism is not like mine, really, at all. My feminism is intersectional, radical, angry, loving, and queered. Mindy's seems to be about being traditionally successful and, occasionally, sexually bold—not bad, per se, but limiting. I loved the fact that she adored her female patients and was a wonderful doctor. I could not stomach, however, the repeated and diverse forms of self-loathing the character performed because she couldn't seem to get and keep a man.

Further, the show did not take these moments to shift the narrative about what women wanted/should want in heteronormative relationships. There's nothing revolutionary about "you'll find someone, someday" and "you deserve better." Especially given that the first season was largely about Mindy being left, repeatedly, by a gaggle of White men. Now, there's nothing wrong with "having a type," but let's not willfully delude ourselves into believing that our notions of what is sexy are not influenced by a mortifyingly racist, sexist, classist, ableist society.

In this context, I return to Mindy's looks and weight—topics she herself, and her character on the show, talked about quite often (in the first episode, one of Mindy Lahiri's coworkers suggests, heartlessly, that she lose fifteen pounds if she wants to look good). I have also not seen a single interview with Mindy Kaling where she hasn't self-deprecatingly mentioned the fact that she's not conventionally gorgeous. That, for me, was exhausting, and mostly so because it was not accompanied by an analysis that critiques those standards of beauty—just by one that wistfully concurs: Mindy (Kaling and Lahiri) might not be beautiful enough.

I realize that I'm being quite hard on the show, expecting a lot from it and from Mindy Kaling herself. Perhaps even too much. I also realize that I cannot expect any given South Asian woman to share my experience, political lens, and perspectives completely. As Mindy Kaling herself noted on NPR, there is not a burden put on Steve Carell, for example, to represent all White men:

> As an Indian American actress playing a lead on a TV show, Kaling says, she's gotten positive early feedback but still feels the burden of people pinning "their hopes and dreams" on her. She says she just has to brush aside her worries, because Dr. Mindy Lahiri is a "real character."

That I lean forward when I see women of color on prime time and hope that they will offer me a respite, a space to both see and be seen as a full(er) human being, is the lesson here. It is, notably, a function of the dearth of relatable characters and a tragic commentary on the state of mainstream Hollywood representations of women that I yearn in this way. That, perhaps, is the central node of my anguish, and it has very little to do with Mindy (Kaling or Lahiri). It has to do with living in a world that refuses to acknowledge my complexity, my skin itself, or create a space for me to foster a sense of self free from racist implications. A TV show can't do that, of course, but it could certainly help. It could certainly do better.

Five Reasons I'm Here for Beyoncé, the Feminist

Brittney C. Cooper

On December 13, 2013, while we were all still trying to get back to our lives after part one of the *Scandal* season finale, Beyoncé stealth-dropped a self-titled, totally unpromoted album. The fact that she managed to pull that off undetected means we can conclude only one thing: #BitchBad!

Yes, I said, "Bitch bad." Didn't even do the watered-down version, "Bish." Sometimes to make a statement you have to use all your vowels *and* consonants!

Since I usually be feeling kinda spent after the weekly rendezvous with *Scandal*, I fell asleep. I woke up the next morning to news reports and a newsfeed filled with Bey's latest feat. The thing that immediately drew my attention was the fact that Chimamanda Adichie was featured on one of the seventeen tracks, so I skipped ahead. Lo and behold, I found a remixed version of Beyoncé's song from the prior spring. On the album it's titled "Flawless," but you might have known it is as "Bow Down, I Been On." Some feminists I know had their panties all in a wad when the first version came out because Bey instructed some generally nameless bitches to bow down.

Look, I don't generally get into debates about whether women can or should say "bitch" or Black people can say "nigga." Because why? The bottom line is we do it anyway, and marginalized groups have the right to self-define. What I will say is that it took feminism to introduce me to real bitches (good and bad).

Anyway, folks said that Beyoncé's choice to do something so demeaning killed her feminist street cred. But then, folks been pulling Bey's feminist card from the beginning. Let us not forget how much folk acted a fool after the 2013 Super Bowl.

The reason I fucks wit Bey so deeply is that she had something for that ass.

The remix. The remix with Chimamanda Adichie spitting a very clear and succinct definition of feminism for the masses: "A person who believes in the social, political, and economic equality of the sexes." Yup. For starters anyway. And that interlude came right after Bey said, "Bow down bitches."

Talk about crunk feminism—percussive, a refusal to fit into particular boxes, a willingness to "fuck with the grays."

So here's a few reasons that I'm here for Beyoncé, the Feminist.

1. She's a work in progress, as are we all. In 2010 she gave an interview saying she was a "feminist in a way" because she valued her female friendships deeply. In the spring of 2013, she claimed she was a "modern-day feminist." Then, by the end of 2013, she was straight up embracing the term in her

music and claiming her right to both tell women to bow down and encourage them to be self-confident from the moment they step out of bed . . . in the same damn song! I rock with that because her feminism is complicated, and ours is too. Tell the truth. If your bed and the folks you shared it with were an indicator of your politics, your card might get pulled too. Moving on.

2. Sometimes bitches do need to bow down. Call that a hip hop generation feminist sensibility, but it's true. It's just like when Papa Pope gave Fitz the read of the century on *Scandal*: "Boy, I'm literally above your pay grade." It's like the swag I don when academic goons try to step to me even though they are clearly less qualified. Sometimes I've been known to tell folk, "You haven't read enough to step to me. Go back and come again." The world would be better if women would learn that we don't have to take everybody's shit. Not the White man's, not the Black man's, not the state's, not the hating-ass next-door neighbor's, not your frenemy's. Nobody's.

3. Academic feminism ain't the only kid on the block. Confession: the first time I identified as a feminist, I was in grad school. I was able to come to an informed conclusion after reading Beverly Guy-Sheftall's *Words of Fire* and Patricia Hill Collins's *Black Feminist Thought*. But we need to stop acting like a radical feminist is the only kind of feminist. I mean look, I'm radical and committed to a robust structural critique, but I appreciate the good few liberal feminists in Congress who show up and actually fight for reproductive rights that can be on the books! As Meek Mill says, "There's levels to the shit." But news flash—everybody didn't (or won't) go to college. So when women of color start waxing eloquent about how our grandmothers and mothers were the first feminists we knew and many of them would "never" use the term, I wonder then why we don't understand Beyoncé's homegrown brand of feminism—one that honors female friendships, one that recognizes and calls out sexism and domination in her industry, one that celebrates the power of women. No, it ain't well-articulated, radical social-justice feminism, but if you need a PhD to be a fem-

inist then we've got bigger problems, folks. And I'll take a feminist that knows how to treat her homegirls before one who can spit the finer points of bell hooks to me all day erry-day.

4. I'm here for anybody that *is* checking for the F-word, since so many folk aren't. (Except Republicans. Ain't nobody here for that.) What we look like embracing Queen Latifah and Erykah Badu even though they patently reject the term, but shading and policing Bey who embraces it? If Bey is embracing this term, that is laudable. If she's figuring out her relationship to it, I embrace that. I will never let my politics be limited by folks' identification with a label, but it is nice when folks are willing to take the risk that comes with the word. Especially when said folks are backing it up by living out feminism in the ways available to them—performing with an all-girl band with visibly queer members, for instance.

5. King Bey always brings her A-game and manages to have fun while doing it. I wish feminism could take some clues here. We don't always bring our A-game, since we spend a whole lot of time trying to figure who's in and who's out, as if that is going to get us anywhere. Time-out for the women of color feminist mean-girls shit. Sometimes folks just be hating. Real talk. Cuz if you ain't critiquing Katy Perry and Pink and alla dem for being procapitalist and in league with the establishment, then back up off Bey. Posthaste. (And yes, we can and should have a robust critique, and that in itself ain't hating. But again, sometimes, folk are just being mean or contrary, and we need to be about building some shit, not tearing shit down. And sometimes folks need to go to therapy and heal from the shit the mean girls in your past did to you. Stop taking it out on Bey. She don't know you. Seriously.)

More to the point, sometimes we take ourselves too seriously. If laughing and dancing ain't a part of this revolution we're building, then you can keep it.

In Beyoncé's words, "Haters hate and I get better."

There you have it. #AllHailKingBey

On bell, Beyoncé, and Bullshit

Brittney C. Cooper

Out of respect for elders, I wasn't pressed to weigh in on why the venerable bell hooks, during a panel discussion at the New School in 2014, found it reasonable to refer to Beyoncé as a terrorist. Yet, I felt compelled to respond after reading a piece from Rev. Osagyefo Sekou on *Truthout* that indicted an entire generation of Black intellectuals for apparently "believ[ing] that the system is a good system that only needs to provide greater access to the historically othered." Who exactly were these people who believed this liberal claptrap?

Because of this alleged belief in the "goodness" of our current racist, capitalist, patriarchal, effed-up system, we supposedly "rush to defend the Black embodiments of neoliberalism—Obama and Beyoncé." This generation of Black intellectuals apparently "directs its fever-pitched critique at the blatant racist and sexist actions of individuals while it is unable to articulate the ways in which Beyoncé and Obama undermine the very possibility of antineoliberal discourse."

First, the critique of structural racism is incredibly strong among young Black intellectuals. Ta-Nehisi Coates, Mychal Denzel Smith, Kirsten West Savali, anybody? Second, does Beyoncé even know what neoliberalism is?

Now Rev. Sekou made a number of important claims, a few of which I agree with, the vast majority of which I think are bullshit.

And my calling bullshit ain't about disrespecting elders, but rather about saying that elders, especially elders as astute and insightful as bell hooks, don't get a pass for making wack-ass arguments. I grew up in the Southern Black Baptist Church, my daddy is a preacher, and I still address senior scholars as Doctor even though I also have a PhD. That Southern sensibility peppers how I do my work, but as much as my mama and grandmother taught me to respect my elders, they also taught me never to sit around and stand for no bullshit. And I won't do that shit in the name of either civility or academic respectability, because if Black women are out here *terrorizing* people, then we ain't got no time to be polite with each other.

So let us be clear: Beyoncé is not a terrorist. She isn't systematically doing violence to any group of people, rolling up and taking folks' land, creating a context of fear in which people must live, usurping folks' right to self-determination, raping women as a tool of war, or turning children into soldiers.

President Obama on the other hand . . . might have been doing some of that.

As far as Bey goes, it seems she's committed to antiviolence, at least in her intimate contexts. And when Black women can manage to rise above the violence happening right in front of their faces in their intimate spaces, there is something liberatory and radical about that posture. But apparently who Black women are when the cameras aren't looking (or when they don't know the cameras are looking) doesn't matter in taking down the neoliberal project.

By the way, I'm so drove with all these intellectuals who think defending bell hooks and Cornel West makes them radical.

Calling Beyoncé a terrorist in a moment when three hundred Black girls from Nigeria were being raped and otherwise terrorized daily, and couldn't nobody seem to come up with a strategy to get them back, is not only intellectually and politically irresponsible— it's ill. bell hooks knows Beyoncé isn't a terrorist.

She was being provocative. And I imagine that the provocation has to do with asking us to think about what kind of work or harm Beyoncé's image does under a neoliberal system. And if that was the question, then *ask* that question. But conflating the potential discursive and psychic violence that Beyoncé's image does with Beyoncé herself is irresponsible feminist theorizing.

Yes, the May 12, 2014, *Time* cover shows a light-skinned, bleached-blond Beyoncé, and to the extent that she has control over the image, it certainly doesn't disrupt White beauty standards.

But I also read it as her playing with the possibility and plasticity of her image. Maybe that means she's complicit with Whiteness, but it could also mean that, like many of us, she is interested in all the ways she can be visually rendered. But when light-skinned women revel in their light-skinned-ness, it triggers deep shit for Black women who struggle with colorism. And that's tough because while it might be reasonable to demand that Beyoncé show some empathy for this cultural Black girl struggle, the reality is that she is, as we say in the South, "bright-skinned." And she has the right to love her skin and revel in its possibilities, too.

Regardless of whether you agree with my reading of the image or not, what we should be able to agree on is that how one chooses to appear on the cover of a magazine does not a terrorist make.

And calling a Black woman a terrorist when nothing could be further from the truth is an act of discursive violence. It is not mere hyperbole. It is not metaphor. It is an act of violence. And what we can't have going down in Black feminism is Black women being violent with other Black women in the name of being radical.

That's that bullshit, and we should call it what it is, even if it means we have to implicate our elders. Elders ain't gods to me.

Sekou's conflation of Barack Obama, a politician elected twice to lead the American empire, with Beyoncé, a self-made entertainer, is intellectually untenable.

President Obama could and did use drones on people. President Obama could and did sanction military action. President Obama could and did deport Brown people in startling numbers. President Obama could and did reason with people on the Right far too often when he should have been bulldozing their shit. President Obama did what he was elected to do, which was to run the American empire. And as someone who voted for him, I'm complicit in what that means. I'm also glad that my unemployed homegirl is able to go to the doctor when she needs to because of Obamacare.

So there's that. Anyway.

President Obama's actions materially impact the lives not just of the US millions but of billions around the globe.

Beyoncé is an entertainer who sings good songs and choreographs routines so we can dance and feel good and fuck well and talk shit with our friends or partners as we navigate our lives in this neoliberal, capitalist machine. She might be a bigger cog in the wheel than most of us, but she certainly ain't driving the bike.

And it is precisely this kind of untenable conflation of her with the denizens of empire that emboldens the Beygency.

Now I'm not part of the Beygency, but where Sekou accuses my generation of intellectuals with having outsized outrage at the wrong shit, I want to call him out for the same. Conflating Beyoncé with Obama is outsized outrage at the wrong target if I ever saw it.

What I'm not going to do is relitigate the Cornel West–Barack Obama debate that Sekou attempted to bootstrap, unfairly I think, to the Bey and bell conversation. So let me untie those two critiques. bell hooks was being provocative about pop culture; Cornel West at least tries to bring some righteousness to his critiques of imperialism, even though his approach works my nerves. And now let us return to the claims that Sekou makes.

Sekou writes:

> Race, sexuality and gender are critical aspects of their work, yet there [is] an outright refusal to say neoliberalism and capitalism are bad. . . . Contemporary black intellectuals strive for a non-sexist, non-homo- and trans-phobic, and non-racist seat at the table versus a construction of a new table . . .

He returns to this point again later, saying:

> Again, the dominant intellectual disposition of contemporary black intellectuals is neoliberal. Their anti-racist, anti-sexist, anti-trans-phobic and anti-homophobic sentiments are easily incorporated into the neoliberal project without critiquing neoliberalism.

To be clear, I think capitalism is a fundamentally fucked-up system that magnifies a hundredfold the effects of racism and sexism. I think Sekou is right that an endless focus on antiracist, antisexist, anti-transphobic, and antihomophobic *discourse* does make the work of contemporary young radicals co-optable. I do think a more explicit critique of neoliberalism in our work is warranted. I do think we have to recognize that fluidity and mobility are not the same thing. Elsewhere I have written about how discussions of performance and fluidity have come to stand in for real discussions about whether people themselves have actual mobility, or options to move around in the social structure. I do think we have to remember that intersectionality was never put forth as an account of identity but rather an account of power. That we have taken up intersectionality as a way primarily to speak about ourselves and endless categories of identity is unfortunate, especially since it often means that we can't think productively about how racism, sexism, classism, heterosexism, ableism, and, yes, neoliberalism interact as social systems to disadvantage people multiply placed along these axes.

But I don't think any of this makes Beyoncé a terrorist. Nor does the defense of her by those of us who think the girl should not be verbally assaulted by fellow feminists make us uniquely complicit with the neoliberal, imperial project.

Beyoncé is in the tradition of mega-superstar entertainers like Madonna, Tina Turner, and Janet Jackson, not Barack Obama (or Bill Clinton or the Bushes or Ronald Reagan).

Why is there such hateration for Bey, even though to my knowledge hooks has never called Janet Jackson a terrorist, even at the height of both their careers in the 1990s? There would be no Bey without Janet. I mean, as my friend Tamura Lomax, founder of the *Feminist Wire*, reminded me, shouldn't we be talking about the neoliberal implications of Dr. Dre reportedly selling Beats By Dre to Apple for $3.2 billion? Or is it only capitalist Black women who are cause for concern? Brother Sekou, why no outrage against the brother?

I work from the assumption that Beyoncé is a human being, not just an image or an icon. That is why her feminism doesn't offend me. I see her adoption of the term as the work of a powerful woman in a very traditional relationship looking for language to understand the power dynamics she encounters. I see the contradictory gender propositions in her catalog of music as evidence of both struggle and process. But that is what granting her humanity allows for. If, however, she's just the image on the cover of *Time*, then it becomes easy to call her a terrorist.

I guess. But if Bey is a terrorist, then how do you justify gleefully dancing to "Drunk in Love" shortly after saying such a thing about her? Are you dancing on the graves of those whom she has supposedly slain with all her terroristic fierceness?

I mean, what the entire fuck?

Neoliberalism has apparently caused Sekou (and hooks) to forget that Beyoncé isn't only what she sells, never merely commodity or product. Surely, Black feminism is the one place where we begin from the proposition that Black women are not reducible to their capitalistic capacity. Making #TerroristBeyonce the monstrous, feminist, Frankenstein straw-woman of our movement, upon whom we heap all our anxieties (and bad arguments) about the momentous generational shifts of this moment, is literally an antifeminist act that denies her humanity. Calling Beyoncé a terrorist is also designed to silence a generation of younger feminists who identify with her work and find something liberatory and productive about it.

Listen: we always navigate questions of power and pleasure within the space of these bedraggled systems not of our own making. Those of us who ride for Bey ride for her because she offers us a language of pleasure, a permission to seek pleasure, in the midst of both struggling to make it and struggling for a different world to come into fruition. An ascetic radicalism that is averse to pleasure is neither just nor healthy. It may embolden us to create a new world, but that world won't be sustainable, and it may become more violent than the one we left.

I have a critique of capitalism. I also have an ugly student-loan tab, bills that need to be paid every month, and habits I want to indulge. What Sekou understands as an abdication of responsibility to critique capitalism, I understand differently. I understand our generation of feminists to be, as Joan Morgan called for, "fucking with the grays" seriously, while calling bullshit on those who are so revolutionary minded that they manage to do no real good.

That critique does not apply to bell hooks or Cornel West. They both make our work possible. But if the rhetoric continues, the two of them may also become a cautionary tale in what it means for revolutionaries not to age well. (Yeah, I said it.)

And with regard to their speaker's fees, "I ain't sayin' they gold-diggers, but . . ." (And check it: I think they should make their paper, because I don't believe revolutionaries should live in poverty.)

Anyway, we are all just trying to find our way here. My generation of intellectuals definitely could benefit from a more radical edge to our critique.

But if the argument is that we have to violently mow down our icons, leaving a trail of their blood on the way to this new "radicalism," then you can keep it. Because something about that sounds alarmingly like the patriarchal, male-centered, Black radicalism of old.

And a "radical" critique that goes as hard at Beyoncé as it does at President Obama tells me all I need to know about the effed-up gender politics that will govern the space of the new world those folks are trying to create. Beyoncé ain't Condoleezza Rice, ya dig? And we can't even conceive a world where Black women have a level of political clout and power like Obama has. So then folks make wrongheaded comparisons like Sekou does and conclude that they are cut from the same cloth.

That's that bullshit.

And time's out for bullshit.

Clair Huxtable Is Dead

Brittney C. Cooper

That Bill Cosby drugged and raped women for sport for many years was not new news in 2014. The story had floated for years with women sharing their testimonies, after the statute of limitations had run out, simply because they wanted to tell their stories. When co-median Hannibal Buress had the courage to take Cosby to task for his conservative, antipoor, misogynist respectability rants, people started listening again. It is problematic that folks only began to believe women were really raped when another man said he believed them, but that demonstrates the importance of male allies and the risk for women telling their truth.

Between the reports about Bill Cosby, rapist, and Stephen Collins, the actor from *7th Heaven* who admitted to being a pedophile, the lovable portraits of family that anchored my childhood in the 1990s went up in smoke and, as represented on the November 2015 cover of *Ebony*, broken glass. And perhaps that's a good thing. For far too long, Black women in particular have been saddled with the representational baggage of *The Cosby Show*.

I say that as an avid lover of *The Cosby Show*. Cliff Huxtable's progressive gender politics and the show's overt rhetoric of antisexism struck me in my adult years as decidedly progressive for the time. But it's a sham. How can a man who is a vicious hater of women get all the rhetoric right, offering up an idealistic view of what a "good, feminist family man" might look like? It turns out that dudes, or their carefully crafted representatives, can sound right, and seem right, and still be all the way wrong. It turns out that you can have progressive feminist politics on the outside and still be deeply emotionally damaged and fucked-up on the inside.

And since Bill Cosby is a rapist, his avatar Cliff Huxtable is a representational terrorist, holding us hostage to a Black family that never was. But let him die. Stockholm syndrome be damned.

I'm reminded of a couple of moments that always struck me as creepy—after Denise got married, Cliff's character felt compelled to have a conversation with Martin about whether she had been a virgin on their wedding night. Martin assured Cliff that she was "inexperienced." And on another episode, when Vanessa got caught sneaking out with her boyfriend, he used the infamous apple demonstration to ascertain whether or not they had had sex. I understand the parent of a teenager wanting to know, for a variety of reasons, about the level of sexual activity of their sixteen-year-old, but he coulda kept the ocular demonstration. And the inquiry into his married daughter's sex life was hella inappropriate, and perhaps offers us a clue into the mind of a sexual predator.

That obsession with Denise's sexual practices was not unlike his row with Lisa Bonet in public after she, a grown woman, married Lenny Kravitz. It makes me think again about whether Bonet was the problem child she was made out to be, and reconsider her choice not to participate in the ten-year Cosby reunion special back in 2002.

It has long been time to slay the Huxtable patriarch. So, Cliff Huxtable, you're dead to me! And perhaps now representations of Black families, and in particular Black women, can live and breathe on television.

The exposure of the utter fictiveness of the portrayal of Cliff Huxtable strikes me as really necessary in a moment where, because of Shonda Rhimes, Black women dominate *The Cosby Show*'s (and later *A Different World*'s) old prime-time Thursday-night slot. Rhimes brought Black Thursdays back.

But these new representations of Black women labor under the old expectations. That's a problem for a lot of folks, one that won't be solved because neither Olivia Pope (Kerry Washington) nor Annalise Keating (Viola Davis) aspire to Clair Huxtable status. That's a good thing. A thing that those of us with all of our respectability feminism would do well to really grapple with.

After the explosive two episodes in which Olivia (and Smelly Mellie) managed to rescue the president's daughter from a sexisode without slut shaming her, and Viola Davis took off her wig and dark, dark, beautiful, earth-toned makeup on screen, everybody should be clear that Clair Huxtable is dead, too.

How meta does Shonda Rhimes have to get for us to see that she's peeling back layers, forcing us to look in the mirror, offering Black women opportunities to deal with our racial and sexual traumas at the hands of White patriarchs and White patriarchy? Black men have traditionally dealt with that trauma by aspiring to the level of power White men have. Black women have experienced much of the trauma of White patriarchy in intimate spaces—though not only there—and it's time we had an opportunity to work out that trauma in (representational) intimate spaces. For once it's about us and our pain, and what "the man" has done to us, specifically. Would I have chosen Rhimes as my midwife through this moment? No. But she's proving to be a far more savvy one than I initially thought.

That she weaved the scene in *How to Get Away with Murder* through a grammar and a vocabulary utterly familiar to Black women (the taking off of wigs, smoothing back of hair, lotioning of skin, removal of foundation—*before* a fight) suggests that she does in fact *see* us, does know us, even if it is not how we want to be known.

We need new representations. And we are getting them. But somehow, our feminist analyses can't seem to wholly catch up. Far too many folk with otherwise good politics and insightful thinking circumscribe Olivia Pope to a mammy-jezebel-sapphire nexus that is both laughable (in its lack of rigor) and infuriating (in its prescriptiveness). Can a sister get it in on TV without y'all calling her a jezebel? Did y'all know mammies are utterly asexualized? And if a Black woman runs shit, but don't take care of other people's kids, why does that make her a mammy? If she was totally unloving and uncaring, we'd call her a bitch. But wait . . . ol' girl Alessandra Stanley at the *New York Times* said some (totally incorrect) bullshit about all Shonda Rhimes's characters embracing angry Black womanhood. So . . . where the hell does that leave us? I mean, on one hand Liv and Annalise might be cautionary tales in what it means to fellate and romanticize White-supremacist, capitalist patriarchy on the regular. I know that's what many feminists want me to say. There I said it. On the other hand, they might be complicated, powerful women in love with complicated, powerful men. On this we probably gone have to fuck with the grays just a little bit.

Perhaps we needed to slay Clair Huxtable to find out. (I ain't even into slaying the mother like that, but Cliff Huxtable has got to die, and unless we can imagine some new possibilities for widowed Clair, I suspect she'll just not be the same without him.)

As someone who on some days aspires to have a partner and maybe a kid, I wish for more opportunities to see badass (cis and trans) Black women in both hetero and same-sex partnerships that aren't emotionally abusive and fucked up. But I know far more professional sisters in "creative" configurations of relationships than ones in traditional hetero- and homonormative partnerships. It's real in these streets.

Shit, even our inability to cut Liv some slack for loving somebody toxic long after they have outlived their usefulness strikes me as deeply emotionally dishonest. I know I have been there. I know what it's like to try to imagine possibilities of relationships beyond the person that has moved you deepest. But maybe that's my shit. I own it. But I also maintain that it seems mad difficult for us to really grapple with what emotionally vulnerable Black womanhood looks like on television.

Liv and Annalise are gonna force us to do it though. And it will take both of them and then some to move us away from our finely cultivated worship of Clair Huxtable, the sister who had the man, the kids, the beautiful home, the bangin' career, fun friends, and hot sex.

Part of the reason pop culture is so important is because it refuses in so many ways to give us characters that conform to the shape of our deepest political desires. In so doing, it forces us to grapple with what it means to want the things we want. It makes us imagine that we could (and perhaps should) want other, better things.

What I see when I look at Liv, when I look at Annalise—they have cultivated options for themselves. I don't agree with all their choices, and I prolly would not run my relationships in the ways they do. But in the ways they seem to exist always adjacent to marriage, almost as the sandpaper rubbing away the facade, they teach us something.

Nah, I ain't saying Black women are only the sandpaper smoothing the walls of other people's marriages. I'm saying that just as sandpaper's rawness and roughness is used to smooth surfaces, these sisters rub our romantic and intimate desires right up against the rough-hewn nature of our most revered social and family structures, allowing us to see them more clearly. Meanwhile, they walk away with the bruises and scars to prove that those institutions are not as smooth and innocuous as they look from a distance.

We could continue to read these sisters as failures of certain kinds of respectable representation, or we could take a different feminist move and imagine what kind of possibilities they open up. And maybe those possibilities are about what they break, and not what they build. Maybe those possibilities are about the graves they allow us to dig, the bodies they allow us to bury, the fertilizer for the soil that those buried bodies become.

Perhaps their purpose is not so macabre as that. Like chocolate truffles broken open, the goodness, the substance, runs out of the center. But like good sex, it's all impossible to enjoy without getting messy.

Maybe they simply inhabit every representation that we have been taught to fear, from the mammy to the jezebel to the overachieving Black lady. And perhaps once we have confronted our ghosts, dealt with the things that haunt us about who we might get to be in America's popular imagination, we can ease up and let these sisters live.

A Scandal and a Lawn Chair: Why Olivia Pope Can't Save Us from Racism

Robin M. Boylorn

In the same week, in 2015, that the Ferguson-inspired "The Lawn Chair" episode of *Scandal* aired, a video of members of the University of Oklahoma chapter of Sigma Alpha Epsilon singing a racist chant went viral. Both events centered race, what Marita Golden describes as "the tar baby in our midst; touch it and you get stuck, hold it and you get dirty, so they say." Perhaps it is the fear of the filth that causes people to ignore or avoid conversations about race and racism, even when events happen out in the open, begging for breath and acknowledgment. The fictionalized account on TV, and the fact-checked video in our newsfeeds, challenged us to reckon with what twenty-first-century racism looks like.

Scandal was both praised and critiqued for its depiction of a "happy ending" to an all-too-familiar nightmare. In Shondaland, we were given a story line where there was justice for a murdered Black body lying in the street at the hands of the (in)justice system. In Shondaland, the White police officer who took the life of an innocent child was exposed and held accountable for his actions instead of protected and shielded from responsibility. In Shondaland, we were offered a temporary tale of what it would look like if Black lives mattered to White people by fictionalizing the continuous reality of Black folk dying at the hands of those who are supposed to protect them and giving us the ending we keep hoping for but never get. In Shondaland, race only matters sometimes.

In "The Lawn Chair" we see Olivia, who is generally racially ambivalent and remarkably "color-blind," recognize and center her race and seemingly, for the first time, understand the impact and persistence of racism, particularly by White men in positions of power (how this feels novel in this episode when she'd been knockin' boots with the White POTUS for the past four seasons is a conversation for another day) and particularly toward Black men. Her sudden recognition of her Blackness is instigated by Black maleness: Brandon's dead body underneath a lawn chair; Clarence, a grieving father, who is guarding his son's body with his own; and Marcus, a protester turned gladiator, who gives Ms. Pope a race read when she implies race is a nonfactor in the case. Eventually connecting the tyranny of racism to the tyranny she experienced by her kidnappers, Olivia inspires the "good" White men to hold the "racist" White men to task.

Meanwhile, in the real world, in the SAE video, we see fraternity brothers gleefully singing a chant to the tune of "If You're Happy and You Know It," proclaiming the intentional segregation of their fraternity.

> *There will never be a ni--er SAE (clap clap)*
> *There will never be a ni--er SAE (clap clap)*
> *You can hang 'em from a tree*
> *but he'll never sign with me*
> *There will never be a ni--er SAE (clap clap)*

Ironically, the racist and inflammatory chant, exposed in part by Black student alliance group OU Unheard, inspired White apologia on behalf of the poor White boys who made "an unfortunate mistake." Parents claimed the video was not evidence of racism, supporters defended their first amendment rights, and pundits scrambled to distort the story altogether. On MSNBC's *Morning Joe*, Joe Scarborough and Mika Brzezinski attempted to transfer the responsibility of racist rhetoric away from White racists and onto Black rappers, claiming hip hop made them do it. They attempted to mystify the meaning of racism and distract us from the blatant racism of the fraternity brothers by hijacking the narrative to make the racists the victims. This backward logic is not unpopular, but it is also not representative of how progressive and liberal White folk interpreted the video.

White allyship is and has always been a necessary ingredient for institutional intervention, and this is reiterated in both the fictional and factual cases. University of Oklahoma President David Boren demonstrated White allyship by calling out the racism, immediately closing the campus chapter of the fraternity, evicting the fraternity members from their frat house, and expelling Parker Rice and Levi Pettit, who were recognizable on the video and leading the chant. Similarly on *Scandal*, fictional POTUS Fitz Grant and Attorney General David Rosen used their power and legal influence to hold the crooked cop accountable and ensure the dead boy's father would not be prosecuted for his demonstration.

While the *Scandal* episode showed us what would happen in a perfect world, SAE showed us what happens in the real world. In a perfect world, Black folk would not be killed in the street, nor would racist chants about lynching exist within the confines of predominantly and historically White organizations. In a perfect world, all Black lives, not only those recognized as cisgender and male, would be privileged and acknowledged in public platforms. In a perfect world, racism would be fictional.

While Black boys and White saviorism are at the center of both narratives, it is important that we acknowledge that gender/sex does not preclude racism. Racism affects Blackgirls and women as much as Black men, and it is important that we not mistake the media absence of reference to Black women (including trans women) in mainstream outlets to mean that they are somehow protected. Racism against Black men is racism against Black women—and even if Olivia Pope can transcend race in her relationships and career, real-life Black women cannot.

Twenty-first-century racism hides in coquettish grins and well-dressed suits; it lives and breathes in the subtle justifications for injustice, and in the silent acquiescence of bystanders who marginally participate in racism by not challenging it, who smile at racist overtures and laugh at racist jokes, but have one convenient Black friend; it cheers for Black bodies on football fields, sells out rap concerts, and borrows Black culture. Twenty-first-century racists may have voted for Obama, listen to Jay Z, and may fuck (with) Black people sometimes. Racism these days is mild-mannered, politically progressive, formally educated, well-spoken, and intergenerational. It denies itself, distorts itself, and apologizes when it gets caught.

But racism (not race) is still dirty and mired in the politics of privilege and willful ignorance. In a culture where racism hides in plain sight, there are some things even Olivia Pope can't fix.

Tyler Perry Hates Black Women:
Five Thoughts on *The Haves and the Have Nots*

Brittney C. Cooper

Welp.

I watched the premiere of Tyler Perry's introductory train wreck on OWN, *The Haves and the Have Nots*, for two reasons: morbid curiosity, and I didn't wanna hear negroes' mouths about how I didn't give it a chance and was therefore uninformed and unqualified to speak on his show (despite the twelve or so movies and two stage plays of his I've *paid* to go see, and time I spent watching episodes of his existing TV shows that I can't get back). Anyway. Here are my thoughts.

1. **Tyler Perry is a cultural batterer.** The cultural equivalent of an unrepentant wife batterer. Why, you ask? Well, let's see. In under fifteen minutes of the first episode there were three Black women: Hanna, a maid, who speaks like she just left the plantation; Veronica, a rich Black ~~lady~~ bitch who throws her coat and hat at the maid; and Candace, the maid's daughter, a scheming, conniving prostitute who tells people her mom (Hanna) is dead, later can be seen raising her hand to her mom, has her own son who is God knows where, is allegedly in law school but paying for it by questionable means, and ultimately by the closing scene of episode two can be seen raping the White patriarch/politician.

   The fact that Mammy, Jezebel, and Sapphire, along with their remixes (Bad) Baby Mama, Gold-digger, Freak, and Hood Bitch showed up in under fifteen minutes is surely a new world record.

   A few caveats: no knock to domestics who speak in Southern dialect—I am from the deep, rural South, love the cadences in our voices, and have a beloved and dearly missed grandmama who cleaned White folks' houses well into her sixties. But I know a fucking controlling image when I see one.

   No knock to sex workers, who I think should have rights, benefits, and legal protections. Black women sex workers in prime time is a whole different deal representationally, though, and we need to OWN that, and take care to portray these sisters without recourse to trite and demeaning stereotypes.

Black women deserve better.

2. **Tyler Perry can only represent Black men positively by throwing Black women under the bus.** Since dude's plotlines are so simple a thirteen-year-old could write them—no disrespect to thirteen year olds—there are of course three Black men to balance out the three Black women. They include the husband of the rich lady—he'll prolly be comparable to *Scandal's* Cyrus, or at least Tyler prolly thinks that's what he's doing; his son, a drug counselor (respectable profession); and the son of the maid, a Shemar Moore look-alike and all-around good guy, whose sole aspiration in life is to— wait for it—drive a tow truck. So one-point-five solidly good guys out of three ain't bad. Why one-point-five? Because of course the rich drug counselor is on the DL, which in Tyler Perry's world makes him a sexual deviant. I don't know how this plot line developed, but since Tyler Perry outs the dude by way of terrible slow pans, meant to simulate not-so-secret longing after the buff White dude, I am not optimistic.

Black gay men deserve better.

3. **I feel some type of way that Oprah would be in league with such foolishness.** And that is because I AM NOT AN OPRAH HATER. And I have little patience for people who are. The chick is doing her thing, and I'm proud of her. And I really want to see OWN do well. That aside, I like to think she has been duped, hoodwinked, and bamboozled. But I know that ain't the whole truth. Really, OWN was struggling. And when networks struggle, they pimp the "urban demographic" for ratings and money. And once they are set financially, they bounce. The Fox Network did it: *Living Single, Martin, In Living Color.* The WB, UPN, and the CW all did it. So I see what OWN is doing, and I resent it.

Why?

I know she and Tyler share that nouveau-riche-Black-Southern-abuse-survivor-started-from-the-bottom-now-we-here connection.

BUT.

Oprah doesn't seem to understand that a rich, independent, college-educated chick like her, who shuns traditional marriage, is in Tyler Perry's world the DEVIL, a veritable conniving bitch who hates babies, men, and old people, needs Jesus, plus a good slap from a sexy Black man, and will still probably catch AIDS and live in misery because she chose not to conform to the dictates of Christian respectability.

Why Oprah doesn't get this is beyond me. It seriously is. OWN deserves better.

4. **On his best day and her worst day, Tyler ain't even in Shonda's stratosphere.** This wack-ass mash-up of *Deception* plus *Scandal* plus *The Help* in no way compares to anything Shonda Rhimes is doing. I can already hear the brothers now, talking about how Candace's character is comparable to Olivia's character. They are comparable in only one way: they both sleep with White men. Comparison over. *And that is how you know that Black men's primary issue with Olivia is not her moral choices, but her racial ones.*

I digress.

My love of *Scandal* should be a clear indicator that my problem with Tyler Perry is not about respectability politics. In other words, I am not advocating for positive representations. I'm advocating for complex, human representations. Tyler Perry doesn't complicate Black women; he demonizes them.

Candace is not just a sex worker but a sextortionist and a rapist. A predator. She does not merely have mother issues but she nearly slaps her mom and can't account for her baby's whereabouts.

We don't hate Liv, because while we might reject many of her choices, we identify with her as a human being with needs and emotions and as a person with the ability to do good in the world, despite the bad she also does.

Tyler Perry just thinks Black women—other than maternal domestics—are bad. That's why he can't complicate his analysis. But they have therapists for that, and I wish he'd see one.

Posthaste.

And this brings me to my final point:

5. **Tyler Perry is dangerous.** He has made Black women mistake hate for love. When his heavy-handedness is still not enough to chastise and discipline us for being independent,

driven, and sex-positive, he will resort to straight-up distortions of history and assume that his working-class audience will miss the sleight of hand. Case in point: that rape scene! Because, of course, history is replete with poor Black women raping rich White men. Not.

And the fact that he would traffic in such an utter fiction—a fiction that is the very basis for centuries of brutality against Black women on the grounds that they are by nature unrapeable, a fiction that drove the creation of the culture of dissemblance and the politics of respectability—makes his cultural production not merely bad but despicable.

And that is why I titled this essay "Tyler Perry Hates Black Women." How can he not?

IDENTITY: INTERSECTIONALITY FOR A NEW GENERATION

Introduction

In the first edition of *The Black Woman: An Anthology*, Toni Cade Bambara asks and answers the question, who is the Black woman?

> She is a college graduate. A drop-out. A student. A wife. A divorcée. A mother. A child of the ghetto. A product of the bourgeoisie. A professional writer. A person who never dreamed of publication. A solitary individual. A member of the Movement. A gentle humanist. A violent revolutionary. She is angry and tender, loving and hating. She is all these things—and more.

Bambara's description is multilayered and varied, highlighting the complementary and contradictory aspects of a Black woman's identity, how she is perceived, and how she sees herself. Bambara's definition of a Black woman is a consistent reminder of how complicated and nuanced identity politics can be, especially for Black women who are routinely negotiating who they know and believe themselves to be with the ascribed identity cast on them by outsiders and bystanders.

In the twenty-first century, Black women are navigating new terrain and enjoying empowerment and visibility unavailable to them in the 1970s, when Bambara initially answered her own question, but we still face the same discriminations. Nearly fifty years later the same labels continue to hold true, but in addition to the list Bambara compiled, Black womanhood and Black feminism has expanded the lexicon of possibilities for Black women and girls to include terms popularized in hip hop vernacular, academic and activist spaces, and everyday speech and colloquialisms.

The "and more" includes: Masculine of center. Cis. Trans. A lesbian. A stud. Femme. Straight. Asexual. Androgynous. Hypersexualized.

A baby mama. A thot. A gold-digger. A side chick. Bohemian. Vegan. Conscious. Self-conscious. Woke. Ratchet. Respectable. God-fearing. Agnostic. Fast-assed. Celibate. Feminist. Womanist. A PhD. A Pastor. FLOTUS. An entrepreneur. A professor. Liberal. Conservative. Queer. Crunk—and more.

We believe that all of these identities can coexist alongside our feminism, alongside our politics, alongside our activism. But we also recognize that as women of color there are and have always been structural and institutional systems of power at work against us. Through crunk feminism we attempt to disrupt those things we can't dismantle and resist those things we can't control.

Intersectionality is an inheritance from Black feminism that informs, but does not define identity politics. Identity politics refers to the political positions and perspectives, as well as theorizations, that emerge from our shared experiences as members of marginalized social groups. As Brittney Cooper articulates, "Intersectionality is not an account of personal identity, but one of power." This section approaches intersectionality by looking at identity through a lens that critiques the power structures that shape it. Writers approach topics including race and ethnicity, color and colorism, body types and fatphobia, and survivorship and tokenism to investigate those identities in the context of what bell hooks calls White-supremacist, capitalist patriarchy. hooks uses the language to represent the interlocking systems of domination that define the reality of people of color. Intersectionality mandates that we cannot consider race, class, gender/sex, ability, and sexuality without first considering racism, classism, sexism, ableism, cisgenderism, and heterosexism (including homo- and transphobia).

Intersectionality, then, does not offer us an account of our identity, it offers an account of power systems that work together to work against us. These institutional and cultural power structures are designed to privilege those who are what Audre Lorde calls "mythically normal" while punishing everyone else. Mythic normality refers to White, Christian, cisgender, heterosexual men who are healthy, wealthy, and well-educated.

Because we believe that our personal and social identities are products of our backgrounds, standpoints, and lived experiences, we know that who we are is not simply located within us, it is also located around us. We also know that as women of color our social identities are influenced by external factors including economics, education, access, regionality, and upbringing. We do not, however, interpret intersectionality as merely an account or representation of our multiple identities. Intersectionality does not do the work of identity politics; it offers us language to theorize the constructions that oppress us because of our identity and politics. We realize that intersectionality has been largely used to account for marginalized identities and the indistinguishability of oppression, but we understand intersectionality also to be a way of critique that Black feminists have used over many generations, before it had a name, to talk about how our oppression is embedded in the laws of the land and the injustice of a system designed to regard us as less than human.

The essays in this section tackle topics that are generally seen as taboo or unspoken and are directly related to identity politics. While not exclusive to Black womanhood, they suggest that women of color approach sense-making and meaning-making as it relates to their identities through a sometimes-distorted lens dirtied by White supremacy and patriarchy. Because our identities are always automatically compared to White, cis, mythically normal representations and presentations, there is always something to prove. We think about intersectionality as an intervention and an opportunity for us to self-define and redefine ourselves on our own terms. As writers, we wrestle with what it means to negotiate a shifting self in the face of multiple and ongoing experiences of discrimination, and how crunk feminism can inform and instruct how we see ourselves in a world hell-bent on only seeing the parts of us they want to see.

You're Pretty for a Dark-Skinned Girl

Robin M. Boylorn

I have heard those seven words too many times to count, from well-meaning elders, Black men with a preference for light-skinned women, family members who haven't seen me in a while, and perfect strangers who are color struck. Folk be acting like I conjured some kind of voodoo magic for being darker than a paper sack— *and* cute. The words, usually stated hurriedly and in that flowery and matter-of-fact voice that lets you know it's seeped in shade, are offered as a criticism and compliment. I never know if I should feel flattered or insulted.

"You're a pretty ol' dark-skinned girl . . ."

The words make me feel proud and hurt my feelings at the same time.

The words mean my attractiveness has caught someone off guard, taken them by surprise. After years of absence, I am at a family reunion, greeted with an invitation for inspection, so I can be looked at up close.

"Come here with your pretty Black ass . . ."

I have the kind of beauty that moves slowly and sneaks up on you. In those few seconds when you are still trying to decide what you think of my face, you realize that the thing that made you unsure was not my features, but my skin. My pretty is a subtle, disarming, vulnerable, newly confident beautiful that comes with self-assurance and a little self-doubt. It is housed in a body that used to sit in bathwater with Clorox mixed in, ashamed of itself. I was a little girl who prayed for light skin at Christmas and resented cousins and best friends who were born with "built-in" beauty, red bones, bright skin, and high yellah complexions.

When people tell me I'm pretty to be dark-skinned they insinuate that one is either pretty or dark-skinned, not both at the same time. They imply that the tendency to be both simultaneously is possible, but not likely, and requires the careful construction of culturally conditioned standards alongside dark skin. Their words suggest I am an anomaly.

My melanin proficiency has often led to color complex(ion) issues brought on by my country upbringing in a community (and country) fascinated (via the hegemonic influences of beauty) with my yellow-skinned sister with loooooooooooooooooooooong hair and generally ambivalent with me. People always knew my sister was beautiful, but for me it took time, years, deep long looks and depth of consideration, to finally determine that I was cute—shit, beautiful even—for a dark-skinned girl. I have often pondered the implications of those terms of my beauty, put on me by society, community, and sometimes myself.

Colorism (or internalized racism) in the lives of dark-skinned women translates to how we see ourselves (as beautiful or not) and how we are seen (desired or not). A dark-skinned sister sighed in surrender as she shared with me that

"dark-skinned women were never in style."

This, of course, doesn't mean that men don't notice when we are "pretty," don't whisper those seven words like sweet nothings in our ears. Still, their short-term seductions transition to long-term sensibilities that tend to send them on quests to find the most exotic, racially ambiguous (or White) woman to take home to mama or make babies with cuz

dark-skinned women ain't trophies.

it's hard to see yourself as beautiful when the epitome of beauty is seen as something like White

i believed the hype

surprised at songs that praised "boricua morenas,"

skeptical when Tupac said, "the darker the berry, the sweeter the juice,"

confused by Lauryn Hill's lyrics saying the sweetest thing she had ever known

was wrapped in "dark skin tone,"

and fascinated with India.Arie's obsession with "Brown skin."

my skin

wasn't ever treasured

Being dark-Brown-skinned in a culture that privileges red bones causes conflicts in my community because of colorism. People stay telling me I am pretty in spite of, not because of, my "dark skin."

Truth is, in the words of Yaba Blay's Brown beauty self-love campaign, I'm "pretty period."

So, from now on, if you're passing out compliments, I'm checking for two words, not seven: "You're pretty ~~for a dark-skinned girl~~!"

Does This Make Me Look Fat?

Susana M. Morris

I own the movie *Phat Girlz* and I'm not ashamed.

Starring a pre-Oscar Mo'Nique, before her one-hundred-pound weight loss, *Phat Girlz* is part Cinderella story, part conventional rom-com about a big girl searching for some love. It's not remarkable in terms of budget, plot, or acting. In fact, a fair bit of it is cringe-worthy. (What immediately springs to mind is the fetishization of Nigerian men. Good Lord.)

Still, despite its shortcomings, the film works for me for some fundamental reasons. I appreciate the fact that big girls are not sassy sidekicks but stars of the show. And while it was billed as a romance, the theme of self-love was perhaps just as important as the romantic plot line. And positive portrayals of a thick sister having sex? Yes, please!

But perhaps one of my favorite moments in the movie happens in the beginning. Heroine Jazmin Biltmore (played by Mo'Nique) is working in a department store when a customer asks her if the outfit she has just tried on "makes her look fat."

The film makes this into a funny moment, but oftentimes this type of interaction is no chucklefest. If I had a dollar for all the similarly inappropriate and downright hurtful invocations of the word "fat," I'd be a wealthy woman. If I had a dollar for all the times thin folks with complexes (bred by the impossible social standards of the mythical norm, I know) wanted me to soothe their fears by letting them project their disdain for fatness onto my larger body . . . you get the picture.

A lot of this behavior is born out of self-loathing and the public shaming that comes along with being even remotely associated with being overweight. I understand. I get it. At the same time, being large, fluffy, plus-sized, Rubenesque, or whatever, does not make one equipped to be the counselor for a family member, friend, coworker, or random stranger's fat bashing.

More and more poor folks of color don't have access to reasonably priced fresh food. This is not a trivial matter. I think living a healthy life is an admirable goal. Losing weight might be an admirable goal for some folks too. Putting folks down or assuming the right to police another person's health (e.g., through fat shaming) should not be a part of this.

So, in light of all this, I'd like to make a crunk public service announcement:

Fat does not equal ugly.
Fat does not equal weak.
Being thin does not make one morally superior to those who
    are not.
Being thin does not make one healthier than those who are not.
Leave your judgment at the door.
Feel free to bring your love right on in.

Does This Make Me Look Latina?

Crunkista

I was recently asked to give a presentation about women in the workforce to a group of Latina undergraduate students. After the panic about speaking in public wore off, I started asking myself, what could I possibly teach them?

I started thinking about my experiences (as a student and professional) and how they have been shaped by the cultural imaginary of Latinxs in this country. Too many stereotypes persist and continue to negatively affect Latinxs. You know them. I will not waste my time listing them here. I will, however, say that after going through the long list of stereotypes that have kept and continue to keep my people oppressed, the next thing that came to mind was the "Latin explosion" of the late nineties. This explosion introduced Jennifer Lopez, Marc Anthony, Ricky Martin, and Shakira to the American mainstream. One of the most frustrating realities of this so-called "explosion" is the idea that these people became famous overnight. Just in case you did not know this, Marc Anthony, Ricky Martin, Shakira, and the newly popular Sofía Vergara were *huge* in Latin America and filthy rich before their "crossover" to the American mainstream.

History lesson: there are thirty-two Spanish-speaking countries around the world. Of these thirty-two, Spanish is the official language of twenty-one: Mexico, Guatemala, Honduras, Nicaragua, El Salvador, Costa Rica, Panama, Colombia, Venezuela, Ecuador, Peru, Bolivia, Paraguay, Chile, Argentina, Uruguay, Cuba, Dominican Republic, Spain, Equatorial Guinea, and Puerto Rico. Each of these countries has a rich and complex history, its own entertainment industry, and again, lots of famous people. Anytime I hear an ignorant statement about Latinxs in this country, I remember Susana Morris's mama's words of wisdom, "We were kings and queens when they were still running around in caves."

But, I digress. Let's get back to my dilemma. What can I possibly tell these young women about being professional Latinas in the workforce? How can I equip them for the challenges they will surely encounter?

In my research I came across an article in a Latina magazine, "Latinas at the Office: Do We Need to Tone Down Our Sex Appeal?" The article focused on Latinas who had been negatively affected by their imagined sex appeal. One of these women, Debrahlee Lorenzana, was involved in a lawsuit against Citigroup. Her allegations: she was fired because her male colleagues and supervisors believed she was too distracting at the office. After seeing images of her in her business attire I couldn't help but marvel at her beauty (she is indeed breathtaking) and my wanting to be her (if only I could rock stilettos like that).

While reading about her case, I started thinking about the current cultural imagery of Latinas. The so-called Latin explosion did in fact open many doors and in many ways solidified that we actually exist. We knew we existed, but apparently White people didn't. It isn't a coincidence that after Jennifer Lopez's rise to fame, several people (Black and White) told me that I looked like/reminded them of Jennifer Lopez. Side note, I don't look like Jennifer Lopez.

So, who are today's mainstream Latinas and what can we say about their representation in the media? On basic television: Sara Ramirez (*Grey's Anatomy*'s resident hot, lesbian Latina doctor), Eva Longoria (Desperate "hot Latina" Housewife), Sofía Vergara (*Modern Family*'s hot, young Latina wife), Rosalyn Sánchez (*Without a Trace*'s hot special agent), and Salma Hayek (Alec Baldwin's hot Latina girlfriend on *30 Rock*). In movies: Jennifer Lopez, Eva Mendes, Zoe Saldana, Rosario Dawson, Jessica Alba, America Ferrera, Penélope Cruz, Paz Vega, Michelle Rodriguez, Rosie Perez, and Christina Milian; all of them often cast as the hot, Latina, light-skinned girlfriends of White men. What do all of these women have in common? You guessed it: they are all HOT Latinas.

So what are these young Latina women about to encounter after graduation? As women and as women of color, the obvious: sexism, racism, and working harder than everyone else because they have to prove they are qualified and deserve to be there. As Latinas: working with people of other backgrounds who very likely have only been exposed to one-dimensional representations of Latina women—hot, sexy, curvaceous, and, my favorite, spicy. They might be even hotter if they have accents, or not Latina enough if they either lack the accent (because maybe their people have been here for over three hundred years) or if, heaven forbid, they lack the curves.

My presentation will of course include a modified version of this tangent and the following list of advice.

1. Dress for the job you want, not the job you have.
2. Respect and acknowledge every individual's contribution to your company/institution. Everyone from the cleaning personnel to the administrative assistants to the company CEO makes significant contributions to your organization.
3. Know the ins and outs of your field.
4. Define clear goals for yourself.
5. Find a mentor.
6. Mentor other young women.
7. Read. Read. Read.
8. Attend seminars geared toward cultivating your leadership qualities.
9. Find support groups for women/women of color in your field.
10. Work should NEVER be your life. Make your physical, emotional, and mental health a priority. No one else will do this for you.
11. Stay connected to your college/university alumni network.
12. After you graduate, make sure you give back to your college/university.

Memories, Survival, and Safety

Crunkista

Warning: This essay contains information about sexual violence that may be triggering to survivors.

I am an extremely private person. So private that even Facebook gives me the creeps. Consequently, it feels like writing for the Collective and speaking frankly about my experiences, thoughts, doubts, fears, and feelings exposes me more than I feel comfortable with. Writing sometimes makes me feel unsafe and vulnerable. These emotions are often difficult for me to deal with. They bring back unwanted memories. The first time I felt this way I was eleven years old.

It was Father's Day and I was at my grandparents' house for the summer. All of the grown folks were drinking and playing card games. I remember going up to my grandparents and saying that I was going to go to bed, that I was scared to be in the house by myself, and asking them not to take long before they too retreated for the night.

I went to bed, fell asleep, and woke up with my grandfather on top of me. His hands were all over me as he licked my face and repeated, "Suck on my tongue." I didn't understand what was happening. I couldn't move. I was paralyzed with fear. I couldn't even scream. At some point, my grandmother opened the door to the house. Once he heard the sound of the door opening, he quickly got off of me and jumped into the bed he shared with her.

He did not rape me. However, he did scar me for life. He stole my childhood and all of the childhood innocence I once had. From that moment on I understood that there was evil in the world. I was so ashamed of what happened that I didn't tell anyone. I wished I had had the courage to tell someone, *anyone*, of what he was capable of. To make matters worse, I blamed myself for years—I was convinced that I was a bad little girl. My child logic told me that God wouldn't have let this happen to me had I been a good little girl.

It took years for me to realize that it was not my fault, that I was just a child, that the adults who were supposed to take care of me failed, and that he was the one to blame. The church taught me that there was great power in forgiveness, and I made an honest attempt to forgive him. I convinced myself that alcohol made him do it. Sadly, that was not the truth, and I received a rude awakening at the age of fifteen. I was at my mother's apartment doing my homework while a movie starring Tom Cruise played in the background. I was sitting on the living-room couch and from the corner of my eyes I could see my grandfather fidgeting in his seat. At one point Mr. Cruise kissed the female lead and my grandfather looked over and said, "Do you remember when we did that?" He said those words with pride. That is when I realized that I could never forgive him for what he did to me. I remember screaming at him, going to my room, calling my best friend, and having a panic attack. After that incident, I decided to tell my mother. When I told her, she yelled at me and asked me why I hadn't told her sooner. She expressed anger at my silence because I had a little sister and he could have done the same to her or to others. (*Note: This is never an appropriate response. It is never the responsibility of children to protect other children. That is what adults are for.*)

My grandfather died of prostate cancer a few years after that incident. I remember trying to console my mother for her loss while being very angry at God for giving him that much time on this earth. Unfortunately, I was not the only one damaged by his actions. Other women have come out and admitted that he fondled them as well.

My story is a very complex one. I was abused by my grandfather at an early age and was later forced to live with him after the abuse had occurred. I couldn't tell anyone, but in hindsight the clues that I was abused were always there; the adults around me just didn't know what to do with the information. We often don't know what to do with child abusers in our families or our communities. That is a sad truth.

The story does not end there. My grandfather was not the only one to abuse me; there were babysitters and family friends who also stepped out of line and fondled me. The memories are fuzzy. For a very long time I was haunted by my lack of childhood memories. In my midtwenties, I inexplicably started crying without reason or provocation and decided to seek therapy. Even at the therapist's office, I couldn't keep it together. I discovered that the crying episodes had to do with the fact that there was so much I couldn't remember. I was horrified that my subconscious had blocked out five years of memories. What could be so awful that my subconscious would lock it all away? What would happen to me if I were to remember all of it? Would the memories break me? My therapist reassured me that I didn't have to remember and that I was safe now. I found that to be quite liberating and only then was I able to stop crying. Thank goodness for therapy.

I am better now, but I often have nightmares. There is no rhyme or reason to when they come; they just do. In fact, a girlfriend once revealed to me that I often quietly sob in my sleep. I want to be clear that there are a lot of details to my story that I am not including here. It is nearly impossible to package our stories in neat and linear boxes. Although, I am a survivor of child abuse, this does not define me. This story is complex. My story is complex. I am complex.

I am sharing this story because I think there is power in sharing your truths. I do not live in fear anymore. I am indeed safe. I hope with all of my heart that other victims of sexual abuse can one day say the same.

The following are some facts about child abuse:

1. While abuse by strangers does happen, most abusers are family members or trusted individuals. Child molesters, pedophiles, and perpetrators are everywhere: they are parents, grandparents, family members, teachers, neighbors, and friends.
2. Oftentimes, survivors of child abuse are forced to see their abusers regularly.
3. Perpetrators know how to identify their victims. Consequently, victims of sexual abuse are often vulnerable to abuse by multiple people.
4. Most child-abuse cases go unreported.
5. There are often many signs that a child is suffering from abuse.
6. It takes a lot of courage to tell anyone that you have been a victim of abuse.
7. It is *never* okay to blame the victim.
8. If you or someone you love has suffered because of abuse, please know that there are resources available to help.

Getting to Happy, or The Myth of Happily Ever After

Robin M. Boylorn

"Is this going to have a happy ending?"

A student asked this question when the documentary we were watching in class seemed to be going awry.

"Well," I said, "it depends on what a happy ending is."

I wanted to resist the student's need for a feel-good ending and the implication that there is only one version of what counts as "happy." Happiness is a fleeting feeling. And endings are subjective.

I knew the real question was: Is everything going to turn out all right? Is everyone going to be okay in the end? Will the merits of meritocracy win out? Will the American Dream be achieved?

There is no real or easy answer to those questions because we weren't watching a Hollywood romantic comedy. We were watching a true story. And true stories are reminders that good things don't always happen to good people. And sometimes, regardless of how hard-working, deserving, good-looking, smart, likable, or enviable real people are, happy endings don't always look the way we have been conditioned to imagine them.

American movies and fairy tales romanticize trauma and hurt by framing them with happy endings where the protagonists fall in love, the villain goes to jail, the poor person gets an inheritance, the sick person gets well, and everyone lives the Disney-esque happily ever after. In the happy endings of privileged lives/eyes, no one dies, no one hurts, pain is deserved, and in the end children are protected, love is enough, and poverty only exists out there somewhere in the faraway distance or past.

But in the real world, many people don't have the privilege of a canonical happy ending. In the real world, people settle for some semblance of fairness in their lives while many others (based on who they are, how and where they were born, the color of their skin, the accent on their tongues, the performance of their gender, their biological sex, who their parents are or aren't, how much money they have, whom they make love to, whether or not they meet societal standards of beauty, etc.) don't have peace, go to bed hungry, don't have sound minds, go to substandard schools, don't get better, live in substandard homes, don't have homes to go to or arms to run to, don't know unconditional love, don't have good health, don't have access to health care, will never be seen as "normal," won't see better days, won't make it out of the bad situation they started in, won't be swept off their feet, survive, or go down in a blaze of glory. Real life endings are not always happy. Real life beginnings aren't either.

In my own life I often ask myself, "Is this (my life) going to have a happy ending?"

And then I think about the Black and Brown folk all over the world who find bliss in the simplest of things, and I wonder what happiness means. I was a melancholy child and I am a depressive adult, so happiness is and has always been something to be attempted or worked toward, not a perpetual state of being. For me, happiness is a possibility, but not a promise.

In our capitalist culture we learn that happiness means owning material things, having material worth, and being in a traditional relationship. It seems like we are always working toward happiness as the reward for hard work, patience, and endurance (sometimes suffering). We never think about how happiness is a commodity that is bought and sold to us if we are gullible enough to think it can be owned. Companies offer us happiness in a bottle if you can afford it. If you don't have the money then you have to settle for hand-me-down happiness, the watered-down version left in a donation box after the holidays or when seasons change. Some folk go broke trying to get to happy.

If and when you are not happy, people feel sorry for you and assume there is something wrong with you. Strangers and intimates alike tend to make you feel guilty for not being happy all the damn time.

Truth is, there is no such thing as happily ever after. There is happy. But there is also sad, pissed off, ambivalent, angry, and disenchanted. We are master pretenders. As seasoned actors we smile when we don't mean it, dress up when we're feeling down, and play the part of "happy-go-lucky" person when we really feel like shit or don't want to be bothered so that other people will feel comfortable. Truth is, happiness is dictated by hegemonic promises that nobody can keep up with. Not even the Joneses.

I take my happiness in degrees and hold it with both hands, but I don't hold too tight. I know it comes and goes like beautiful weather, good sex, and bad attitudes. To me, happiness is knowing that the people I care about know I care about them. Happiness is utilizing my gifts to make people smile. Happiness is calling Blackgirls beautiful. Happiness is feeling beautiful. Happiness is being able to donate my time, money, energy, and endorsement to worthwhile causes. Happiness is teaching my students to see and consider standpoints beyond their own. Happiness is hearing my mother and grandmother's voices on the phone. Happiness is looking back over my life and recognizing how far I have come.

But every day is not happy. Every moment is not happy. And that is not failure. That's life. Some days will be punctuated by sadness, anger, resentment, frustration, confusion, and disappointment. Some days will be blissful, whimsical, damn near perfect.

It has taken me years to give myself permission to not be happy all the time. To admit my humanity. To embrace my vulnerability. To appreciate all of my emotions. It is a brave confession, but when I'm not feeling happy, I am at least feeling brave. I am learning not to be invested in a life without tears, sadness, or disappointment, but I am down for a life fully lived.

When You're "The One"

Susana M. Morris

It was the summer of 2004. I was a grad student with experience in resident life, and I had taken on a job as codirector of a summer program hosted at my university. The pay was good, and it gave me time to read and prep for my first go at teaching that fall.

At first, the job was cool. I was codirecting with one of my best friends and the high-school kids I worked with were sweet. That is until my boss, a surly, hapless White man who spent most of his time avoiding work, decided to show out. We'd be at staff meetings and he would literally act as if I wasn't there. He would look past me and pretend I wasn't speaking. It was infuriating, disrespectful, and petty. I had suffered ill treatment for being a young Black woman before, but this took that experience to a whole other level.

To say that I was angry would be an understatement. This lazy fool refused to speak to me, actively obstructed my job, and was generally an asshole. And he thought he could get away with it because I was "the one"—the scapegoat, the garbage dump, the only sista in the room.

This happened over ten years ago, when I was a wee crunk feminist. But please believe I was crunk as hell. Trust. He didn't break my spirit—in fact, with the help and support of my codirector, my friends, and my loved ones, I finished out the summer with my coins, my sanity, and my spirit intact.

I mention this story because it reminded me of Sasheer Zamata, the latest cast member to join *Saturday Night Live*, which has been under fire for its lack of Black women comedians. (Remember the tragicomic skit with Kerry Washington during season thirty-nine, in 2013, where she had to act as every famous Negress there was, while *SNL* added some wacktastic disclaimer because if we all joke about it it's not racist, right?)

Zamata cut her teeth at the Upright Citizens Brigade and has had a promising career, so I hope she'll do well. But, as so many women of color know, being the one in the room can be a heavy burden and, sing it with me, "I'm Not Your Superwoman!"

While I am heartened by the news that two other sistas (LaKendra Tookes and Leslie Jones) now work as writers on the show, there is still cause for concern, especially considering the fact that Zamata is only the fifth Black woman to join the cast and was only added after *SNL* was convinced to hold a casting call for Black women comedians, and after ol' trifling-ass Kenan Thompson flapped his gums out of order about the supposed lack of talented Black women comedians. Brotha, go sit down and have a stadium of seats. (Let's not even mention Don Lemon's shenanigans, wherein he stated that Zamata would "have to be a whole lot funnier than she is Black." The hell?)

Now, some of you may be thinking, "Girl, please. I don't even watch *SNL* like that." Well, me neither. I've never been a huge fan of the show. Back in the day, *In Living Color* and *Mad TV* were my go-to shows in terms of sketch comedy. And, today, there are so many excellent web series (see Chescaleigh and really any of Issa Rae's productions), hilarious websites (*Crunk & Disorderly* is an old fave), and gutbusting podcasts (*The Read*—need I say more?) with Black women front and center, I'm not really studying *SNL* like that. I do think, though, that it's important for Black women to have as many opportunities as possible to live out their dreams. And I'm glad Sasheer Zamata is on *SNL* for that reason alone.

Currently, I am the only queer Black woman at my job. Well, I'm also only one of two Black people, period. And while I certainly am not experiencing the tomfoolery of 2004, being the only one can be, well, lonely.

I hope that Zamata knocks it out the park and makes me DVR *SNL* because she's so fucking funny. I hope that in meetings and interviews folks don't talk to her sideways, and ~~when~~ if they do, she takes a lesson from our sista Laverne Cox on how to get someone together right quick without even breaking a sweat (I'm talking to you, Katie Couric). I hope that when folks say, "Do you know Sasheer Zamata?" they respond, "Oh yeah, she's the funniest one on *SNL*."

SISTERHOOD: SHE'S NOT HEAVY, SHE'S MY SISTER

Introduction

The lie is that "you can't trust females." That women can't be friends. That women are naturally catty, petty, and messy. That women gossip too much. That women are mean.

The lie is that femmes, queer women, straight women, and non-binary folks can't be comrades or allies. Or friends. That our issues and concerns are too different. That there is no way for us to connect.

The lie is that trans women are not women. That women-only spaces are only for cis women. That when folks say "women," they mean only those who are cis or straight or White or middle-class or able-bodied—or all of the above.

The lie is that sisterhood only looks one kind of way. That sisters need to policed, checked, silenced, and controlled. That carefree womanhood is dangerous and a threat.

The lie is that women of color are the worst offenders of them all. That we should be disciplined, exoticized, and erased—not respected, supported, or understood. That sisterhood is a sorority for White girls only.

These lies about women and sisterhood can even creep their way into so-called feminist spaces. People believe these untruths and treat one another like the enemy. We become mean and petty. We use hurtful language. We are antiqueer. We are transphobic. We are ableist. We erase one another's experiences. We do harm to one another, break each other's hearts and spirits when we believe the lie.

Truth is, the real lie is that patriarchy is over, racism is dead, and that feminism is past its expiration date. And this is why we need sisterhood and solidarity among women and femmes more than ever.

Quiet as it's kept, being a sister is not just something you are, it is something that you do. Sisters can be biological, chosen, or a combination thereof. Sisters have bonds that transcend normative labels.

Sisterhood is deliberate love and solidarity in action.

Sisterhood is showing up and showing out for your friends. Sisterhood is saying what you mean and meaning what you say. Sisterhood is trans, gender nonconforming, nonbinary, and cis. Sisterhood is rejecting mean-girl cliques. Sisterhood calls out and calls in. Sisterhood is quiet, tender, loud, and joyful. Sisterhood is hard. Sisterhood is rewarding. Sisterhood gives the side-eye when someone says, "You know how we are" or "That's why I don't really fuck with females." Sisterhood is leading with love and letting go when love's lost. Sisterhood is celebrating womanhood in all of its forms and facets.

That is not to say that sisterhood is not in trouble. Besides all the internalized self-loathing that often threatens to tear us apart before we can even get together, there are stronger and more sinister threats that women of color are facing. And this is not because we are terrible crabs in a barrel that would rather tear each other down than lift each other up. Rather, we are threats to White supremacy and heteropatriarchy because of our fierceness, beauty, intelligence, and fortitude.

While women of color face increasing rates of incarceration, Black and Brown girls face rising numbers of suspensions and school discipline, all the while being tracked into the school-to-prison pipeline. Eviction and unstable housing plague our communities. Equal pay is far from a reality for Black and Brown women in the United States, who continue to have to work twice or three times as hard to get half as far. Although the passage of the Affordable Care Act opened up many doors, far too many are still closed; women of color are still in many cases grasping for proper medical care. Childcare costs are astronomical, and many working-class women of color do not have the luxury to choose between staying at home and having food and shelter for their families.

Mike Brown, Freddie Gray, and Walter Scott, among other men of color, have become the face of police brutality, and rightfully so. Each man was brutally murdered by law enforcement intent on killing people of color with impunity. But the truth is that women of color are assaulted and murdered by the police in sickening numbers. Women and girls such as Sandra Bland, Loreal Tsingine, Rekia Boyd, and Sarah Lee Circle Bear all died in police custody. Oftentimes these women's stories create little more than a blip on the news cycle, despite the fact that Black and Brown women are attacked and murdered by the state in alarming numbers.

Trans women of color are in a particularly urgent state of emergency. The average life expectancy for a trans woman of color is thirty-five years, while the average life expectancy of a cis woman of color is over twice that. Issues ranging from homelessness, job insecurity, inadequate health care, intimate partner violence, hate crimes, and more can whittle down the years of a trans woman's life. And while (wealthy, White, Republican) trans women such as Caitlyn Jenner may be more visible, visibility has not necessarily translated into more empathy or progressive policy change. In fact, antitrans legislation—often marketed as an attempt to "protect" cis women and girls—is on the rise, making trans folk more vulnerable than ever.

So, you might ask, what does all of this have to do with sisterhood?

Sisterhood literally means being our sisters' keepers, #SayingHerName, and fighting for all of us to have the resources we need, to have the access to the means to improve our lives, and to be able to live with the dignity that is our human right. Women of color and femmes are leading the charge when it comes to prison abolition and disrupting the school-to-prison pipeline. Women of color and femmes are at the forefront of the housing equity and environmental justice movements. Women of color and femmes, from economists to activists, are speaking truth to power about equal wages. Women of color and femme health-care advocates and practitioners have agitated and continue to fight for affordable health care and reproductive justice. Trans women of color and femmes, in particular, have been the vanguard of social change, fighting not only for visibility but for stable and secure housing, jobs, and health care. It was women of color and femmes who kept the story of serial-rapist cop Daniel Holtzclaw in the news and who lifted up the names of the survivors of his assaults. And it was three Black women who founded the Black Lives Matter movement that has swept the nation and changed the face of activism. Sisterhood is not an empty word or a clichéd phrase—it is a way of life.

Sisterhood has been a core tenet of crunk feminism. We have always been very interested in how women understand themselves and one another. As a feminist collective founded in the tradition of the Combahee River Collective and other feminist organizations, we have been focused on our relationships with each other above all else. And this interest has spilled over to the blog in a whole host of important ways. Over the years, we have covered virtually every aspect of sisterhood—from calling the names of our marginalized sisters, to celebrating the relationships between women, to calling out sisters who don't do right by one another.

We reject the lie that sisterhood is dead. Sisterhood is powerful. Long live sisterhood!

Antoine Dodson's Sister: On Invisibility as Violence

Chanel Craft Tanner

One day he was just a regular guy, and the next day he was famous for fighting off the intruder that climbed into his sister's second-story window in the middle of the night and tried to attack her with her daughter present. Remember his reaction? Hilarious right? I mean, he's pissed off that his sister was attacked! LMFAO! He was so hilarious that the Gregory Brothers made a song remixing the news clip and turned it into the summertime hit of 2010. It even made the iTunes Top 20 so we could purchase sexual assault for $1.99 and jam all day! And the star of all this was, of course, Antoine Dodson, for his "comedic" reaction to violence, and the Gregory Brothers for their creative innovation of putting it to song. Sarcasm aside, I must admit that to remix a news story like that is pretty amazing. But what does it mean to remix violence against Black women when our stories are already left behind?

See, usually when a Black woman is attacked, we find some way of making it her fault. We ask questions like, what was she wearing? What does she do for a living? How many sexual partners has she had in the past? You know, the typical stuff that removes accountability from her attacker. But in this case, where a Black woman was minding her damn business and awoke to an attacker in her second-story apartment, normal victim blaming would not work. So now what do we do, because we obviously can't take a Black woman's story of violence seriously? Well, that's simple. We marginalize the attack and focus the story on her brother, whose anger we can exploit because it fits into stereotypes of queer masculinity that provide comic relief. The producers used the footage to lock Antoine in a frame, to capture him in place, in order to tell a story that fits their truths—Black women's confrontations with sexual violence are either not real or not important. Framed under the guise of "news," this masquerades as a story about a woman awaking to an intruder in her bed, but it is really a story about a funny Black man, hilarious even in his anger. It was never about her.

I think we have to talk about the power of invisibility. As a child, I participated in the normal debates about what superpowers were the most desirable. For me, invisibility won hands down. To be able to be invisible was the most super of all the powers. See, I was nosey, so being invisible would allow me to know exactly what my mother and her sisters talked about when I was shooed out of the room. It would allow me to see what the forbidden boy's bathroom looked like. And those moments of being in a new place wouldn't have felt nearly as terrifying if I could turn on the power of invisibility.

Invisibility also afforded protection. Remember Violet from *The Incredibles*? Invisibility not only protects her from being noticed by the young man she has a crush on, it keeps her safe as she travels though the evil lab in search of her father. Or Harry Potter and that banging invisibility cloak. It not only allowed him to freely explore the campus but also often saved his life.

But as invisibility oscillates between power and protection, the ways in which it can be used as a tool of oppression become, well, invisible. For women of color, invisibility is often forced, and along with hypervisibility, it is used as a means to discredit and oppress. This is indeed the case with Kelly Dodson, made invisible through the hypervisibility of her brother. Her invisibility is highlighted by the numerous "Antoine Dodson for President" T-shirts and parapher-nalia that exist in the same space where we don't even remember Kelly's name. (In fact, I had to go back and watch the video to even remember her name, a video I found by merely typing in "Antoine Dodson.")

Kelly Dodson's experience of violence gets reduced to a frag-ment of the news segment and even further condensed to one line in the song: "I was attacked by some idiot in the projects." And while Antoine is central, that too is nothing to be celebrated. He is hypervisible as a caricature for public amusement. We all know Antoine's name thanks to the "Bed Intruder Song." But the Gregory Brothers have taken his voice, chopped it up, synthesized it, and put it to a beat so that it is no longer recognizable as his own. An-toine Dodson wasn't looking for fame. He was angry that he had to save his sister from being attacked!

When it comes down to it, Antoine has been made hypervisible in order to make Kelly invisible. This is not the invisibility of Harry Potter, free to put it on and take it off—this is an act of erasure. There is a difference between choosing invisibility and being made invisible. See, the choice of being invisible also comes with the recognition that you're missing. When Harry and the crew would return from their invisible outings people often asked where they were. When you are made invisible through processes of erasure, people don't even acknowledge that you're gone. It's like you never existed. So in a story that begins with the headline "a woman awakes," we don't even acknowledge that the entire segment focused on a man—her brother. We don't even acknowledge that the moment she is the most upset and telling us that her young daughter was in the bed with her, the news reporter is talking over her, so this reality exists as background fodder.

As women of color, we have long yearned for Black women's experiences of oppression to be paid attention to. Our stories of sexual assault, inside and outside of our communities, never make the evening news. And now, when we finally are awarded a few minutes of attention, we are simultaneously erased. We are further erased through the music that has increasingly been used to enslave rather than liberate us. It is the music that has put us in a trance, and even *we* are singing along to a Black woman being attacked. Singing along until we agree with her erasure. Until her erasure becomes more of a reality than the attack. Every note we sing erases Kelly Dodson.

I demand a remix to this remix! One whose beat doesn't influence your body to sway and your lips to smile as you sing the words. One that, instead, causes your body to curl over in pain and your eyes to water. One that makes you feel sad, or, better yet, angry that this happened. Can we remix this remix into a story that centers the Black woman who was attacked?

So here is my letter to Kelly Dodson that does just that.

Dear Kelly,
We know that in these conversations about this Internet sensation, YOU are missing. We know that when they're jamming to the music they aren't thinking about YOU. We know that you were never central, not in the original news story, not in the song, and not now. All of this has been about trivializing your brother's anger (characterizing as "emotions running

high" instead of emotions running normal for someone whose family member was attacked), the creativity of these White boys (a group that has always profited off the abuse of Black women), and the power and creative force of technology. Well the Crunk Feminist Collective says it's all about you.

We are sorry that this happened to you. We are sorry that when you should have been at peace in your home you were attacked. We are sorry and angry that your little girl had to be present for that. We are sorry that you no longer feel safe in your own home. We are grateful that you had someone home to help you and we are sorry that this is happening to your story. We want to center you. We want this moment to be used to talk about the realities of our communities as spaces of vulnerability and danger for women of color. We want to remember you as we work to build the communities we want to see, because let's be real, we have learned to make do but our neighborhoods are often scary as shit. We live in a state of violence that is so common that people can sing along to it.

We understand that you live in a community like many of ours, one that is so far lacking in social safety nets that your brother had to envision a mechanism of accountability that would hold up regardless of a response from a police state that more often than not disregards violence done on the bodies of Black women. We completely understand the realities that would make your brother tell your attacker, "You don't have to confess. We're looking for you, we're gonna find you" and when he does that he's "gonna beat his ass and then call the police while I beat his ass because I want you to feel what you made my sister feel." And we don't think his or your anger is comedic, and we keep his statements in mind as we attempt to build an antiviolence movement that doesn't combat violence with violence while recognizing the difficulty of doing so.

From this point on when we hear the "Bed Intruder Song" we will force ourselves to center you, and we will think about where we stand in our antiviolence movement. We will dedicate a moment of silence to making a safe world for women and girls like you and your daughter. We want to let you know that this is not okay and we are fed the fuck up.

The Joy(s) of Being a (Black) Woman

Robin M. Boylorn

When speaking with a Black woman scholar whom I both admire and respect, I shared some of my concerns about a course I was teaching on the stories of Black women. While Black women's stories are certainly powerful, many narratives of Black womanhood, including my own, oftentimes concentrate on pain. I shared that I was excited about the class because it allowed me to collect all of my favorite Black girl/woman stories and teach them, but I worried that students would walk away feeling like Black womanhood is an altogether negative experience. I was concerned that the stories we tell and write about are so saturated in disappointment and disillusionment that Black women in the class would feel defeated rather than visible, and students who were not Black women would miss the miracle inherent in our testimonies.

After listening to my fears and acknowledging the importance that such a class exist, particularly in an institution that might otherwise render Black womanhood invisible and insignificant, my mentor looked me in my eyes and asked a poignant question:

"What about the joy of being a Black woman?"

I was surprised by her response to my musings, but I was mostly disappointed in myself because it had not occurred to me that there was joy and pain in our experiences, like Rob Base and DJ E-Z Rock sang in my childhood, *"Joy and pain, like sunshine and rain."*

"With all the struggles attached, I have never wanted to be anything other than a Black woman," she continued. "I have never wanted to be a man. And I have never wanted to be White."

I shrank in my seat as I realized that only half of what she had said rang true. I had never wanted to be a man, but I had fantasized, many times as a child, about being a White girl, or at the very least light-as-White. As a dark-skinned child in a light-Brown family with a light-skinned sister, I couldn't help but absorb a color complex that made me long to be something altogether different. In my mind, not being Black would have been altogether wonderful.

But that was before I read *The Bluest Eye*. Before I knew Alice Walker existed. Before I was exposed to the ways Black women beautifully write (about) Black womanhood in such a way that you learn to love the Black, the funk, the blues, the rejection, the hope of it all.

Without responding I considered how I had never consciously thought about the joy(s) of being a Black woman, and I recognized it as a failure in my curriculum. My mentor's question challenged me to challenge my students to find the deliciousness of Black womanhood in our stories, somewhere betwixt and between the struggle/s and oppression/s, the loss and the heartbreak, the nappy roots and ashy elbows, the half-assed apologies from no-good N-words, and good gossip shared alongside brown liquor and spades games. Every book written by a Black woman about being a Black woman contains this bliss—even though it is sometimes hidden and tucked around survival and sacrifice.

While there was a repetition of pain fostered in an inability to not break (resisting or embracing strongblackwomanhood stereotypes, ambivalence about love/relationships/life, witnessing loveless partnership, experiencing passionless sex, fearing forced celibacy and loneliness, the inner workings of incest, uses for anger, shared secrets, abandonment, mama and daddy issues, and depression), the stories and books we read contained declarations of joy. It just wasn't sitting out in the open on the page.

From Pearl Cleage's *In the Time before the Men Came* to Barbara Smith's introduction to *Home Girls*, from Audre Lorde's *Sister Outsider* to Joan Morgan's *When Chickenheads Come Home to Roost*, we analyzed Black women's experiences of discrimination but also their experiences of pleasure and hope.

On the last day of class, remembering the exchange I'd had with a joyful Black woman, I asked my students to think back to everything we had read and pull out the joy. On each side of a whiteboard I wrote the words "pain" and "joy," inviting them to contribute to both sides. We assembled in a circle calling out how the stories teach Blackgirls to be unapologetically themselves and find joy in friendships and relationships with other Black women, even and especially unconventional Black women. We talked about surviving as joy and remembered laugh-out-loud scenes from the books we'd read.

We talked about how romantic relationships begin with hope and anticipation, anxious waiting, and "good loving," even if it is a cotdamn lie.

We remembered sisterhood and friendship and moments of escape and dreams—finding love, inspiring love, writing love, loving yourself, loving our bodies. We recognized that, for Black women, self-love and being loved is a revolutionary act. We talked about ways of being revolutionary.

We discussed the power—yes, power—in loving Black men (and women) as friends (and lovers). We confessed our insecurities about "getting chose" and becoming mothers without romanticizing the unconventional relationships we had regrettably and sometimes unknowingly participated in. We talked about the possibilities of polyamory but attempted to imagine it for heterosexual women who desire to be in relationships with heterosexual men, and how despite men's expectation that women deal with being side chicks they could not handle being side dudes.

We shared secrets about secret touches that made us grow up too soon from people we trusted and who knew better. We spoke out loud, for the first time, about secret hits we took, promising not to tell, desperate to believe it would really be the last time this time.

We talked about art as an escape and poetry as a medium. I shared my interest in creating things, and they talked about their own methodologies of peace. We appreciated sex, sometimes before one is grown, and the complication of consent for Blackgirls, ourselves included. We remembered, together, being called fast, hot, ho-ish, and grown long before we truly understood what the words meant, learning together to resist labels that attempt to shame our bodies, our sexuality, our freedom and possibility. We marveled at how Blackness defines Blackness and the pride and purpose we feel being Black women feminist revolutionaries. We said being free and beautiful in your own self is a manifestation of joy.

There were tears in my eyes as our class time slowly came to an end with each student giving an offering of Blackgirl joy and hope, recalling the retelling of stories as their own, as mine. We realized as we stared at the board, now a backdrop behind me, filled with words and expressions about Blackgirl joy, sadness, and hope, that there was joy there all along, hidden beneath pain and purpose, in the everyday experiences of our lives.

Is It Ever Okay to Tell a Sister to Go Kick Rocks? Black Women and Friendship

Brittney C. Cooper

This week I met a Black girl who doesn't want to be my friend. Well, let me take that back. We didn't meet this week. We met a couple of months ago, both of us newcomers to the university where I'm doing a postdoc. My custom in academic spaces is to make sure I meet and try to get to know every sister in the space, because there are so few of us. However, my interactions with this one particular sister have been inexplicably terse and strained. I had hoped we might be friends because we are both junior academics, new to this space, and we share the same alma mater, although by several years' difference.

After attempting to get to know her through casual conversations that never seemed to quite work, I was hoping to make a connection with her at a brunch over the weekend with a couple of other sister academics. Instead, she continued with her terse, uneasy, awkward social manner, a forgivable offense, particularly knowing that many academics tend to be awkward. But then, without warning, she made a rude, uncalled-for, off-the-cuff remark to me, the contents of which I'll leave unsaid.

I played it off and changed the subject, but it was definitely off-putting. Ever the optimist, especially when it comes to Black women and friendship, I still thought that perhaps what she said had come off the wrong way or that I had taken it the wrong way. So when I saw her at a holiday party this week, though I was a little wary, I made it a point to speak to her . . . though she had already looked at and ignored me one time. But when she then gave me her customary halfhearted wave of acknowledgment (or dismissal depending on your vantage point) and proceeded to have a lively conversation with the (White) colleague standing next to her, I had to accept that, for whatever reason, she dislikes me or at best is indifferent.

Though her rejection and her rude remarks have stung, it is good to be at peace (or actively making peace) with the fact that every Blackgirl academic that I encounter won't be my friend.

Though I'd be lying if I said I didn't wanna tell ol' girl to #GoKickRocks. (And a few other things.) But that is generally not productive.

I think twelve-year-old me—the me that struggled to find Blackgirl friends, accused as I was of "acting White" and being a nerd (and thus uncool); the me that made the girls in the *Baby-Sitters Club* series and the *Sweet Valley Twins* series my friends because I identified with them, Black though they were not—would be both excited and surprised to find that thirty-one-year-old me has all the Black girlfriends I can stand (and more). Thirteen-year-old me would love to know that there are Black girls in the world who don't make mistreatment the price for friendship.

I was that girl who put up with being talked about and bullied, apologized first in fights I didn't start, and hung around with girls who occasionally liked to make me the butt of mean jokes, just because they knew I was desperate to be liked. To be affirmed by girls who looked like me, girls who understood why I couldn't get my perm wet in the swimming pool (and whose parents wouldn't give my mama and me the side-eye for insisting so), girls who knew what it meant to talk one way at school and another at home, girls whose choice of adolescent crush was either the bad boys of Jodeci or the good boys of Boyz II Men.

The grown-up version of myself knows what my girl-self couldn't know:

1. Everybody won't like you, and that ain't your problem.
2. If you show yourself friendly, friends will come.
3. Just because others have an issue with you, doesn't mean you have an issue.

On most days, I still see Black women as part of a Divine Rah-Rah Sisterhood. I know it's a fiction, but given the popularity of *Girlfriends*, *Living Single*, and their warped parallel universe counterparts *The Real Housewives of Atlanta* and *Basketball Wives*, I'd say I'm not the only one invested in that fiction.

I still believe in Black women and friendship. For when we are in a healthy and loving place, it is Black women who are my air, who give me space to be, and who breathe life into me when others would suffocate me into silence.

Black women have been my salvation. But we can't save those who don't wanna be saved.

In relieving myself of the expectation that I befriend every Black woman (especially ones with issues a mile wide and a soul deep) and relieving other Black women of those expectations, I create the room to receive the wonderful life-sustaining friendships that I'm meant to have. And in choosing not to focus on the one sister who has treated me badly, I celebrate the wonderful sister scholars in this space who have embraced me with open arms and made my journey here a joy. I'm thankful for them.

In the face of this rejection, I don't have to succumb to the intra-misogyny that Black women inflict on each other. Because in the face of all the Black women who have loved me, I simply know better.

So the first great commandment of my Black girl feminism remains, "Thou shalt love thy sister as thyself," but in being my sisters' keeper I now take the time to know who my sisters are, and I make sure that the relationships I insist on keeping are in fact worth having.

Beauty Parlor Politics

Robin M. Boylorn

The first time I "got my hair done" was in the kitchen of a church lady who did hair on the side. She was not professionally trained or licensed, but her clientele graced her threshold every other Saturday and she "did" hair for a few extra dollars. Getting my hair done was a womanly ritual that blended self-care with community building.

Women of all sizes, colors, backgrounds, and religions gathered together at the salon, waiting patiently, all day if need be, for their two-week fix. In between appointments they would talk in hushed tones, cross their legs, flip through Black hair magazines, and shoot the breeze. It was the only time in my childhood when I was not banished from a room full of grown women talking, laughing, just being.

The all-woman space, smelling like Jean Naté and scorched hair, made me feel empowered. It was nothing for women to share secrets, give advice, get into friendly debates, laugh, and listen to each other while offering a bite from their plate or a drag of a cigarette while we all sat around, watching the transformations from new growth to relaxer, split ends to goddess braids, or bald spots to hair pieces. "At the shop" we were sisters, even when we were strangers, because being without a done 'do was like being naked. Between our sing-alongs and gossip, no one noticed what our "before" hair looked like. The salon was a meeting place, the great equalizer—like church, but without the judgment.

Unsolicited compliments between strangers are rarely overheard between Black women in public. In the salon, though, we saw each other as beautiful and said so—out loud and proud like. That was what drew me to it, and still does. For me, hair salons are bonding places. Salons have, over the course of my life, served as safe spaces for talking through everything from heartache to home remedies, recipes to religion. It is a safe space for social critique and casual conversation, a place where women gather together in one place unseparated by their differences. These public-private spaces, almost exclusively occupied by Black folk (this is equally true for barber shops), transform strangers to sister-girls, if only for a few hours every two weeks.

A recent visit to the hair salon resulted in misunderstanding and maliciousness. I learned, after returning for my next appointment, that upon my exit I had been verbally assaulted by another Black woman.

I routinely initiate and/or participate in provocative hot-topic discussions in the salon. The stylists and I, along with various other patrons ranging in age from midtwenties to midseventies, have shared laughs and wisdom about topics ranging from politics and sex to interracial relationships and popular culture. While I don't remember the specifics of the conversation I had that day, I know two things for sure about any- and everything that I ever say publicly: 1. It was truthful (at least my truth); and 2. It was not (intentionally) offensive (I am very intentional with my words and mindful of correcting myself, immediately, if I feel I have spoken out of turn or inappropriately). I am also a communication professor who has had years of training in public and professional speaking, so I imagine that despite codeswitching and my country drawl (which comes out when I am especially comfortable), I am easily outed as an academician.

I was warned, when I returned to the salon, that an unnamed Black woman had asked "who I thought I was," and then announced her intention to "get me in trouble" on my job for things I said in the salon. I work at a public institution where I study, research, and teach taboo topics, and as an auto/ethnographer, part of my job is to write about and critique social encounters. In other words, it is my job to speak my mind and say whatever I damn well please. My stylist was apologetic and concerned as she explained what happened. "I confronted her when she said that," she said. "It upset me that she came in here and wanted to get you in trouble."

I assured my stylist that my job was not in jeopardy and that anything I say in the beauty salon is, not only personal and private, but inconsequential to my day job as a university professor. I was, however, bothered by the audacity and nerve of a Black woman to enter the sacred space of the beauty shop with the intention of causing harm to another Black woman. This encounter, the first I have had in a salon, disrupted my narrative of support and jeopardized the ethic of care I had come to expect (and need).

My past experiences taught me that there is no jealousy or competition in the Black beauty salon, no attitude and resentment, just Blackgirl magic moments and seeing each other beautiful. The beauty shop was one of the few spaces I felt at home away from home. It was a space where I have trusted Black women I didn't know with my unmasked and unfiltered self.

Every two weeks, I will continue to make my way back to the salon. When I open the door I will be greeted with the warmth and welcome that radiates from the women who are already there. In a world that despises Black women, I refuse to give up the necessary experience of sharing intimate space and time with Black women despite the possibility I will encounter someone who means me no good. Beauty parlors are spaces of Blackwomanlove at its finest!

Remember Their Names: In Memory of Kasandra, Cherica, and Others Gone Too Soon

Robin M. Boylorn

I am sure that by now you know the name Jovan Belcher. He is the Kansas City Chiefs player who shot and killed his girlfriend before taking his own life in 2012. Headlines and news stories focused on the tragedy from his lens (including speculation of potential brain trauma, his involvement as an undergraduate in a Male Athletes

Against Violence initiative, and his standing as an all-star athlete), dismissing or overshadowing the lens of his victim, who in headlines is simply referred to as "(his) girlfriend."

Her name was Kasandra Michelle Perkins. She was twenty-two years old, a new mother, and an aspiring teacher. Her picture showed off a beautiful smile and her friends described her as selfless, kind, and generous. She was excited about being a mother to her newborn, Zoey, and was optimistic about her future. You should know her name.

Do you remember Cherica Adams? Eight months pregnant, she was gunned down in a drive-by shooting on November 16, 1999, when Rae Carruth, a then wide receiver for the Carolina Panthers, conspired to have her killed because he did not want to pay child support (she had refused his insistence that she get an abortion). Remarkably, Cherica had the fortitude, while suffering multiple bullet wounds, to call 911 and name Carruth as her murderer. She gave birth to her son (who was born with cerebral palsy as a result of the shooting), slipped into a coma, and died a month later. Did you know (remember) her name?

Tragic stories of death and murder, like Kasandra and Cherica's, push the often-silenced and taboo issue of intimate partner violence to the forefront. When the perpetrator is famous, attractive, rich, or charming, people don't want to believe that they are guilty and shift the blame and responsibility for the assault or murder to the woman, insinuating that she had to have done something to trigger the man's violence.

In April 2014, Columbus Short's wife Tanee McCall went public with allegations that he choked her, put a knife to her throat, and threatened to kill her. In response, comedian D. L. Hughley called her a "thirsty bitch" who should have kept her mouth shut. Later in 2014, Ray Rice was suspended and later fired from the Baltimore Ravens for knocking his then-fiancée Janay Palmer unconscious and dragging her limp body from a hotel elevator. The couple quickly married and participated in an ill-timed and ill-advised press conference in which Rice offered a half-assed apology and Janay expressed regret for "the role" she played in the incident, taking responsibility for inciting her husband's violence. This perspective was further supported by ESPN analyst Stephen A. Smith, who was suspended for a week after saying that women oftentimes provoke men to violence.

In 2012, when Chad Johnson (Ochocinco) head-butted his then-wife, Evelyn Lozada, the public had little empathy for her because of her infamous attitude and penchant to fight when she starred on *Basketball Wives*. Folk assumed that she must have "started it" and got what she deserved. And, of course, there was the backlash Rihanna experienced when Chris Brown was arrested for beating her to the point of being unrecognizable. Instead of vilifying Brown for his violence, many fans, Black women included, speculated about what she must have done to cause him to go off on her.

Our culture has a problem with silencing victims and protecting men. While I don't think men who participate in antifeminist, misogynist, and/or violent acts are irredeemable (many Black feminist men I know have problematic pasts), rehabilitation and genuine change is only possible when these men are called out and required to take responsibility for their actions (or lack thereof). Abuse is not normal and need not be normalized.

I did not write this piece to offer a commentary on the dangers of hypermasculinity or to insinuate a direct correlation between NFL athletes and violence (though those are conversations that are worthy of discussion). I wrote this piece to adjust the focus away from the famous athlete who "snapped," and to put it on the true innocent in the case. I wrote this piece as a clarion call to remember Kasandra and Cherica and others by their names and not by their relationships. I wrote this piece so that we don't forget that, although victims may fall into statistics, they have names. I wrote this piece as a reminder that Kasandra and Cherica existed before their relationships with the men who literally took their breath away. I wrote this piece as a reminder that when a tragedy like this happens, it is not the perpetrator's name we should remember, but the victim's. And since Kasandra Perkins's name was hidden somewhere between the facts of the case and the eulogy of a man deemed the tragic, martyred hero, I wrote this piece to call out her name. And since Cherica was presented as a nameless, faceless gold-digger looking for a payday instead of a young ambitious woman looking forward to raising her son, I feel like you should know her name—and the name of every other victim who gets lost in the shadows of a murderer's limelight.

Mama's Feminism

Robin M. Boylorn

I don't have a lot of friends who identify as feminist. My nonacademic, nonactivist friends don't see themselves as feminists, don't call themselves feminists, don't all the way understand what it means. They spend a lot of time trying to resist myths around being Black and a woman, and don't have the energy or motivation to also resist myths of feminism—of bra-burning White women who hate men and stand in picket lines, or bourgeois Black women who understand the theoretical nexus that connects their lives to "the cause" but become disconnected from movements close to home.

Feminism as a term was born in academe (in an environment that polices people's behaviors to dictate who can and cannot be feminist and what is and is not feminist). Feminism was conceived at my mama's house (in a space that made woman power and intentional equality a survival strategy and mechanism to make up for oppression, the absence of men, and lifestyles that were without the luxury of adhering to strict gender scripts).

I learned feminism from my mama and them, rural women who did not have the benefit of formal college education or fancy words for how they lived. They would, no doubt, by strict standards, in the vulnerable moments of their lives that were necessary for sanity and survival, have been called unfeminist while the world called them unfeminine. They would have had little investment in either label, learning from experience how dangerous it is to let outside people dictate your inside thoughts. They would have been resented by traditional feminists for the way they were conditioned to desire men and canonical lifestyles while being single parents to multiple children, fantasizing about whitewashed happily-ever-afters. Their lifestyles were feminist, but their dreams and desires, for being kept women with White women's problems, would have been read as problematic. They would have rebelled because they wouldn't let a label like feminist tell them what to do. They wouldn't give a damn what people thought about them.

I learned/realized I was a feminist from a teacher who described my mama without saying her name, gave her secrets away without giving her credit, and put struggling on a pedestal. Feminism became a metaphorical stepping stool, giving me access to the self-actualization I would have otherwise not known to reach for.

I got my feminism from my mama, even though she doesn't know it. And my grandmother. And my aunties. They had a feminism that would fight back and hide behind the mask of smiles or scorn. My mama's feminism was wrapped up in God and respectability politics she could never live up to. She taught me to have mustard-seed faith. My grandmama's feminism was housed in her meanness and caution. She carried it with her for emergencies and protection, like the cigarettes in her pocket and the gun in her bra. She taught me how and when to fight. My aunties held their feminism in their laughter and occasional anger. They used it to cover up pain. They taught me to get mad, but not stay mad. My mothers didn't know they were feminists. They didn't mean to pass it on to me but they couldn't help it.

My mama's feminism is inherited but unnamed. She taught me how to own my feminism like I own myself. She taught me how to be a feminist by being herself.

My feminism needs space to breathe and room to stretch out. My feminism never gets old. It is quiet sometimes. It listens to hip hop and gospel music, watches soap operas, and likes to be listened to. My feminism shows up in the bedroom and the classroom. It asks for what it wants, doesn't apologize for what it needs, and isn't afraid of being alone. My feminism is androgynous. It loves football and basketball, and dances when no one is looking. My feminism is soulful and historic, sexual and conscientious. It is standoffish and suspicious. My feminism needs to drink more water.

My feminism has daddy issues. It talks back, snaps back, hits back, and doesn't take any shit. My feminism kicks ass and takes names. My feminism says no. My feminism cries and doesn't cover its eyes in shame. It gets mad and doesn't try to explain it away. My feminism is peaceful in practice but ready for war. My feminism is in conversation with other feminisms and makes room for difference. My feminism takes mental-health days and moves on when people walk away. My feminism loves Jesus and critiques the church, wears black fingernail polish and red lipstick, and loves reality TV. My feminism is homegrown. Rebellious. Reckoning. Evolving. Unapologetic. And beautiful. My feminism is opinionated. It questions everything.

My feminism is not always right, but it's never wrong. My feminism has insomnia. My feminism gets tired. My feminism is antiracist, antisexist, and conscious of class issues. My feminism knows what misogyny means. It takes days off. It tells people off.

My feminism, like my mama, is braver than me, stronger than me, and keeps me grounded. My feminism, like me, is complicated and full of contradictions.

My feminism is crunk.

My feminism has dreams.

So, Two Feminists Walk into a Bar . . .

Susana M. Morris

For some, the title of this piece would indicate that what follows is most certainly a farce, but it's a bit more complicated than that.

Once, I took a trip to New York to visit my girls and celebrate finishing up my book manuscript. I was dead tired but so, so glad that I had booked a vacation. Far too often I have fallen into the trap of going, going, going, even when my body and spirit are telling me, "Sit the hell down."

So, for once, I listened. I hung out with Eesha and Crunkista and other folks who are near and dear to me. I ate, drank, and was very merry. (There was even karaoke involved.) And this is when feminist barhopping comes into place. E and I decide to head to one of her neighborhood haunts, a sweet bar with mahogany and marble throughout, killer nachos, and delicious lemon drops. As the night progressed (and we got delightfully hammered), there was much laughter and fun, including pulling bar patrons into an impromptu dance to the tune of "The Way You Make Me Feel." It was at this point that a couple of brothers sidled up to the two of us. (I mean, with dance moves like ours, it was only a matter of time.) And hey, I'm cool with an attractive fella kicking game and being flirtatious, even if he is dressed like Diddy in the Hamptons. So while CJ* (a Wall Street "financier"—I'm just repeating what he told me) was doing his best James Brown/MJ footwork, and I was doing a classic shimmy and shake (watch out now!), I was indeed having lots of fun. I spied E from the corner of my eye and saw that she was engaged in earnest,

*Names changed to protect the foolish.

and probably philosophical, flirty conversation with CJ's boy, Duke* (a brain surgeon—again, verbatim from the surgeon's mouth), who was giving the pensive blerd (complete with short Maxwell fro and glasses) in a big way. Extra cute. We end up kicking it with these boys (okay, thirtysomething-year-old men), talking about race and ethnicity, having some more drinks, doing a little more flirting. CJ and I exchanged info, with him claiming he "wanted to talk about my book." <Side-eye> But I get the game, and I appreciate the nominal interest in my intellectual life.

Things were going well, but, as they sometimes do, they took a decided turn for the worst. Dr. Duke was all like, "It's a disgusting habit that I rarely partake in, but . . . would y'all like to smoke a couple ciggies with me?" Then he pulls out a pack of Camel Lights. I agree it's a disgusting habit, but I don't apologize for my yearly ciggie, so we go out there. E and CJ are off using the restroom, settling tabs, dancing the conga, I dunno. I just know I went outside, and Dr. Duke and I smoked and chatted. We're talking about how the world is not postracial and I'm thinking, All right, E, he might be cool to kick it with, when this fool says, "And you know my wife . . . and my kids . . ." Um, what? (Later, CJ reveals he has a fiancée who is pregnant with twins.)

Now, we were far from heartbroken, but with enough drinks in a sister, what was a fun night could've turned tragic, real quick. E and I exchanged glances with each other and kept it cool, wrapping up the convo (which included a strange detour into a chat about feminism that was extra ridiculous). After one last round of lemon drops (hey, they had to pay for their foolishness), we settled our tabs and headed out into the rising dawn. This is when those fools wanted to know what we had planned for the evening. How about *not* doing you? Ha! We turned on our heels and sauntered off, giggling perhaps a little too loudly, leaving blue balls in our midst. Deuces, suckas!

So, what does this have to do with feminism? Well, E and I are crunk feminists all day long, so a trip to the grocery store could be a tale of feminist praxis. Still, after this experience I am left with less of a "damn, dudes are trife" kind of feeling (although some indeed are), and more of a "thank goddess I got my girls" kind of feeling (as I hum the theme to *Living Single*). I have some amazing women in my life for whom I am so grateful. They read book chapters and talk about teaching with me. We debate politics and politricks. We talk about family: biological, chosen, and all kinds in between. We cry, we laugh, and we love. So, I rebuke the notion that women can't get along or that "chicks are so damn catty." And, let me tell you, it's not that I have some rosy view of interpersonal relationships. I went to a women's college, taught at another, and have two sisters. I've had a range of experiences. What I will say is that being a feminist has enabled me to have richer experiences with other women (and men for that matter) because it helps me to recognize and honor affinity in expansive ways. Even after several lemon drops.

How Talking to Your Homegirls Can "Liberate" Your Sex Life

Brittney C. Cooper

Over the summer, while I was visiting Crunkadelic, she and I ended up brainstorming methods for positioning oneself at an optimum angle for penetration in the missionary position. Yes, that means what you think it means.

The conversation went a little like:

ME: The thing is, when we do it in missionary, I'm having this problem lifting my ass up enough for him to hit it at the right angle. (*Sigh.*) I'm officially too fat to have good sex.

HER: Nah girl. You just gotta use pillows. And ain't he grown? He needs to help you lift it and help you get in the right position. If he don't know what he doin', that ain't on you.

ME: Maybe. But I still think me being so large is causing a problem, and I gotta figure out a better angle because the angle he was at . . . he wasn't staying in.

HER: What you mean he wasn't staying in? He ain't got a "teenie weenie peenie" problem does he?

ME: Nah. I ain't never fucking with a little dick dude again. That ain't the problem. So maybe I could try the pillow, but what kinda pillow do you think would hold up all this ass?

HER: You know, B, I think I saw some kind of pillow or something they make for that.

ME: Really? What's it's called? What should I look up? Would it be under "sex pillow"?

And off the two of us nerds went on a Google quest to find a sex pillow, one that could help me lift my ass into a more optimal position. I don't know if you talk to your girls like I talk to mine, but no conversation is off-limits. And this is a good thing. For professional Black and Latina women who are often dogged by long periods of forced celibacy, "getting it in" cannot be merely a declaration. Sometimes there has to be a pragmatic conversation about how to, um, get it in and keep it in.

After a little sleuthing, a Google search confirmed our suspicions. This store called the Liberator sells both a ramp and a wedge (and the ramp and wedge combo, if you're adventurous). These firm pillows are designed to help you lift your behind into an apparently optimal angle for penetration. The great news for big girls is that they also provide support for your back and your knees in other positions (e.g., doggy style).

And you can thank/blame Crunkadelic for all this extra information (TMI) and for putting me on to the Liberator wedge and ramp and all the other goodies that they boast at their website.

The thing is: in my experience, having close homegirls to crowd-source information from has made all the difference in the quality of my sex life. And apparently I'm not the only one.

A few months after Crunkadelic helped me get "liberated," imagine my pleasant surprise to discover via my Facebook newsfeed that three of the cast members of The Real Housewives of Atlanta visited the newly opened Liberator in Atlanta on the season four premiere. I didn't know the Liberator was an actual brick-and-mortar place. Field trip!

I found Sheree, Kandi, and Phaedra's trip to the sex store important for a couple of reasons.

1. Black women are prosex, notwithstanding the bad reps we get as denizens of respectability. Plus, every grown woman needs (and deserves) sex toys. Seeing representations of the ways that grown Black women negotiate their sex lives and prioritize their pleasure is hella important.
2. If you want to have better sex, you should discuss it with your homegirls. I'm serious! Frankly, I would venture to say

that the good sex I have had is as much a result of "consul-
tations" with my homegirls as it is a result of my bedroom
skills and the skill sets of my chosen partners. It is my girls
who have encouraged me to be bold in asking for what I
want and to try new things, disabused me of my investment
in being a good girl in the bedroom, helped me to know
what is "normal" (namely anything that my partner and I
willingly desire and consent to do) and what is not acceptable (e.g., being used as a partner's masturbation machine,
being pressured, and being in pain [unless BDSM is your
thing]).

Me and my girls routinely have intense conversations about our
intimate lives, what it looks like to have the kind of sex we want to
be having in our twenties, thirties, and forties, and the nuts and bolts
of the acts, when necessary. I have helped my homegirls plan whole
seduction schemes from the lingerie to the breakfast menu, and they
have reciprocated. (The hilarious part is that none of the sex partners
who are beneficiaries of all this planning know just how much the
work homies put in to help them win. Gives total feminist meaning
to "ain't no fun if the homies can't have none.") When it comes to
getting it in, my motto is "be intentional."

So of course, I was slightly offended when one of my Facebook
friends had the nerve to question why anyone would need a pillow
during sex. Either they're gymnasts or they must be having pretty
boring sex if they have never needed to prop a limb in an unconventional place. It reminded me, too, that in a culture which privileges
smaller body types, it rarely enters into the purview of the slim (and
the able-bodied) that all bodies can't and don't (want to) have sex in
the same ways. Posting shit like that is a dangerous form of fat shaming that seeks to make fat people believe we aren't worthy of pleasure
too. (Fuck all that.) Because fat people aren't seen as sexy, most folks
think that fat people aren't having sex, or at least not good sex. And
that is lie number one.

Lie number two comes from big girls who are fronting and faking
like sex happens for us in the same ways as our skinny counterparts.
Yes, there are some big girls who are flexible and acrobatic, and they
are my sheroes. But it's not a leap to recognize that physical acts
work differently on bodies that are 120 or 150 pounds versus bodies
that are 300 or 350 pounds. Can we be real about that? Extra weight

requires extra creativity about most things, from fashion to sex. And ain't no shame in admitting that.

I talked to Crunkadelic about this flexibility issue too. Because she is entirely more flexible than me.

ME: Girl, but he want me to try this position and that position, and um, it's unclear how any of that is supposed to work.

HER: B, you just gotta do your stretches. Take some yoga. Stretch every day. That's a problem you can solve. Flexibility can be achieved.

ME: *(Starts stretching.)*

So if the Liberator pillow (or any other similar product or strategy) can offer support for F.A.T. (fabulous and thick) girls or people with disabilities who may be less flexible or need additional support for the elbows or the posterior, then I say get free! And never forget—*talk to your homegirls!* They'll help you win.

SELF-CARE:
THUS SAITH THE LORDE

Introduction

Self-care, the catchall phrase that refers to the intentional acts of mental, physical, and spiritual care that you do for yourself, is a common enough term today, but many of us never heard it growing up. So many women in our communities did not seem to be spending time intentionally caring for themselves. Sure, these women were caring for and nurturing countless people at their jobs, in their families, and in their communities. These were superwomen who were only missing their capes. In fact, these were folks working themselves to death. We never really saw too many of them taking time to sit down, step back, or even breathe. Not on purpose, anyway.

But, as kids growing up in the seventies, eighties, and nineties, we were all pretty familiar with the concept of self-help. Sitting cross-legged on the floor in front of our mamas' television sets, we devoured episodes of *Oprah*, learning how we could "lose the weight!" and "live our best lives." Oprah, Iyanla Vanzant, Dr. Phil, and any number of other talking heads rhapsodized daily about how to cure all that ails the postmodern woman.

What we didn't realize then but what we know now is that these conversations about self-help usually operated from the assumption that the viewer had some sort of deficit, that something was wrong with us. And that buying a certain book, or following a particular talk-show guru, or losing a specific amount of weight would make things better. Make things right. Make ourselves right. These things would fix us.

What followed were the on-again off-again cycles of doing right and then being wrong that required more self-loathing and more self-help. There is always something else to fix, right?

Admittedly, many of us have fallen for the self-help trap more than once. And, truth be told, some of the advice not only was not entirely wrong but was even at times quite helpful. Then again, even a broke clock is right twice a day.

Truth is, women of color are under a ton of stress. Zora Neale Hurston famously quipped that Black women are "the mules of the world," and the adage has not become less true over time. In the face of the seemingly unrelenting demands of work, family, and life, women of color and nonbinary people are often forced to choose between taking care of ourselves and taking care of others. But, quiet as it's kept, we are not born superheroes. Over time, we either choose that mantle or it becomes our cross to bear if we are unwilling or unable to reject it. Self-help has been advertised as a healing strategy, one that can lift our heavy burdens, when in reality it is a bill of goods intent on keeping us hooked on its empty promises.

Self-care, however, moves away from the epistemology of lack and brokenness that self-help often embodies toward a way of navigating the world that emphasizes the right to take up space and the right to have joy despite pain.

Self-care invites us to consider our needs, first and foremost, not because we are selfish, but because taking care of ourselves is a supreme act of self-love.

When we move from just trying to survive to aiming to thrive, focusing on self-care also compels us to both recognize the histories and recover the practices that our ancestors did to take care of themselves, even when they lacked resources and stability. As Alice Walker writes in "In Search of Our Mothers' Gardens," enslaved Black women had histories "cruel enough to stop the blood," yet they found ways to nurture the creative impulses inside of them that ached to be released. Spiritual practices around music—whether the sacred gospel or the profane rhythm of the blues, soul, and hip hop—and alternative healing practices are undoubtedly part of what we would today call self-care. Additionally, while we might have once dismissed homespun practices like sewing, gardening, quilting, or cooking solely as burdensome chores, the reality is that so many artists were fueling their creativity in every seemingly mundane stitch, homemade pie, and patch of flowers they planted. For, as Audre Lorde reminds us, "Poetry is not a luxury." And we nurture ourselves by finding the beauty in our worlds.

Sometimes the lines between self-care and community support are blurred, which is not necessarily a bad thing. Communities of color sometimes stigmatize mental illness, but that doesn't mean it always goes unrecognized or necessarily unsupported. Take, for instance, the way some folks describe having "bad nerves." Folks often refer to having "bad nerves" as a way to describe everything from mild anxiety to full-out depression. And while these folks—us, them—sometimes get the side-eye when they have to receive "special" treatment, there is often an understanding that some people have bad nerves. So, even if you can't go to the hospital when a friend is sick, you may take care of that friend in another way, show up in a way that is more manageable, and folks understand. Remembering how under-resourced, marginalized people show up for each other (or don't, for that matter) is another way to recognize the value of self-care.

Audre Lorde, perhaps the paragon of feminist self-care, once wrote that "caring for myself is not self-indulgence, it is self-preservation, and that is an act of political warfare." It is this sentiment—self-care as an act of defiance, transgression, and revolutionary self-love—that has been a guiding practice at the Crunk Feminist Collective since its inception. Ultimately, we are about loving ourselves and loving on one another unapologetically.

Over the years, we have figured out all the ways in which we can perform self-care. Self-care can look like a range of things—spending time with friends, spending time alone, sleeping, cooking, watching TV, reading, writing, laughing, dancing, making love, and so much more. Truth is, most of us have a list of tried-and-true but perhaps not-so-feminist things that we do to let off steam and keep it together, especially when feminist community can be scarce.

Self-care can be getting your mind right and gathering a crew of feminist health professionals that honor your body rather than finding fault with it, taking care of yourself despite all of the obstacles to doing so.

Self-care can be shouting out another sista and letting her know you see her shine. Self-care can be loving yourself fiercely in the face of loss and disappointment.

Self-care can be social media breaks and turning your phone off when the relentless onslaught of bad news is just too much. Self-care can be banishing negative self-talk and treating ourselves with kindness and compassion, rejecting imposter syndrome and self-loathing, and embracing self-love.

Ultimately, much of self-care boils down to navigating how to create and maintain boundaries in a world that seeks to marginalize women of color's agency, health, and joy.

With self-care, the possibilities are endless.

Still, despite all the good there is in emphasizing self-care, the term does have its limits. In fact, in some ways the binary between self-help and self-care might very well be understood as a specious one. Both rely on individuals to do most, if not all, of the work or make all the changes and demand little, if any, structural accountability as a matter of course. Self-care, despite its roots in a past devoid of or severely lacking in resources, often requires a certain level of socioeconomic privilege. This is a huge drawback because it often asks people who are already depleted to do the heavy lifting in both their personal and professional lives. Indeed, because self-care is at its heart focused on individuals, we, as folks in community working to change our society, must incorporate accountability and care into our social frameworks so that this vital work does not continue to fall solely to the most vulnerable among us.

Life Is Not a Fairy Tale:
Black Women and Depression

Robin M. Boylorn

I have a confession to make. Some days it is a physical struggle to get out of bed. At least once a month I cry myself to sleep and wake up with puffy red eyes and hiccups. I experience bouts of depression that range from simple sadness to life reconsiderations as predictably as the season changes. It has become more manageable as I have gotten older.

This feels like a confession because while I am only admitting to having moments of vulnerability, as a Black woman, these realities are oftentimes seen as weaknesses.

Fantasia Barrino's 2010 confession of her suicide attempt sparked a realization that Black women are as susceptible to depression as anyone else. At nineteen, Fantasia rose to fame as the 2004 American Idol. She was a survivor of rape and intimate partner violence and was raising her daughter as a single mother. Despite her undeniable talent, she only enjoyed moderate success, and within five years she had largely dwindled her fortune, starred in a Lifetime movie based on her autobiography, and had a short-lived VH1 reality show, *Fantasia for Real*. But Fantasia, for real, was hidden from the spotlight. Fantasia, for real, had never had the space or opportunity to work through the traumas and insecurities of her childhood. Fantasia, for real, was carrying the responsibility of taking care of herself, her child, and her extended family, while being unlucky in her love life and attempting to recalibrate her career. Everybody had a hand out.

When I heard about Fantasia's suicide attempt, I wasn't particularly surprised. In an interview on *Good Morning America* she stated, "Everybody feels like I'm so strong . . . and it just became heavy for me . . . to the point that I just wanted to be away from the noise." It would take both hands for me to count the number of times, in my life, I have pondered the same dilemma, come to a similar conclusion. I did not immediately admit I could relate to Fantasia's hopelessness because there are precious few friends who won't judge or chastise you (a Black woman) for not being strong. Or who won't attempt to encourage you (a Black woman) by reminding you that, AS A BLACK WOMAN, YOU ARE STRONG.

Blackgirls are taught to be strong from an early age, and we have that expectation reinforced by everyone in our lives, from other Black women, to church folk, to White folks, to the (wo)men we love or want (to love). It is further complicated when our (supposed innate) strength is celebrated and memorialized in ways that make us territorial of it. We are encouraged to embrace it. Black women's strength is the single stereotype that is disguised as a compliment, and we oftentimes don't want to relinquish it. But what does it mean to be strong? What happens when we don't feel it, when we are tired of it, when sadness and strength trade places?

Interestingly Fantasia, while trying to give up the superwoman facade that plagues Black women, reinforced it. Without giving herself more than a week to recover from wanting to die, she reemerged to face her demons, her critics, her family, and her fans. In what can only be interpreted as her demonstrating and proving her Black woman strength, within two weeks of her suicide attempt, she was promoting a new album and appearing on a *Behind the Music* special, which premiered almost two weeks to the day of her suicide attempt. Like other Black women, she likely didn't feel like she could afford to be depressed and didn't have time to recover from her emotional breakdown.

I understood the instinct. Following suicide tries I would often get up, get dressed, and go to work/school/church/dinner as if everything was fine. I understood depression as White women's shit and my uncontrollable tears and obsession with death as un(Black)ladylike. We (Black women) didn't have time to cry over crises or break down from a broken heart. There were bills to pay, mouths to feed, ways to make (out of no way). Over years of watching and witnessing women hurt (from unsuccessful relationships, struggling with finances, dealing with discrimination, and simply waiting for something better for themselves or their children), I saw them struggle, but I never saw them "feel." So my feelings (of unspeakable, unexplainable sadness) didn't make sense. And while the women I knew never demonstrated the reality of depression in their lives, the reality of my experience tells me that there had to have been tears in the dark, surrender in prayer rooms, wishes of ending lives over seemingly mundane struggles. I think we all sometimes or at some point, like Fantasia, just want the noise to stop.

Superwoman syndrome has the capacity to take us out in myriad ways. Fantasia's story, while tragic, is not unique. While not all of us will attempt to "silence the noise" by unaccidentally swallowing a bottle of pills, there are those of us who isolate ourselves, over-work or overcompensate, overeat or don't eat, trade sleep for worry, say yes when we need to say no, stay in unhealthy relationships, self-medicate, and concentrate on everybody but ourselves.

There is a danger in being strong because ultimately we are all human, and Black women do not have superpowers of physical, emotional, or mental strength. We have to let ourselves off the hook so that we don't feel like we are failing (others or ourselves) when we simply get tired. While Black women have the benefit of our ex-periences, the training to cope in particular ways (with racism and sexism), and the wherewithal to expand our capacity to deal with bullshit (racism, sexism, classism, etc.), we are not invincible.

These Days I Hate Going to the Gynecologist

Sheri Davis-Faulkner

Oftentimes women complain that they hate going to the gynecologist because they don't like the procedures. Sometimes a GYN visit is likened to a dentist appointment, but much more uncomfortable and personal. I cannot say that I dislike the intimate discussions about my personal life and habits. I also can't say that my reasons for hating gynecological visits are related to the exam procedures. In fact, the only reason I am uncomfortable with the vaginal speculum is the history of James Marion Sims experimenting on Black female slaves, torturing them in Alabama for research, but I digress. Ideally the gy-necological space should be like going to a mental-health therapy session where I also have an opportunity to learn about my body, dis-cuss my habits, and explore my sexual and emotional health without feeling less than or abnormal. Unfortunately, this is not what tends to happen.

Why do I have such idealistic notions about the great possibilities of a gynecological visit, you might ask? Well I had phenomenal ex-periences early in my life that set a high standard for gynecological safe spaces as "the norm." Nurse Fuqua, a Black woman at the Spelman College Health Center, taught me to feel powerful as a sexual being while also advising me to be cautious. She kept a basket of condoms, male and female, in the common area so students never had to have an appointment to pick up as many as they wanted. She had a care ethic that included listening first, without interrupting, and then talking through my concerns. I never felt like she told me what to do, but she offered options and discussed pros and cons with me.

Dr. Martin Dukes, a Black male doctor in Washington, DC, always made sure there was a female nurse or assistant in the exam room whenever he examined me. He was deliberate about making me feel as comfortable as possible throughout my visit. When I had a "missed miscarriage" he was gentle with my partner and me; he sat with us as long as we needed him and prepared us to move forward with the next steps. Unfortunately, he only had hospital privileges at a Catholic hospital; he could not perform the D&C. We had to find an abortion clinic. It was traumatic, but he continued to support us through the process of healing.

The Feminist Women's Health Clinic in Atlanta was a "breath of fresh air" after numerous bad experiences. At my last visit I had a White female nurse practitioner. She treated me like a grown-up worthy of extended dialogue and not "health-insurance speak." I've never had the same person for my exams, but I've always felt like I was in learning and healing spaces. I asked direct questions and got thorough answers and resources. The visits felt tailored to me, not standard or routine, like I was on a conveyor belt. I never felt abnormal or broken even when something was wrong. They explained that my issues were typical occurrences for women and provided various reasons like stress for what was happening to my body and vagina. I never left feeling violated or that I had unanswered questions or concerns.

I shared my good experiences. Now these are the horrific encounters that made me hate going to the gynecologist:

In 2008 I had pain in my pelvic area and decided to see a "holistic" Black female doctor. After doing an ultrasound, she explained that one of my ovaries was attached to my uterine wall and that I needed a pelvic laparoscopy, an invasive outpatient procedure, to take a closer look. I was skeptical because her diagnosis did not match where I felt pain. Plus, I did not want another incision so soon after having an emergency cesarean section in 2006. She was indifferent about my concerns and basically told me to make a choice with very little explanation. It wasn't until after the procedure that she determined the problem was my estrogen levels, which were high because I drank soy milk regularly. This could have been determined with some discussion. She admitted that I did not need the invasive treatment and that another ultrasound would have revealed that the ovary wasn't attached, but prior to the procedure my complaints and concerns were not considered so I left her practice and never returned.

In 2009 I went to a new Black female doctor. During my examination I requested an HIV test. She promptly responded, "But aren't you married?" Strike one, two, and three. She couldn't possibly be my doctor and ask such ridiculous questions. My partner and I were very clear that we trusted one another to be monogamous, but we agreed that as adults we were responsible for our own sexual health, including getting STD and HIV tests annually. I needed my doctor to be concerned with my sexual health regardless of my marital status.

In 2011 I saw a Black female gynecologist at a clinic that served mostly refugee and immigrant communities. She was so rude and rough that I literally left the office in pain, and for the first time ever I feared returning for my test results. When I returned I brought a friend, partially for support and also to witness. Once again the doctor was so rude that my friend had to ask her to leave the room—I wanted to do violence! On my way out I looked around the waiting room and saw Black and Brown families and my heart sank.

After these experiences I started talking with other Black women about my difficulty finding a good gynecologist and learned that they'd had similar experiences. I also had a few women share with me that they'd stopped going to the gynecologist altogether because they were getting lectured on their weight and size during their annual exams. Now it is one thing for a doctor to have a holistic discussion about healthy bodies, but it is something totally different to have weight-loss programs peddled in a gynecological space unless weight is directly related to the concerns raised by patients in the exam room.

Based on my experiences and discussions, I determined these baseline requirements for what I am looking for in a gynecological relationship:

1. **Access.** I want to be able to see a doctor or nurse practitioner about a yeast infection without waiting six months.
2. **Dialogue.** I want "me-conscious" explanations to my questions that are not canned messages provided by pharmaceutical or insurance companies. I want to know why my doctor is asking particular questions about recreational drug use and other habits, and how they are related to my uterine health.
3. **Kindness.** I want recognition that typical gynecological procedures and treatments are oftentimes invasive, and that these intimate investigations can have emotional costs. If I am treated well I am more likely to continue to pursue care, so I want a health-care practitioner who values women as thinking and feeling human beings.
4. **Do No Harm.** If I am in good health, I want my body esteem left intact. I am not interested in the latest and greatest weight-loss program, products, or diet. I want to leave the visit feeling whole, supported, and encouraged to be my own health advocate.
5. **Respect.** If I have specific concerns I want the health-care practitioner to address them to the best of their ability or to refer me to someone else. Furthermore, I don't want to be made to fit into a "normal lifestyle" to receive excellent care. I expect them to know their craft and treat me based on my medical history and my family medical history and deal with my explicit concerns.

Even though there was a stretch of time when I hated going to the gynecologist, I kept going. I kept searching until I found the care I deserved. Doctors, nurse practitioners, and other medical professionals need to hear in plain language how important it is that their practices are inclusive, encouraging, supportive, and mindful of the women they encounter. My horror stories are not nearly as severe as those of the Black women experimented on by James Marion Sims, but these experiences haunt the medical histories of me and other Black women. Seeing a Black woman doctor is not inherently the solution, especially when most doctors are trained in the Sims medical tradition. Honestly, I believe medical professionals whose patients are predominantly women should be required to earn a minor in women's and gender studies (wishful thinking).

Living in a major metropolitan area I am privileged to have options, but it is essential that we assert our right to quality women's
health care for all women. We must break our silence and tell our
stories so we can open up real dialogue about receiving, as well as
providing, excellent gynecological services for all women.

Back-to-School Beatitudes:
Ten Academic Survival Tips

Brittney C. Cooper

Graduate school was nothing short of an emotional and physical
roller-coaster. I spent the first semester depressed and homesick, and
years two to four battling a stress-induced stomach condition that
caused me to lose not only seventy-five pounds but also a whole semester of work. I healed just in time to begin my dissertation, wherein I gained back most of the weight I lost, and experienced a nasty
case of stress-induced shingles just as I was rounding third. I love
my work, and I'm glad I made it, but here are a few things I wish I'd
known:

1. **Be confident in your abilities.** If you feel like a fraud, you
   very likely are suffering from *impostor syndrome,* a chronic
   feeling of intellectual or personal inadequacy born of grandiose expectations about what it means to be competent.
   Women in particular suffer with this issue, but I argue that
   it is worse for women of color (particularly Blacks and Latinxs), who labor under stereotypes of both racial and gender
   incompetence. The academy itself also creates grandiose
   expectations, given the general perception of academicians
   as hypercompetent people. Secret: Everybody that's actin'
   like they know, doesn't really know. So ask your question.
   It's probably not as stupid as you think. Now say this with
   me: "I'm smart enough, my work is important, and damn it,
   I'm gonna make it."
2. **Be patient with yourself.** Be patient with your own process
   of intellectual growth. You will get there and it will all come
   together. You aren't supposed to know everything at the be-

ginning. And you still won't know everything at the end (of coursework, exams, the dissertation, life . . .).

Getting the actual degree isn't about intellect. It is about sheer strength of will and dogged determination. "Damn it, I'm gonna walk out of here with that piece of paper if it's the last cotton-pickin' thing I do." That kind of thinking helps you to keep going after you've just been asked to revise a chapter for the third time, your committee member has failed to submit a letter of rec on time, and you feel like blowing something or someone up.

3. **Be your own best advocate. Prioritize your own professional needs/goals.** You have not because you ask not. You have to be willing to ask for what you need. You deserve transparency about the rules and procedures of your program, cordial treatment from faculty, staff, and students, and a program that prepares you not only for the rigors of grad school but also for the job market (should you desire a career in academia). But folks won't hand it to you on a silver platter. You have to build relationships, ask questions, and make demands.

Figure out your writing process and the place (home, coffee shop, library), time (morning, afternoon, night), and conditions (background noise, total silence, cooler or warmer) under which you work best, and try to create those conditions as frequently as possible during finals, qualifying exams, and dissertation.

Your self-advocacy will often be misperceived as aggression and anger, entitlement, or selfishness. Don't apologize.

4. **Be kind to yourself.** Reward yourself frequently. Most of us need positive affirmation of a job well done, but for long stretches (especially during exams, dissertation, and the job market) the rewards elude us, and often given the time crunch, once we conquer the mountain, there is little time to enjoy the view before it's time to trudge back down and start climbing the next one. All that hard work in high-stakes conditions for anticlimactic ends can take a toll on your psyche. So be kind to yourself. Figure out the things you really like and make sure to enjoy them as much as is possible and healthy.

5. **Be proactive about self-care.** Figure out your nonnegotiables. For me, sleep is nonnegotiable. I must have it. I don't do all-nighters. I also generally don't do weekends, so I adjust my schedule accordingly. What are your nonnegotiables?

    Take advantage of on-campus therapy services. My last two institutions also have had women of color thesis and dissertation support groups. Consider joining.

    Cultivate a spirit-affirming practice. Grad school/the academy is a mind-body-spirit endeavor. So meditate, pray, exercise, do yoga, go to church, cook a good healthy meal. Do whatever you need to do to keep your mind, body, and spirit in balance.

6. **Be a friend/comrade to others and let them do the same for you.** Build community with colleagues inside or outside your department.

    Build community with nonstudents/nonacademics. You need folks who live life outside the dungeon. They will affirm you and help you keep things in perspective.

7. **Be willing to get *crunk*!** If the environment is hostile, it is most probably characterized by *microaggressions* of various sorts. Racial microaggressions—brief and commonplace daily verbal, behavioral, or environmental indignities, whether intentional or unintentional, that communicate hostile, derogatory, or negative racial slights and insults toward people of color—are quite common for women of color, but microaggressions can be used in sexist, heterosexist, or ableist ways as well. A microaggressive environment demands resistance of various sorts. So do you and be you. Unapologetically. Keep a copy of Sister Audre nearby so you can make sure you're channeling your legitimate anger productively, and then, get crunk if necessary.

8. **Be better, not bitter.** Fail forward. Being the overachievers that we are, we tend not to deal with failure well. It tends to become an indicator to us of our intelligence, worth, and competence (see #1). But failure is a part of the process. Unless you are incredibly, exceptionally lucky, you will hit a snag in a course, while writing the proposal, on the dissertation, submitting a journal article, or submitting a book. Two tips: Take the time to process, particularly for big issues

like proposals, dissertation chapters, or books. Cry, scream (not at your committee or editor), go to a kickboxing class. And then dust yourself off and try again. Look at the suggestions offered; determine their validity. Heed them or disregard them depending on your best judgment, and then proceed to the next step. And one more thing: don't let the resentment fester. It may be well-justified, but it simply isn't productive. Just think of it as hazing, and for your own sake, let it go.

A lot of anger comes from bitterness at mentors who have not met our expectations. But all mentors are not created equal. Some will build your confidence, some will give you hell, some will go above and beyond, but a mentor is there to illuminate the process and give you tools to be successful, not to be your friend. So have multiple mentors, know the difference in function, and adjust your expectations accordingly.

9. **Be tight. Bring your A-game.** This is self-explanatory. Honor your gifts by doing your best work. Period.

10. **Be a light.** As you make your way, show the sisters and brothers behind you how it's done, so maybe they won't have as many dark days as you've had.

Love Me Like You Love Your Lover

Aisha Durham

Self-love is the foundation of our loving practice. Without it our efforts to love fail. Giving ourselves love, we provide our inner being with the opportunity to have the unconditional love we may have always longed to receive from someone else. We can give ourselves the unconditional love that is the grounding for sustained acceptance and affirmation. When we give this precious gift to ourselves, we are able to reach out to others from a place of fulfillment and not from a place of lack.

—bell hooks, *All About Love*

I ate the yam. I ate the yam between a pair of greasy chicken-fried-colored legs and well-worn hands that carved hair plots for my budding locks beneath the buzz of Blackgirl talk and a fluorescent flicker. For some of my stay-woke hip hop sistren, our return to feminist roots was all (about) the rage. I believed my minute meditation, speed journaling, and manicured Badu hairdo were the seeds to recovering my Black self. (Commercial-break makeovers were fashionable in the nineties.) So, when I changed my (out)look and my worldview with her four words (read: White-supremacist, capitalist patriarchy), this candied-yam-fed feminist felt personally betrayed by bell hooks, who now seemed hell-bent on some love kick. What's self-love gotta do with it? I ate her yam—brushed over her book. But, how was a series of self-help survival guides gonna save me?

I was young.

Yesterday, I ruminated about Love Day. I unearthed hooks again along with other Black feminists writing about self-love as a meaningful political act of resistance and reclamation for Black women, who are trained to be the first responders to other folks, to be the bystanders of our own crisis. Love—rooted in a unique, emotive, empathetic ethic of care—is the hallmark of Black feminist thought. I was reminded that to do the work of feminism is to do the labor of loving ourselves.

Changing my hair has been much easier than changing my heart.

On a day when we are encouraged to shower someone else, I want to turn love inward too. This ain't ego trip. For some of us, it is a lifelong journey just imagining what love feels like. To starve my all-consuming rage that used to poison me and those I cared for, I have practiced patience and forgiveness, learned empathic listening to hear with my spirit, and devoted time to cultivating dreams for my lovers. After another day of guilt-grabbing drive-through food between on-the-book and off-the-clock meetings, I see myself flopping fully clothed and headfirst on the bed, falling back out of love with myself because of my inner people-pleaser. Still growing. The outsider-within still needs to nurture love from the inside out. I do know how to love. Yet, each day I must remind myself to give to myself what I willingly offer others. I gotta love me like I love my lover. We, sisters of the yam, have strong roots. Let's plot and nurture the kind of revolutionary self-love that Black feminism has sown.

As Toni Cade Bambara said in her essay "On the Issue of Roles":

> Revolution begins with the self, in the self. It may be lonely. Certainly painful. It'll take time. We've got time. That of course is an unpopular utterance these days. We'd better take the time to fashion revolutionary selves, revolutionary lives, revolutionary relationships. If your house ain't in order, you ain't in order. It is so much easier to be out there than right here. The revolution ain't out there. Yet. But it is here.

Loving Ourselves: The Case for Radical Empathy

Susana M. Morris

Certainly, it's never easy to be a person of color, but it has felt, at least to me, particularly egregious lately. We have a lot of work to do to get free and stay free, but in the meantime I'm really concerned about how we love (on) ourselves and each other—because the business of liberation is not for the faint of heart.

Y'all know that *Beloved* is a sacred text to me. I can always open it and find something that will move my spirit. And I've been thinking a lot about how Morrison imagines Blacks in the nineteenth century navigating a hostile world not unlike our own, a world where "white-people believed that whatever the manners, under every dark skin was a jungle. Swift unnavigable waters, swinging screaming baboons, sleeping snakes, red gums ready for their sweet white blood." But, as the novel suggests, the time we spend convincing racist Whites about our own humanity is not only an exercise in missing the point, it is a clear path for participation in our own dehumanization.

I want to make a call for radical empathy within communities of color. Yes, coalition building and allyship are important, Lorde knows. But how we see, trust, and love ourselves should be at the core of our understanding in these times, as we are continually under surveillance, battered, and hunted down in the streets as if our lives were worth less than nothing.

This is a time for fighting, agitation, mobilization, and organizing for systemic change—yes. Absolutely. But this is also a time for reflection, reading, soft beds, self-care, and saying *no!* to time wasters and soul crushers. This is also a time for laughing, lovemaking, singing, crying, wailing, dancing, and holding on to each other tight. This is a time for potlucks, cookouts, BBQs, picnics, cocktails, karaoke, concerts, house parties, blue lights in the basement, slow jams, and dutty wines. You feel me?

How am I practicing what I preach? Spending time with the people I love. Eating copious amounts of roast pork, fresh corn on the cob, and Italian ice. And listening to great music, like Blackgirl genius Alice Smith.

I'm also daydreaming about cuties. Watching bad movies with my mama. Reading novels about zombies. Organizing ways in which I can foster support, self-care, and healing in the communities I live and love in. But mostly, I'm loving myself and those I hold dear fiercely and unapologetically.

Black Autumn: On Black Anger, Tiredness, and the Limits of Self-Care

Brittney C. Cooper

The turning of autumn is one of my favorite times of year. Having been on an academic calendar my entire life, fall is the season of new beginnings, a time to turn up the intensity of scholarly production, teaching, meetings, school. But that intensity is also greeted with the changing of fall leaves and, hopefully, a cool respite to a swiftly passing hot summer.

The summer of 2014 was unusually cool in terms of the weather, but inordinately hot in terms of the toll taken on the lives of people of color. We started that fall mourning Eric Garner and John Crawford and Michael Brown. We started that fall in mourning of the two teen girls, Tjhisha Ball and Angelia Mangum, whose murdered bodies were dumped unceremoniously by the side of a Florida road.

We began the fall bracing ourselves for a long season of waiting and hoping that the grand jury in Ferguson would decide to bring charges against Darren Wilson, the police officer who murdered Michael Brown. We were hopeful that the cold season would not cool our rage.

We started the fall—football season—giving a side-eye to the NFL, which can't seem to recognize the connection between violent cultures of sport and violence enacted against female partners and children in the home. We sighed at the brothers *and* sisters who spent the last couple of weeks defending Ray Rice for putting his hands on his wife, and Adrian Peterson for beating the ish out of his four year old.

We started the fall having run up against the limits of our cultural fascination with violence against Black bodies, both the kind that the state takes the prerogative to enact and the kinds that we justify and use against each other.

All of this is to say that we started that fall tired. Tired of the physical and emotional assault on our humanity and personhood. Tired that a "turn down for what" approach in the hands of state actors means assured Black death. Tired that the violence that is sometimes closest to us comes from the hands of those who look like us.

I taught Sara Ahmed's great book *The Cultural Politics of Emotion* in my graduate feminist-theory course for a two-week unit on affect theory. I'm glad that this book and Melissa Harris-Perry's book *Sister Citizen* open up space to think through how we use emotions in politics. Ahmed, for instance, uses Lorde to think about how anger can energize social movements. She writes:

> Crucially, anger is not simply defined in relationship to a past, but as opening up the future. In other words, being against something does not end with "that which one is against." Anger does not necessarily become "stuck" on its object, although that object may remain sticky and compelling. Being against something is also being for something, something that has yet to be articulated or is not yet. As Lorde reminds us, anger is visionary . . .

I find it necessary to reclaim anger as visionary in a moment in which the trope of the angry Black woman is deployed by a writer at the *New York Times* as evidence of the truncated nature of Black female vision, such that Shonda Rhimes would or could be visionary if only she could more deftly navigate Black female anger.

This is, of course, bullshit. Shonda Rhimes shows are only minimally about Black female anger in the first place. But one of my issues with Ahmed, and one of my sometimes issues with the community of online feminists of which we are a part, is the way that the Black feminist project gets constructed at the site of anger. Ahmed challenges the idea that feminist movements, beholden as they are to anger over patriarchy, are necessarily reactionary, by suggesting that everything is a reaction to something. Still, angry things, valid as they are, are not the only things we have to say.

And what happens in a world where, having been in a continual rotation of anger, you wake up tired?

Cuz I know I woke up like dis. Tired that is.

Tired of having to be angry. Angry, nonetheless, but tired of trying to muster the energy to write from the place of anger.

So I think that if we are going to talk about emotions and affects and the ways they inform movements, let us think about what Fannie Lou Hamer's famous quote, "I'm sick and tired of being sick and tired," invites us to think about in terms of our politics.

Tiredness might not be an emotion, but it is affect. I feel it, I sense it, it exists on the surfaces of my skin and underneath, it contours my relationships—political, professional, and personal.

Usually tiredness is debilitating in the sense that it makes you want to sleep or rest or simply stop and call time-out. But tiredness can also energize in the same way that the elder lady during the Montgomery Bus Boycott said to Dr. King, "I don't feel no ways tired."

So I want to say simply today, I write this from the space of feeling tired and feeling at some level "no ways tired" all at the same time.

In the midst of anger and helping those in Ferguson and us who stand with them cast a fully articulable vision of Black freedom, I write this as an invitation to care for yourself and those you love.

As I write I am aware of—
my house which looks askew,
the to-do list that won't quit,
the homecooked meals that I don't even have time to prepare,
the sex I need to have,
the hugs which I would refuse but probably need,
the book that's giving me fits,
the bills I need to pay,
the loneliness that sometimes tugs insistently around the edges of an outwardly appearing orderly overachiever's life—
the limits of self-care.

I am thoughtful about what it means to build communities in which others have the capacity and opportunity and means to show up for us when we have reached the limits of ourselves.

But we are loved. We are angry. We are tired. We are sick of it. And we are cared for. In the midst of this, we find purpose. That purpose is to fight for the world we want to see. To teach others to see it, too. To commit to learning until we know how to cast a better vision.

I write this from the space of tiredness. I write it from the space of subdued anger. I write hoping that as we move from the green hues of summer into the golden hues of fall, we meet it with ripening political consciousness and possibilities for a robust Black Autumn.

Disappearing Acts, Unreciprocated Interest(s), and Other Rhythms to My Blues

Robin M. Boylorn

On the crevices of my thirty-third year, if you listen hard enough and look long enough, you might hear the rhythm of my blues. This is not a blues to sashay to, but rather one that leaves you listening to your heartbeat while sitting on the floor, legs folded, with crossed arms and neck pushed back, eyes closed. This is the kind of blues that leaves you unsure about life and reflective about the ways that life folds in on itself after a while. This is a Nina Simone–like blues. A fear-of-being-alone-type blues. A blues that sustains and suffocates at the same time.

As I sit here I imagine myself fully strong and round, and rise to perform myself accordingly. In reality, this week especially, I have been struggling, disappearing on myself the same way others have seemed to vanish from my life, silently but intentionally, and without warning. I had imagined the post-thirty blues would be different, unrelated to the things that marked the ambivalence of my twenties. Instead I find these emotions are inextricably linked to the past. My blues are still sometimes about the ignorant acts of White folks in the South, the fear of abandonment and loneliness, the residue of bad choices and regret, the rejection and unreciprocated (and unexplained) interest of romantic possibilities, the insecurity of not being/having/becoming enough, the pressure of performance on my job and in my life. This, as they say, is not supposed to be my life. I had imagined it different, post-thirty, as if I would miraculously wake up with all of my shit together and all of my issues in order. Instead I trade war stories with friend girls about broken hearts and hurt feelings when sex is intermittent, love is underrated, dreams are drowned by disappointments, and the expectations and random requests of others outweigh my time, energy, and interest. My unintentional blues and forced celibacy come back at me like unintentional celibacy and forced blues. These are grown-woman problems.

But I walk around, thick thighs and wayward hips, back tall, chin up, eyes open, just like my mama taught me, acting like I have it all together when only me and my big legs know it is a lie. A performance. A walk that reads as confident. A smile that looks the same whether I mean it or not. Truth is, I have gone eleven days without smiling . . . on the inside. I told my homegirl it was probably just postbirthday blues. The fog of reality we settle into after the euphoria of waking up into the first day of another year of life. My life is vibrant and predictable and beautiful . . . I am not ungrateful . . . but I don't know what to do with the sadness that reverberates in my life like rhythms.

There is sadness in the world made manifest through the perpetuation of isms and ignorance that I face on a daily basis, sometimes within inches of my own life's breath. There is unjust justice that snatches away the innocence of life by those whose skin color and gender make them constantly in the wrong place at the wrong time. There is the discrimination and disrespect I oftentimes have to negotiate in classrooms with White men and Black women, respectively. There is sadness.

Then, there is sadness of the spirit that lingers like cigarette smoke and stays wherever it touches for days, sometimes weeks, until I have the energy, focus, and mind to clear my headspace. The sadness of knowing that despite my best intentions (and other people's misgivings about my abilities and availability), I am not superwoman (or strongblackwoman), and holding it together for everyone else's benefit is an exhausting, oftentimes unreasonable endeavor. There is the sadness of feeling inadequate and replaceable. There are the multiple memories of mistreatment and the embodied memory of pain. There is sadness. And sometimes sadness is inevitable. And perhaps instead of concentrating so much on pushing it away, I should pull it in. Embrace it. Utilize it. Cocreate with it until the blues slip away, to keep myself present, so that I don't disappear.

There is power in my blues (sometimes), untapped potential, reservoirs of resources and creativity. Maybe instead of chasing my blues away I should invite her in for a while. Have a cup of hot chocolate or a glass of wine and patiently pay attention to her. Hear her words, heed her warnings, and listen to the rhythms of her blues.

How to Say No and When to Say Yes

Robin M. Boylorn

It took me years to unlearn the habit of automatically saying yes when someone asked me for (or to do) something. Over time people assumed I owed them a response of agreement, no matter how inconvenient and unreasonable the request. To this day when I tell someone no, even a stranger, they seem surprised, almost offended, at my nerve.

And perhaps it is nerve. And the fact that saying yes all the time got on my last damn one. I would say yes because as a self-described superwoman and strongblackwoman, it was the only word I knew to say. I would say yes because I was flattered at the request(s) and anxious to people-please. I would say yes because it felt like the right thing to do, the polite reply to any well-intentioned question, and evidence that I was a good-nice-sweet-reliable-thoughtful-friendly-generous person. I would say yes because I felt like people were taking score, and I always wanted to be on the plus side (even though, as is usual with people who perpetually say yes, I hardly ever asked anyone for anything). But the yeses nearly took me out. Saying yes to everyone else was, in essence, saying no to myself.

When I learned to say no, I realized it did not require an explanation, and that no is an adequate one-word response. There didn't have to be a substantial reason why. I didn't need an excuse or legitimate reason. Sometimes I say no because I am tired, overwhelmed, depressed, moody, PMSing, jonesing, or otherwise distracted. And sometimes I say no because I simply don't want to, don't feel like it, can't afford it, don't have any interest or desire to, and would prefer to indulge in doing something else or nothing at all.

In the spirit of knowing how to say no, I have the following suggestions:

1. Always say no first. Do not allow yes to be your default answer. It is easier to go back later and say yes than it is to go back and say no.
2. Never agree to do something on the spot. Always take some time to think about it and consider whether or not it is going to be an imposition. If it is, say no.
3. Limit yourself on how many things you agree to do (beyond your comfort zone) every month/semester/year, etc. I say yes to three things beyond my regular responsibilities every academic semester. After that, I almost always (depending on the request) say no.
4. Never compromise your peace. If you have a full plate, acknowledge it. Don't try to overcompensate for a previous no with a present yes. Never agree to do something you are not comfortable doing or that will cause you distress. Never feel obligated to do something for someone because you have declined in the past. You do not owe anybody anything!
5. If you have a choice (and clearly, sometimes, whether it be for personal or professional reasons, you don't), reserve the right to say no.
6. Save some yeses for yourself. Women have the tendency to put other people's needs and priorities above their own. Self-care is not selfish, and even if it were, we deserve self-indulgence every now and then. Don't say yes to something that is essentially saying no to yourself. Take care of yourself.
7. Don't apologize for saying no. You have every right to decline a request or refuse an opportunity. You should not feel like you are doing something wrong, being rude, disrespectful, or obstinate. No is the other option to yes. It is a neutral response, neither positive or negative (regardless of the requestor's reaction).
8. It is not a sin to change your mind. Don't feel locked into something just because you may have agreed to do it in the past. Circumstances change. Your number-one obligation should be to yourself.

While it is important to know how to say no, it is equally important to know when to say yes. Here are some reasons to say yes:

1. Say yes if/when you are being offered a once-in-a-lifetime opportunity. Consider the uniqueness of the opportunity and whether or not you will ever have the same chance again. If not, say yes.
2. Say yes when saying yes makes you feel good. Whether it be indulging in a sinful dessert, buying the badass shoes, or making love, give in to your cravings when possible. And let others love on/take care of you.
3. Say yes when saying yes can/will make a positive difference in someone's life (including your own). Sometimes something seemingly insignificant to you can have a lasting impact on someone else. And sometimes the smallest effort on your part can make a significant difference in your future.
4. Say yes when you really want to say yes. While I don't think we should ever say yes out of some sense of responsibility, if you want to say yes, you should! There have been times I have been tempted to say no just for the hell of it, or because I was already overcommitted, or because I didn't want to seem too available, or because I didn't want to seem over-eager, or because I wanted to give someone else the opportunity, or because I felt guilty for having declined a different invitation, or out of concern about what someone else may think/say. At the end of the day, if it is something you want to do, something that will make you happy, do it!
5. Say yes when you have the chance to experience something new or do something you have never done before. Be open to new experiences.
6. Say yes when it can benefit your overall health and well-being (i.e., yoga, juicing, massage, exercise). Sometimes saying yes is saying no. For example, saying yes to healthy choices is saying no to unhealthy ones (this includes relationships).
7. If it has anything to do with your mama . . . say yes!
8. If there is ever a conflict between the yeses and the nos (meaning you feel conflicted or uneasy and/or ambivalent) say no! A guilt-inspired or unenthusiastic yes is really a silent no. Say your nos out loud so people can hear them.
9. Always revert to numbers 1, 2, 3, 6, 7, and 8 of the No list.

Outro

This book is the culmination of hopes, dreams, and years of dedicated hard work. When Brittney and Susana started the CFC they had really big goals. They wanted to open up space for a larger range of feminist conversations. They wanted women of color to have a place to speak their peace and to shine. They wanted to say things they were unable to say anywhere else. And they wanted to be part of shaping feminist and pop culture discourse. The CFC has done that and so much more. It has carried on a legacy of feminist thought and helped blaze a trail alongside other bloggers to create the vibrant Black feminist digital space there is today. It has created a fierce on-line community that has become a lifeline for us and for our readers. It has brought together a group of people and changed them forever.

The blog lives on for now, but at some point we will reenvision what the work of the CFC looks like online. We plan on continuing other projects individually and as a collective. Be on the lookout for more writing from us from various corners of the Internet and in print. Look for us in front of and behind the camera. Look for us giving talks and workshops at various venues. And holler at us when you see us at conferences and in movement spaces.

The virtual landscape has shifted dramatically since we began blogging in 2010. We have seen a whole new social movement emerge, precipitated by the reach and power of Black Twitter. We have social media platforms—Snapchat, Periscope, Instagram—that didn't exist when we began working. We have seen sister sites like *Feministing*, the *Feminist Wire*, and *For Harriet* continue to grow and direct the tenor of profeminist conversation in productive ways. In the Collective, we have moved our own work out from the contained space of the CFC to other venues like *Salon*, *Ebony*, the *Guardian*, the *Nation,* and a range of radio and TV shows as well. But for the conversations that matter most to us, we keep coming back to this space, because it is home. Even when our community of readers disagrees, challenges, and trolls us, even when we are exasperated and overwhelmed, it is home.

The social landscape has shifted, too. We write this book in the thick of a persistent and growing #BlackLivesMatter movement. To date, more than twelve hundred protests on behalf of the movement have occurred since the killing of Michael Brown in Ferguson on August 9, 2014. We have undertaken this project in the midst of what feels like a rise in the callous police disregard for Black life. They ain't never loved us. But most of us came of age in the era of "make pretend," the neoliberal era where we watched White progressives *pretend* that shit had changed. We write this book to you in the midst of a series of stark and deadly reminders that the world done changed, but the game still the same—the game being the devaluing and taking of Black life in service of White dominance. The academy, out of which most of us come, is not exempt from this structural devaluation of Black life. We started the CFC to counteract the silence and violence that kills far too many Black women academics way too soon. Before this movement, led by queer and trans people of color, made it explicit, the CFC was one place where sisters could come to hear other sisters affirm that "our Black lives *MATTER.*" *All* Black lives do.

In this regard, we should remember that before the #BlackLivesMatter movement became a reality, for more than a decade Black feminist women cultivated digital space through blogs, Twitter, and Tumblr, making these places productive for the work of social justice. Digital Black feminism is to be credited for the work of turning social media into a technology of racial and gender justice. We don't claim credit for that, but we are glad to have been one set of voices among the many, one crew on the grind helping to grease the wheel upon which this current movement rides.

We do this work not only for the sisters to come but for the sisters who were here, who didn't make it to Freedomland with us. For Sandra Bland. Gynnya McMillen. Latasha Harlins. Renisha McBride. Kindra Chapman. Aiyanna Stanley-Jones. Rekia Boyd. Keisha Jenkins. Penny Proud. Islan Nettles. Eyricka Morgan. Hadiya Pendleton. Natasha McKenna. Miriam Carey. Tanisha Anderson. Mya Hall.

This work is our collective dream for a world in which all women, girls, and femmes—cis, trans, and nonbinary, Black, Brown, queer and straight, formally educated and not—get to live and thrive, to move safely through space, to build families and partnership, to shine as bright as they possibly can. The work of the CFC is our particular remix of both Black feminism and hip hop feminism. But we surely need more. The CFC is not a blueprint, but it is possibility—the possibility that sisters of color can tell their stories on their own terms and be heard. There is room for every sister at the table.

#YouCANSitWithUs even when you can't sit with anybody else. So we hope you see this book as an invitation to enter the cypher and spit your rhymes, sing your song, or do your dance. We'll be two-stepping and showing love and maybe getting some younger sistren to show us how to Hit the Quan and Dab.

There are so many young sisters and siblings, not to mention colleagues and peers that we are checking for, looking up to, and following—folks like Candace Yonina Simpson, Candice Benbow, Arielle Newton, Lourdes Ashley Hunter, Charlene Carruthers, Samantha Master, Janet Mock, Patrisse Khan-Cullors, Opal Tometi, Alicia Garza, Cherno Biko, Nakisha Lewis, Kimberly Foster, Luvvie Ajayi, Issa Rae, Amandla Stenberg, Marley Dias, Quvenzhané Wallis, Blue Ivy Carter, Nia-Malika Henderson, Elle Hearns, Jamilah Lemieux, Brittany Ferrell, Alexis Templeton, Kayla Reed, KiKi Williams, Alexis Pauline Gumbs, and Rachel Jeantel. These girls, ladies, femmes, and so many more are building the world we want to see.

We only get free when every sister recognizes that she has a stake and a place in this project. So where you at? Who you wit? We'll be checkin' for you.

As always, keep it CRUNK.

—**Brittney, Susana, and Robin, 2016**

Crunk Glossary

Ally A person with social privileges related to their identity who publicly supports and advocates for marginalized groups of which they are not a member. (E.g., a straight person can be an ally to LGBTQA+ people, or a White person can be an ally to people of color.)

Blackgirl A term coined by CFC member Robin Boylorn to represent the inextricable experience and oppression of marginalized race and gender/sex. By removing the space and separation between the terms "Black" and "girl," she attempts to demonstrate the connectedness of being both Black and a girl simultaneously as a lived experience; definition is inclusive of grown Black women.

Chosen Family Kin that are unrelated to you. Family that you choose for yourself. Sisterfriends, brothers from other mothers, siblings, play cousins, aunties and uncles who are not biologically related to you but whom you claim and honor as family all apply.

Cisgender A gender identity and performance where an individual's experience of gender follows the sex they were assigned at birth. (E.g., male genitalia accompanies masculine gender performance; female genitalia accompanies female gender performance.)

Clapback Refers to a rhetorically combative way of responding to people who criticize—or in contemporary parlance, shade—you. It is direct, aggressive, and to the point.

Colorism Skin color discrimination or preference/privilege for having light skin; usually refers to prejudice against people who are dark-skinned by other people of color.

CRUNK A Southern hip hop term originally used beginning in the 1990s by Lil Jon and the East Side Boyz. Refers to excitability, hyperness, and high energy. Some argue that the word is a mash-up of "crazy" and "drunk." It also refers to the high energy of cranking something up.

Crunk Feminism Our brand of hip hop (generation) feminism, which centers the high-energy and percussive nature of crunk music together with a clear commitment to dismantling patriarchy.

Disrespectability Politics A term coined by CFC member Brittney Cooper. It refers to the strategies that Black women use to resist the persistent disrespect they receive culturally and to the ways they "dis" and dismiss the polite dictates of respectability politics. Rather than responding to disrespect by acting "respectable," Black women who use disrespectability politics often talk back, go off, vocalize their anger, or otherwise let their displeasure be known.

Down-Ass Chick A woman (usually a Black woman) in a relationship with a man (usually a Black man) who is willing to tolerate any behavior or disrespect without leaving; her allegiance to a man may lead to her willing participation in acts of criminality (e.g., Bonnie to his Clyde).

Family Those closest to you, who have your back no matter what. Blood kin, play cousins, family of origin, chosen family, crew, and/or squad. See also "chosen family."

Formenism A term coined by scholars Sarojini Nadar and Cheryl Potgieter referring to a belief in the inherent superiority of men. However, this version of sexism and patriarchy is propagated by women. (And ain't that a shame?)

Genderqueer An identity in which people perform and present themselves outside the binary of men and women; may or may not refer to someone who identifies as both trans and queer.

Hip Hop Generation Feminism Our riff on the term "hip hop feminism," coined by Joan Morgan in 1999. We add the term "generation" to reflect the fact that we grew up as members of the hip hop generation and are shaped by the terms of this historical and cultural moment. Unlike hip hop feminism, hip hop generation feminism does not demand any particular allegiance to hip hop culture beyond acknowledging how the moment has shaped our politics and worldview.

Identity Politics The political positions, perspectives, and theories that emerge from the shared experiences of members of marginalized social groups (e.g., race, ethnicity, gender identity, sexuality, ability, etc.). First used by the Combahee River Collective in their famous paper, "A Black Feminist Statement."

Intersectionality Coined by Prof. Kimberlé Crenshaw in 1989, this term captures the ways that systems of power interlock and interact to create multiple forms of structural oppression for people of color and queer people. It means that Black women don't just confront racism, but also sexism and very often classism. Though many use the term "intersectional" to refer to the many facets of their identity (e.g., race, class, gender, sexuality, ability, religion, nationality, etc.), we insist that the term be used as it was originally intended—to foreground the interacting and interlocking nature of systems of power on marginalized communities, particularly Black women.

LGBTQAI+   Acronym for a range of nonheterosexual or nonnormative identities related to gender and sexuality. Stands for lesbian, gay, bisexual, transgender, queer or questioning, asexual, intersex. The plus represents additional and emerging identities.

Misogynoir   Coined by Dr. Moya Bailey in 2010, this term refers to the unique hatred that Black women and girls experience in American visual and popular culture.

Neoliberalism   Refers to a shift in both social and economic policy that began in the 1970s that is characterized by redistribution of wealth upward, an increasing focus on personal responsibility as a solution to social ills, a hyperregulation of gender and sexual norms, and a shift to the carceral state and policies which criminalize communities that confront a shrinking social safety net.

Nose Open   Old-school phraseology that means to be in love.

Percussive   The productive possibility that ensues from placing competing ideas, intellectual traditions, or activist strategies together (e.g., hip hop and feminism).

Queer   A term often used to refer to people who identify as nonheterosexual or on the LGBTQAI+ spectrum, including people who are attracted to many genders or who resist cultural norms around sexuality and gender expression; queer may also refer, politically, to a transgressive resistance of the status quo.

Ratchet(ness)   Refers to a Southern working-class mode of both play and resistance that is unconcerned with social propriety, often engages in profane social behaviors (like overtly sexual dancing or unapologetic use of profanity), and adamantly refuses the aspiration to be respectable. The term in its current iteration was first used by Anthony Mandigo of Shreveport, Louisiana, in a 1999 song called "Do the Ratchet," but has in the ensuing years been taken up as a class-inflected slang term characterizing behaviors that lack respectability or decorum.

Ratchet Feminism Coined by CFC member Brittney Cooper in 2012, this term refers to critiques of sexism and patriarchy that happen in otherwise "ratchet" (see above) spaces. Also refers to unlikely female friendships forged in the midst of complicated romantic relationship situations (e.g., between a man's girlfriend and his "baby mama").

Ratchet Respectability A term coined by CFC member Robin Boylorn. It is defined as a hybrid characterization of hegemonic racist, sexist, and classist notions of Black womanhood. Ratchet respectability is a form of resistance popularized by Black women on reality TV shows like *The Real Housewives of Atlanta* and *Love and Hip Hop Atlanta*, wherein Black women simultaneously challenge and accept stereotypic characterizations of race, gender, and class. Ratchet respectability allows Black women to coalesce ratchet behavior (often linked to race and class) and politics of respectability (often linked to race and gender), performing and enacting both ratchetness and respectability at the same time. See "disrespectability politics."

Respectability Politics A nineteenth-century term and ideology, coined in the decades after slavery, which argued that if Black people acted chaste, pious, and frugal and comported themselves properly in public, they could prove their fitness for American citizenship. Today, respectability politics are often used to police Black people for nonnormative behavior. See, for example, Bill Cosby's "pound cake" speech.

Self-Care The radical act of resistance and healing that is women of color taking care of themselves. As Audre Lorde wrote, "Caring for myself is not self-indulgence, it is self-preservation, and that is an act of political warfare."

Siblings/Sibs A gender-inclusive way to invoke kinship and love among Black communities; frequently used as a replacement for the more gender specific "brothers and sisters."

Side Chick A woman who (knowingly or unknowingly) is in a relationship with a man who is already committed to someone else.

Strongblackwoman A stereotype that refers to Black women's supposed impenetrable strength and capacity to withstand pain, disappointment, loss, and responsibility for others.

Transgender, Trans* When one's gender performance does not correspond to the biological sex one was assigned at birth. The asterisk also refers to the variety of groups of people who find the term "trans" meaningful, including but not limited to transgender, gender nonconforming, gender nonbinary, and intersex people.

Woke   A term used to reference one's awareness or consciousness about issues of racial and political injustice, first popularized in Erykah Badu's 2008 song "Master Teacher."

Contributor Bios

ROBIN M. BOYLORN was born and raised in rural North Carolina by Black women who unintentionally taught her feminism. She is associate professor of interpersonal and intercultural communication at the University of Alabama, where she teaches and writes about issues of social identity and diversity. She is the author of the award-winning monograph *Sweetwater: Black Women and Narratives of Resilience* and coeditor of *Critical Autoethnography: Intersecting Cultural Identities in Everyday Life.* Her next book, *Blackgirl Blue(s),* is forthcoming from Routledge. She enjoys old-school hip hop (and, eri uh, a lil' Drake sometimes), ~~ratchet~~ reality TV, poetry, soul food, and sports. Her favorite things include organic soap, scented candles, and earth tones. To unwind she crochets blankets and watches football, sometimes simultaneously. See more about her work and words on her website, RobinBoylorn.com.

BRITTNEY C. COOPER is cofounder of the CFC. She is assistant professor of women's and gender studies and Africana studies at Rutgers University, where she specializes in Black feminist thought, Black women's intellectual history, hip hop studies, and digital feminisms. Brittney is best known for calling folks on their racist and sexist BS in her impassioned posts about gender politics in the hip hop generation, convergences of faith and feminism, dating while feminist, and contemporary feminist movements. Her first book, *Beyond Respectability: The Intellectual Thought of Race Women,* is forthcoming from University of Illinois Press. She is also a sought-after public speaker and commentator. Her work and words have appeared at the *New York Times,* the *Washington Post, Salon, Cosmopolitan, TV Guide,* the *Los Angeles Times,* PBS.org, *Essence, Ebony, The Root,* MSNBC's *Melissa Harris-Perry Show,* and *All In with Chris Hayes.*

CRUNKISTA is a Caribbean-born first-generation immigrant, a true city girl with a real country heart. She resides in the Southeast and daydreams of being on the beach daily. Crunkista blogs anonymously. She is still very skeptical of the Internet and is very protective of her privacy. She is feisty, Latina, queer, sustained by her chosen family, tired of the homophobia she encounters all too regularly, can't stand patriarchy (is so over him and wishes he would just stop calling), was raised by a community of fierce women, gets angry quite often, sometimes has unfeminist moments, has had her heart broken . . . a few times, loves to spoon, is often told she looks like Jennifer Lopez—does not in fact look like J. Lo—loves Sonja deeply and is working on being better for her, is a child of Yemaya, has learned a whole lot of lessons from past relationships, loves DIY holiday gifts, is always ready for love, won't ever deny that she is a f#@%g feminist, is addicted to swag, is a survivor of child abuse, and is done with bullshit apologies. Most recently Crunkista was given the title of baby whisperer.

SHERI DAVIS-FAULKNER is the director for the Westside Communities Alliance in the Ivan Allen College of Liberal Arts at Georgia Institute of Technology. She works closely with faculty, researchers, alum, students, and project staff to facilitate engagement with a variety of community partners living and working in Atlanta's Westside. A native Atlantan, Davis-Faulkner completed her doctorate in American studies in the Graduate Institute of the Liberal Arts at Emory University. She also holds an MA in women's studies from the Ohio State University, and a BA in psychology and political science from Spelman College. She has experience working in national and international arenas for social justice and currently lives in west Atlanta with her family.

AISHA DURHAM is a cultural studies scholar. Her research about Black popular culture explores the relationship between media representations and everyday life. She examines how controlling images or power-laden stereotypes are produced by media makers and interpreted by media audiences to make sense of Blackness in the "post" era. Durham uses auto/ethnography, performance writing, and intersectional approaches honed in Black feminist cultural criticism to analyze representations of Black womanhood in hip hop media. This scholarship contributes to an interdisciplinary field called hip hop feminism. Her recent work on Black womanhood is featured in her 2014 book, *Home with Hip Hop Feminism: Performances in Communication and Culture*. This book extends earlier discussions about hip hop culture, media representations, and the body in her coedited volumes, *Home Girls Make Some Noise: Hip Hop Feminism Anthology* and *Globalizing Cultural Studies: Ethnographic Interventions in Theory, Method, and Policy.*

SUSANA M. MORRIS is cofounder of the CFC. She is associate professor of English at Auburn University, where she teaches African American literature. Her book, *Close Kin and Distant Relatives: The Paradox of Respectability in Black Women's Literature*, was published by the University of Virginia Press in 2014. She is currently at work on a book-length exploration of Black women, Afrofuturism, and feminism. Susana also currently serves as the cochair of the board of directors of Charis Circle, the nonprofit programming arm of Charis Books and More, one of the nation's oldest feminist bookstores, located in Atlanta, Georgia. Writing as Crunkadelic on the CFC blog, she covers a range of topics, from politics to self-care to sizeism to reality TV, often irreverently. She has written as the women's issues expert for About.com and for *Gawker, Cosmopolitian*, and *Ebony*. She has also been featured on NPR and HuffPost Live and in *Colorlines* and *Essence*. You can always find her live tweeting your favorite shows for the blog @crunkfeminists.

EESHA PANDIT is a writer, activist, and consultant to antiviolence and reproductive justice organizations. She's a regular contributor to *Salon* and the CFC. You can read her at *Feministing*, the *Nation, Rewire, Feministe, In These Times*, the *Texas Observer*, and *Bitch* magazine. Eesha has worked as executive director of Men Stopping Violence, women's rights manager at Breakthrough, and as director of advocacy at Raising Women's Voices. Eesha currently serves as copresident of the board of directors for the National Network of Abortion Funds. She has a BA from Mount Holyoke College and an MA from the University of Chicago. Follow her work and writing on Twitter @EeshaP.

RACHEL RAIMIST was born with the New York version of crunk, which brought her to hip hop. Needing armor for all the racism and sexism she experienced, led her to hip hop feminisms. She is coeditor of *Home Girls Make Some Noise: Hip Hop Feminism Anthology*. She holds a BA and an MFA in directing from the UCLA School of Film and Television, where she made the first film about women in hip hop, *Nobody Knows My Name*. She holds an MA in women's studies and a PhD in feminist studies from the University of Minnesota, where the Rachel Raimist Feminist Media Center was named in her honor in 2009. Currently, she is associate professor at the University of Alabama. See more about her work at rachelmakesmovies.com.

CHANEL CRAFT TANNER is a doctoral candidate and a university administrator. She sees herself as a scholar-activist with areas of specialization in US third world feminism, hip hop feminism, cultural studies, critical media literacy, and critical prison studies. She is currently completing her dissertation, "Police Stay on Us Like Tattoos: Constructions of a Prison State in Hip Hop." Her dissertation uses a US third world feminist framework to analyze the ways in which hip hop artists use their cultural productions to construct their lived environments as borders between confinement and freedom. She is a mother, wife, sister, and an amazing auntie! She hates being put in boxes and often enjoys blasting gangsta rap in inappropriate places. If you ask her, she'll rap Biggie's entire verse on "Notorious Thugs."

Acknowledgments

Collective work is hard work, and we are grateful for the remarkable ways we have grown with and because of each other. We have supported and celebrated each other, caught each others' tears in our hands, held each other up while holding each other down. This book, this work, this collective would not be possible without the continued commitment, support, and love garnered within the Crunk Feminist Collective itself. This is what feminism looks like!

First and foremost we would like to thank our CFs Eesha Pandit, Sheri Davis-Faulkner, Crunkista, Chanel Craft Tanner, and Rachel Raimist, whose work is included within these pages. We would also like to thank Aisha Durham, whose poetic prose is also featured in the collection. You are beautiful writers, thinkers, and doers in the world, and we could not be more proud of you or what we have cultivated together. Our love has no limits.

Our support system and community expands beyond the elite eight of the CFC. Our nuanced understanding of feminism, politics, relationships, friendship, and social justice is connected to an amazing group of folk, chosen family, and Black feminist elders and foremothers, too numerous to name, whose work and advocacy inspires and creates space for the work we do. In particular, we want to thank Joan Morgan for paving the way for crunk feminism through hip hop feminism, and for being such a tremendous, beautiful, badass role model for us; Ava DuVernay, who has supported our work since 2010 and whose feminist ethic reminds us of what is possible when a bunch of brilliant women get together; DoVeanna Fulton, who offered us a platform to share our work at the genesis of our project; and Gwendolyn Pough, who invited us to our first gig as the CFC and whose work on Black women, hip hop, and popular culture offers a foundation for the work we do.

We would also like to thank Jennifer Baumgardner for her editing eyes and (pro)vision for this book, and Elise Peterson for designing our dope-ass cover.

Last, but not least, we deeply appreciate our readers and followers. Over the years you have kept us grounded and accountable. We see you and we are ever grateful to you for "seeing" us! It's all love.

The Feminist Press is a nonprofit educational organization founded to amplify feminist voices. FP publishes classic and new writing from around the world, creates cutting-edge programs, and elevates silenced and marginalized voices in order to support personal transformation and social justice for all people.

See our complete list of books at

feministpress.org